THE MEASURE OF A DREAM

A PEACE CORPS STORY

Lora Parisien Begin

A PEACE CORPS WRITERS BOOK

A Peace Corps Writers Book.
An imprint of Peace Corps Worldwide.

FIRST PEACE CORPS WRITERS EDITION, May 2012

The Measure of A Dream. © 2012 by Lora Parisien Begin

ISBN 978-1-93592525-5
Library of Congress Control Number: 2012937102
Oakland, CA

FOREWORD

Tunisian Arabic is not a written language. Therefore, when Tunisian Arabic is used in this book, an italicized phonetic spelling of the word(s) is used. "Translations" were provided by the Peace Corps English-Tunisian Arabic Dictionary, printed July 1977.

Of the people who appear in this book, a few names have been changed.

Cover artwork was designed by John Thomas and Jan Segna for Peace Corps Tunisia (group 1988-1990) and used with permission.

Additional artwork is printed with permission by the creators.

All photographs were taken by the author, or are property of the author, with the exception of the photos heading chapter 36 and chapter 62; these were taken by Kelly Korte Prokes.

For Mom

and dedicated to my Peace Corps family & friends

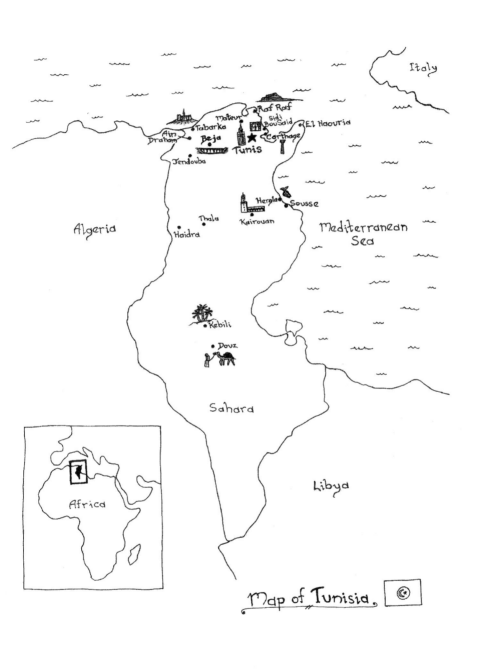

Italy

Raf Raf
Mateur   Sidi
Tabarka   BouSaid   El Haouria
Ain
Draham   Beja   Carthage
Jendouba   Tunis

Mateur

Algeria

Thala   Hergla   Sousse
Haidra   Kairouan   Mediterranean
Sea

Kebili

Douz

Sahara

Libya

Africa

Map of Tunisia

CHAPTER 1

June 1989

Getting there is half the challenge

With my feet on the tarmac I take in my first breath of Africa, a long and deep inhale of gratitude and celebration. But the air is hot and thick and is rapidly beginning to smother me. My first vista oscillates in the sun's smoldering rays. An uninspiring panorama of concrete ripples and merges into the washed out landscape until there is nothing. Okay, not what I pictured. How many times had I imagined this? My Africa had lush trees and refreshing tropical breezes, a mountain range, and camels grazing far off in the distance. But I remind myself, this isn't Africa—this is an airport.

I am swept into my group. In the terminal we are reunited with our gear—enough to fill a house—and begin to pile it onto carts. Like a herd of lemmings, we maneuver our overloaded carts along two black lines through a series of stark corridors, one turning into the next. No one knows exactly where to go. En masse we lumber through a set of swinging doors and are met on the other side by a sea of dark eyes, emotionless, staring at us. Dark penetrating eyes. I feel each and every one of those eyes deep in my gut. Again, not what I imagined. My Africa was warm and fuzzy.

I stay huddled in my group. Together we represent a good cross-section of America, as dissimilar from one another as many of us have ever encountered. Yet with our feet barely on foreign soil, we are suddenly homogenous, a single life form. There is us. And there is them. I have more in common with the Texas rancher among us than any of those intimidating Tunisians who pierce me with their steely gaze. I feel most unwelcome in Africa. In the distance a hand waves the Peace Corps logo and another dangles sprigs of jasmine in the air. I aim for the beacon.

The story of how I got to Tunisia, North Africa began one summer night some years ago when I went cruising with my buddy Paul in his shiny black muscle car. We drove eastbound through Detroit until we found ourselves on Grosse Pointe's Lakeshore Drive, a world that might as well have been a million miles away from home with its palatial estates all in a row, each one with a perfectly manicured lawn and a front row seat on Lake St. Clair. We wandered into Jefferson Beach Marina to ogle moored yachts worth more than the whole of my family's assets. We found a picnic table, climbed atop and sat in complete silence while we stared dreamily into the blackness of Lake Saint Clair. The air was crisp. On the waves the full moon drew a feathery line that appeared to lunge at me from the black mass. I was mesmerized. In this setting I experienced a brief moment of absolute clarity; I fumbled for a pen and forged my plan to venture beyond the feathering of the moon and to be fearless in the doing of it. Sounds corny, but that was my moment. After many nights of wandering I got serious and decided from that night forward, I would wander with purpose. I joined the Peace Corps.

"The Peace Corps? They still around?" Comments rolled in as news of my decision to join hit the ranks of friends and family. "Tunisia? Where is that?" "You want to go live with Arabs?" "Isn't that where women walk six feet behind their husbands?" "What about a paying job?" "Oh the Peace Corps, I wanted to do that once…" "They eat dogs there don't they?" "Plenty of people right here in the U.S. need help, why not do something here?"

My eyes glaze over at the skepticism and the dubious commentary, for I am a starry-eyed optimist floating in the ether of anticipation. The true measure of a dream is the degree to which its inexplicable power holds sway over all one's energy and my dream has me but good—I am a young woman possessed. For two years I have been singularly infatuated, fixated enough to push through endless hoop-jumping, paper-chasing, and medical-probing (including the mandatory removal of three impacted wisdom teeth). Not to mention there was a medical snafu that nearly prevented my going because somewhere in my history someone noted that I had an allergy that I did not—and I had to disprove it. None of this weakened for one moment my stamina or resolve. Whatever was required, my plan was to exit what I have known for a dream that could not be explained away or articulated to the satisfaction of any of my inquirers. So that's it. Now I've made it! I've come blindingly to wherever in the world my government decided, to a small country in North Africa…an Arab country…a Muslim country.

Tunisia sits at the top of North Africa. It is a little over 63,000 square miles, roughly the size of Florida and Connecticut combined. The country is long and skinny and averages just 150 miles across. The northern edge and most of the eastern border is scalloped by the Mediterranean coastline that includes promontories and three sizeable gulfs. To the west Tunisia shares a border (one that runs roughly parallel to the eastern border) with Algeria. At the bottom of the country is the Sahara Desert and the other neighbor, Libya. Tunisia is part of the "Maghreb," the Arab West, dominated by about eight million Arabs whose religion is Islam. I have to admit, I had to search for Tunisia on the map (worldly girl that I am). That is after I had already accepted the assignment. Tunisia. It's where my life is going to begin, now that I have fled the nest.

The dreamer and his dream are the same...
the powers personified in a dream are those that move the world.
Joseph Campbell

CHAPTER 2

You can take the girl out of Detroit...

Art by Paul Domick

I leave behind a family fresh from the aftermath of being obliterated. At twenty-one years of age I abruptly learned that my Brady Bunch childhood was anything but. Ours was the quintessentially happy picture of an American family...until six months ago, December 8, 1988, when my parent's marriage blew up. It is not why I left. But it did set the stage for an awkward departure.

There we were sitting side-by-side in four chairs at the airport gate in Detroit. I can't remember why, but my brothers were absent, having said their goodbyes earlier in their own way. The eldest sibling "gets" me. He is genuinely excited for me, though he somehow has the notion that I will be living on the Serengeti. The other has a track-record of unfortunate mishaps involving Arabs. His opinion of my venture is well known. In the airport terminal, my sister Ann and my dad were a giggly playful two-some, holding hands and clearly operating in their own orbit. Then there was Mom, limp except for the clenching of her fists around wads of tissue. She wore her defeat openly. She slumped in her seat and gazed at the floor. Her face was blotchy and swollen. Her red-rimmed eyes oozed unshakable grief. She leaned into me and whispered simply "I wish I could go with you."

Mom's spent her life in two places. The first was Argyle, Wisconsin (population 673) where she endured a tough childhood, more physically and emotionally challenging than most. She was the oldest of five girls raised on a large dairy farm. She was expected to rise with her father very early every morning before school to help milk the cows and return home in the afternoon to labor in the barn. Her best friend from childhood once told me how Mom used to fall asleep at her desk in school. She also told me that her teachers understood Mom's home life and never once disturbed her while she slept. Everyone in that small town knew everyone else's business, including the fact that one of Mom's sisters was born with a hole in her heart. Every day for months on end, my grandmother made the two hour drive to visit her sick child in the hospital. Mom, as the eldest, became mother to her siblings. Hers was a hard life.

Mom married at twenty and moved to Detroit where she got stuck in a dinky house raising four freakishly close-in-age kids—not so easy either. Hers has been a static, consistent and predictable life, but one she's fully embraced. That is until she found out a few months ago about Dad and his decades-long affair. Since then, the atmosphere in that dinky house has been toxic, saturated with heart-ache and anger and blame. For months now, we have been the walk-ing wounded, shell-shocked and damaged. And Mom is our most critically wounded. In the airport she leaned heavily into me and openly cried. Part of her sorrow was for me, but mostly I think it was grief over the loss of her unremarkable life. But there was hope there, too. Mom has always hoped that my journey will be different.

Ann: tanned, beautiful and looking blindingly bridal. Sending her Maid of Honor off to Africa—on the eve of her nuptials—put a bit of a wrinkle in her plans. We're Irish twins; born only eleven months apart. Even though we are not full-fledged "twinkies" we are every bit as cosmically linked. Yet in the looming of those last hours, we found less and less common ground. In the throes of pre-matrimonial mayhem and familial disaster, I was but a blip on her radar but for the disruption to and dismantling of her wedding party.

The convergence of these events created high drama. And I bailed out of all of it. I left my tribe behind. I took my leap of faith, believing my future was out there.

LIFE BECKONS...

You've done a lot of traveling, child,
From womb to world, tightly curled—
To follow dreams, sweet flags unfurled...
Unbridled, free, you stretch yourself with giddy glee
To reach for the stars undauntedly...
Go for it, child, without reservation
And carve out your own bright constellation.

written by Corinne Adrian Bariteau

Mom had tucked this into my pocket. I found it during my flight.

I hear you Mom.

CHAPTER 3

Gateway to the Sahara

Hamdullah House

The logistics of moving thirty-five people overseas began many hours ago. We are on the final leg of our very long journey, a two-hour bus ride toward an increasingly drier south. The bus immediately fills with the expectant chatter of rookies, all merging head-long into the same Peace Corps dream. We are as divergent as our motivations for being here. A plumber who grew up farming. A liberal arts grad who wants to be a lawyer. A lawyer who wants to be something else. Some of us are starting out. Others left lives in progress or escaped from them. What *is* common is that we have decided to shed those skins and create something else, to step out onto the ledge and dive in head first.

I commandeer a seat, paste myself to the window and feast on the view unfolding outside, adding nothing to the excited buzz around me. I am in a rarified funk, not because of the grapefruit-sized bruise on my hip from the gamma globulin shot I got yesterday, or even because of the walnut-sized lump on my left arm which has started throbbing (a common reaction to the typhoid vaccine), but because I should be witnessing Ann making her grand walk on Dad's arm down the long center aisle of St. Robert Bellermine Church. I'm wallowing in guilt, which I conveniently ignored until now...now that the deed is done. If I summon my most loving vibes and direct them to her, does it count at all?

I wonder, as I slip into this giddy reality, how long will this numbness continue to creep in and how often will the desire to connect with home surface? The nightmarish vision of Mom—the grief clinging to her and swallowing her whole—is stuck in my head. That is not my Mom, the rock, the stabilizing force. She helped me go...but I still feel tethered. This combination of complete exhilaration and intense sadness is not a state of being that can be borne for very long.

I turn my attention outward to the bustling capital which soon gives way to rolling hills, to plains and to increasingly parched topography. Towns and random structures appear fewer and farther between. Olive groves fill the terrain. Then, barren stretches of scrub brush. The arid terrain renders everything dusty. Grime coats the bus. It billows in our wake. It clogs my new world. We enter the gateway to the Sahara.

Outside my window is a monochromatic blur of endless brown earth. I begin to feel intense thirst. My hair is drenched with sweat. My clothes are stuck to me. When our bus crests the final hill, we meet something completely unexpected: a stunning expanse of the Mediterranean Sea. Endless layers of blue supplant the palette of the previous two hours. Turquoise. Indigo. Azure. Cobalt. Sapphire. The breath that I have been holding for months rushes out. To look upon the Mediterranean for the first time is to be mesmerized to the point of ecstasy. The image imprints forever. Finally, an Africa I can get along with!

The village of Hergla, gem that she is, is perched on the edge of a cliff that drops abruptly to the sea. The concrete houses are immaculate. They are crisply whitewashed with turquoise doors, shutters and iron scrollwork, elements that pop against the clean white backdrop. The architecture is uniform and low lying with flat rooftop terraces all clumped together within high-walled private enclosures. The overwhelming presence of the Mediterranean, with its thousand layers of blue, is the undisputed queen of this place. I am awestruck.

Upon arrival, we are scattered among five houses, each bearing an Arabic name. I've been assigned to the *Hamdullah* (thank God) House. There are twenty other single women and one married couple crammed, three or four to a room in this unfinished villa. The exterior is dark gray. Not-yet-cured and not-yet-painted, its walls will someday bear bright white, the distinctly Mediterranean palette of the village.

A quick note about the worldly goods that accompanied me to Africa. They include a trunk that weighs in at sixty-five pounds and one thirty-pound bag, plus a host of gifts that were thrust into my hands at the last minute. I well exceeded the eighty-pound limit. What exactly does one pack for a two-year stint in North Africa? At twenty-two, I am now a person without a fixed address. I own diddly and my priorities at this point in my life revolve mostly around getting to the next point in my life. Maximally uninformed with minimal space, I limited my packing choices thusly:

Priority one, information about Islam, reality being I don't know squat about it, and two, a few professional reference books for my new teaching career that should be useful since I don't know squat about teaching either. Additional items include a sleeping bag that weighs in at less than two pounds, my journal and a shortwave radio for news and information. But one curiously perplexing dilemma I faced as I was packing was the question of how many tampons I should stockpile for a two-year sojourn to a Muslim country. Not for sale anywhere in North Africa, I've been told. Turns out, this matter was of great import to Ann who fervently demanded I should not go without. She stuffed them into every nook and cranny in my suitcase. Thank God I didn't have to open it at customs when I arrived.

I share a room with New Yorker, Pam and the newly law-degreed Beth (who, incredibly, managed to bring her guitar). My bed for the next seventy nights is a four-inch thick foam mat with a decidedly retro patterned polyester cover, on a terrazzo floor. No closets. No drawers. Square footage only and limited at that. We've pushed our trunks against the wall to maximize our meager space. It's cozy enough, if not reminiscent of indoor camping…for the next…ten…weeks. Welcome American. I see you brought a lot of "baggage" with you. Soon enough you'll see it for the burden it is. But, these things take time. Let's begin by reconfiguring (annihilating) your sense of personal space and privacy; such notions do not exist here. Entitlement has no home here either. Well, I'm used to operating with little maneuvering room. I can keep within my perimeter and confine myself to my little foam "island"…for a time. Adaptation is the name of the game. Of the many shifts to be made, each has one point of origination: between my ears. This is no hardship.

Though our room lacks amenity, it boasts a generous balcony fully open to hues and hues of blue—the sea is completely ours. Beth is strumming and singing John Lennon. Perfect melody and lyric meet sea and sky without end. I lack nothing.

CHAPTER 4

Culture shock: let the games begin

Allah

On the first morning in Hergla, I am blasted out of my sleep into darkness by a decibel-packed other-worldly sound, a voice resembling an exotic droning yodel. The voice is a broadcasted over loudspeakers. It pierces the night like earsplitting thunder:

"*Allah hu akbar. Allah hu akbar.*"

"Allah who what?" My roommate screams.

"What in the hell is that?" Questions the other roommate.

Thus I (along with my roommates) am initiated, given my first peek into the world of Islam by way of this early morning collision. Church bells, more my area of acquaintance, do not wake the sleeping dead but serve as gentle reminders to the living. Church bells do not carry the weight of obligation, of command, like this song of the East. This is "call to prayer." It has urgency, if not serious volume, and optional doesn't seem to be the message it is conveying.

The call to prayer is a practice that unites Muslims, millions of them the world over, who beckoned by song abandon their sleep, their chores, their other preoccupations, to engage in prayer. "God is the most great. I testify that there is no God but God. I testify that Mohammed is the prophet of God. Come to success. God is most great. There is no God but God." Punctuating this morning and every morning hence, and four more times throughout each and every day, shall be this hauntingly spiritual voice rousing me along with the devout. This is how I meet Islam—in my face, with a hammer, no...with a bulldozer. An entity all its own demanding attention. I have a feeling Islam is going to affect more than my sleep.

Tunisia is steeped in Islam, which means "peace" and "surrender." Islam is pervasive: it cannot be separated from the culture. It is the very fabric of life. Islam is the official state religion of Tunisia, practiced by 98 percent of its population. The country's constitution requires that its president be a Muslim. Religious holidays, which generally celebrate events in the life of the prophet Mohammed, are national holidays. Islamic religious education is mandatory in public schools. Islam is articulated in everyday language, gestures and practices.

Islam regulates how men and women relate with one another and how people behave in general. Men and women in this country are born of a religion—a way of life—that systematically segregates them: separate duties, separate expectations, separate schools, separate rules. As a result, the underlying tension about what men and women should or should not be doing is palpable.

Because Islam is such a dominant force, infused also in many things unseen, it cannot be ignored. To comprehend Tunisia, understanding the Islamic values upon which all life is based is crucial. This non-believer, make that this neophyte female non-believer, is acutely aware that all this understanding is going to take some time and a wee bit of work. It is after all why I am here. It's not my job to be a big snag in the social fabric. It's my job to try, and to try to understand.

At the core of the Peace Corps philosophy is the belief that you cannot know a people, truly, honestly, without diving in headfirst. If you don't immerse yourself in the culture, learn the language, share meals with the locals, work among them and live among them as they live, then you're just a tourist making a truncated investment and lacking critical knowledge. To know the unknowable Arab and to penetrate the impenetrable Islam in precious short time—this is the agreement I have made.

Peace Corps has three goals:

1) Helping the people of interested countries in meeting their need for trained men and women.

2) Helping promote a better understanding of Americans on the part of the peoples served.

3) Helping promote a better understanding of other peoples on the part of the Americans.

This is my mandate. As for the transferring of skill, it's better to not dwell on my clear lack of qualifications. All I can do is hope that my "can do" spirit will bolster a very serious deficit in this area. I think I have a little wiggle room vis-à-vis the two remaining tenets, promoting understanding—with the caveat that my opinions are not necessarily reflective of all Americans. I am confident I can be a good ambassador for my country. Plus, I am wide open to narrowing my significant gap of ignorance with regard to all things Tunisian. So I admit there is work to be done on the piece in question: just what tangible skill(s) do I bring to the table? Otherwise, I've got my mission.

Figuring out *where* things are leads to figuring out *how* things are. So today I tackle the necessity of my orientation. If I learn the location of the post office—my tether to home—I will have one little victory I can savor and build upon. Something concrete as I begin to take in my surroundings, my hosts, and contemplate the concept of adaptation. I can't just be an American living here. I am going to have to morph. Just what that means, I don't yet know.

About the tiny fishing village we have overrun. Excluding us, it is peaceful and orderly with its pristine uniform white buildings and simple layout. It is such a beautiful place. It is oh-so-easy to find a secluded spot in which to confine myself in that beauty. My spot is in the grasses above the beach, or on a rock overlooking it. I am reminded of Michigan's Mackinac Island, well, in the way this place contents me as the island did. I spent two full summers there during college. Anyone who knows Mackinac Island, knows that its magic is revealed after the "Fudgies" (the tourists) have been ferried back across the straits at the end of the day, when quiet and stillness is reclaimed by the few who remain. Hergla is tranquil, too, and shares something else in common with Mackinac Island—the occasional waft of unpleasant odor ebbing and flowing on the breeze, robbing the view of its purity. On Mackinac, closed to motors of all kinds, horses are to blame. It's fair to say the aroma lends to the charm of the place. However here in Hergla, the existence of open sewage and garbage strewn over the bluff is a contradiction difficult to reconcile. Trash is discarded mostly wherever, on the streets, over walls. Cans, plastics and all manner of organic and inorganic material ac-

cumulates on the cliff side where just beyond, the dazzling sea begs
to be seen. I don't understand how an entire village can be complicit
in its defiling, especially one boasting world-class assets. A soft constant wind bears the odor hither and yon, alternating between what
is and is not palatable.

Hergla is a slow place consisting of perhaps three hundred residents and the few streets they inhabit. Nothing happens with any
great urgency. Nothing really happens at all. Men spend the casual
afternoon in the shade, seated side-by-side on the low wall that runs
through the town center. Children scamper freely. Taking note of
the few women I have seen, though they are brightly veiled, they
are *not* covered from head to toe in black shrouds. They do *not* walk
six paces behind their men. The depth of what I don't know about
Tunisia is staggering. As previously instructed, I am careful not to
make eye-contact with men of a certain age. But this bothers me
and seems aloof behavior at best. Eyes communicate in universal
ways and speak more truthfully than the mouth ever could. Plus,
diverting my eyes effectively cuts me off from a whole segment of
the population and the better part of meaningful communication.
If I don't look at them, they become invisible and no undesired interaction can transpire. Or, is it…if I don't look at them *I* become
invisible? No such luck when you live in a fishbowl.

I didn't completely wrap my head around the fishbowl concept until I became the fish. My glow-in-the-dark white skin, my
clothes—shapeless yet obviously western—and nearly everything
about me screams "foreigner." In a village that enjoys pure sunshine
during daylight hours, the Peace Corps trainees are the only ones
wearing sunglasses (the darker the better). More than attire, it is our
behavior that is a magnet for attention. We are boisterous, obnoxious and unaware of the exhibition we are, drawing eyes wherever

we go and often trailing small groups of children behind us. In a country where the rules of eye-contact are keenly observed, we are the best eye candy around and no amount of blatant staring at us is considered too much. Everywhere we go, we are a curiosity, even in our dwelling at the edge of town. Hamdullah House is the last house on a road where no one except us "occupiers" would otherwise travel. Yet people casually wander past our house at all hours of the day. I can't imagine what is going through the minds of the inhabitants of this tiny village now that it has been overrun by Americans.

CHAPTER 5

I don't know what I don't know

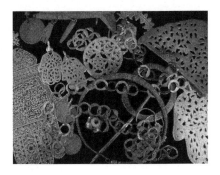

Antique jewelry, an eye, hands of Fatima & a hallal

I cannot call myself a Peace Corps Volunteer until I successfully complete a ten-week in-country training period entitled "stage," pronounced "*staj*" oh-so Française. Training actually started in Philadelphia, where half of our group spent four days in a pre-departure orientation. This orientation set forth to accomplish a number of things. Among the more important was our introduction to Tunisian culture. There was hardly sufficient time in those few days to outlay the breadth and depth of any culture, but what I witnessed was potentially problematic. The fleshing out of the landscape was provided by former volunteers who performed skits and role plays, all very dramatic and all with one overarching theme directed primarily at the women: say goodbye to freedom. Scenes included women being completely ignored by men, disregarded even when their jobs required them to interact with one another. There were directives like "make no eye contact with men beyond the age of puberty," "…learn clever phrases in Arabic so that you can tell men off in unique and humorous ways," and "never speak to men on the street." Yes, this seems problematic indeed. There were intense enactments showing Tunisians trying to convert the volunteers to Islam, or the less obvious performances that demonstrated that Tunisians couldn't speak of anything else save religion. Without benefit of context or discussion of values, our instructors seemed to have one objective: to scare us. Their assertions, which were both ambiguous and ominous, sketched repellent pictures in my head where none had previously existed. I am not a die-hard feminist, but I do savor my independence and appreciate my (perceived) equal status. I don't know what to make of the religious overtones either. One thing is for certain, I do not relish the struggle and frustration that my trainers paint as inevitable. That being said, this cannot weaken my stamina or resolve.

The men of our group were also warned against making eye contact with Tunisian females of a certain age. In defense of the trainers (who have my gratitude for their best intentions for us), it is highly unlikely that the last-minute information dump aptly prepared us for what lay ahead anyway. Truth is, pre-departure we were like amped-up teenagers in an emotional tempest—not the most receptive state of being. Information at that juncture was pointless. On the cusp of my magnificent adventure I absorbed impressions only. Except there are a few troublesome considerations, like the small matter of living in the crosshairs of leering men under conditions which make me the perfect target; and the suggestion that most of my energy will be expended negotiating this. I should expect also to get knocked down a peg or two on a fairly regular basis. These things linger but do not dissuade. Another universal suggestion from our trainers: learn the language. Learn the language. Learn the language. Amen. This is what I left the United States with... this and $15.00 in my pocket.

The state-side training also included the first of fifteen immunizations. I confidently presented my official immunization record to the Peace Corps nurse, positive it would render me exempt from the requisite endless poking of needles.

"Obsolete!" He gloated. I took my place in line looking ahead to those getting boosters in the arms and hips—two at a time, assembly-line style. One girl was so terrified she began to hyperventilate. Man, she's going to have to get over that. The roster of boosters ahead is long and features such goodies as the once every three months, medically necessitated, "it's for your own good so you better report for it or we'll come looking for you locked and loaded" vaccine: gamma globulin. It packs the odd sensation of peanut-butter-being shot in the hip. We're going to be shot up but good-and-regular for the next two years. Our federal government is making damn sure we are protected from all manner of disease and what not. We are an investment after all.

Now that we have arrived in Tunisia, the next three months will focus on intensive Arabic language lessons, technical training relating to our work assignments and an in-depth introduction to Islamic culture. I suppose I should be more concerned about my credentials or lack thereof: specifically, the fact that I'm not an English teacher and the fact that I don't know a lick of Arabic. Regarding the language (the key to my survival) I am eager to learn it, even one so difficult as Arabic. I don't regard my total ignorance of it at this moment as an obstacle—pretty incredible given my exasperating foray into college French, which I barely passed. One would think with a last name like Parisien and a heritage reflecting a fairly dominant strain of French Canadian, I would spew perfect flowing French. Think again. I've left my foreign language failures behind me where they belong. My mind is open. I *will* learn Arabic.

I don't know one iota about Islam either. To me, Islamic culture is my Mom's best friend Jamilla, known to us as "Tootsie," who has a copy of the Qur'an, prepares brilliant Lebanese food and peppers her speech with words like "*smallah*" and "*habibi*." She is the only Muslim I know, and religion is something that never seems to come up in conversation. I got here (recall the hoop-jumping I endured) said goodbye to everyone, including a none-too-supportive boyfriend, walked away when my family needed me most, and arrived on the African continent! How hard can Islam be? Or Arabic? Or Teaching?

"Islam is very much like Einstein's theory of relativity.
Everyone talks about it, but very few truly understand it."
Dr. Azizah Y. al-Hibri

CHAPTER 6

A day in the life of a Peace Corps trainee

Hergla

The largest palmetto bugs I have ever seen camp out in small groups on our ceiling throughout the day. The nasty things are reddish-brown, shiny and about the most horrid insect the natural world could produce. When night falls they break from their clusters, clumsily promenade across the ceiling, lose their grip and fall to the floor—or onto our sleeping bodies. Plunk! Screams erupt in the dark and nervous laughter echoes throughout this cavernous concrete house as North Africa's creatures acquaint themselves with the Yanks. "No-see-ums" feast greedily in the night and incessantly buzz in my ear. My legs are a patchwork of bites that pop-up as tiny pebbles just below the skin in a delayed reaction throughout the day. They appear and disappear only to reappear again later. They itch like hell. In the dark I struggle to keep every inch of my flesh beneath the sheet, leaving only the tiniest hole around my mouth for breathing. Upon venturing to the loo in the night, I've encountered red scorpions, *Androctonus australis,* on the stairs. These lovely creatures pack a sting that is potentially lethal, especially to children and the elderly. Total embrace of all this land's inhabitants is not forthcoming.

It's time to revive a habit postponed since leaving home. I need to start running. The only practical route available is the dirt road that travels in front of Hamdullah House and heads south to nowhere, following the desert as it hugs the long edge of the sea. Outside the realm of physical education for school girls, females do *not* jog here. Period. So I opt not to cruise through town as it is best to avoid becoming more of a spectacle than I already am.

It is 6:00 a.m. The bright orange orb of the sun is just beginning its ascent. With each step a puff of dust springs forth from the dry earth. Not yet stifling outside, I feel at peace until I notice the pack of mangy growling dogs closely observing my every stride. One scruffy dog in particular is especially aggressive. Moving gradually in my direction, he growls menacingly, bearing his teeth, provoking confrontation. I grab two large rocks, turn off my headphones and stop to meet the oncoming attack. It never comes, but those shithead dogs make for an anxious outing. No wonder people don't run here.

• • •

Our training begins today in earnest. We have commandeered the local school which is closed to the regulars for the summer. Spread out all over school's courtyard, each with a desk and a blackboard, we have been assigned into small groups. There are three students per teacher—an excellent ratio. My group meets near the garden, right next to the largest geranium bush that I have ever seen. We begin in the cool of the shade. By noon the sun beats down on our notebooks, making them uncomfortably hot to handle and us, well, equally warmish. The bulk of our efforts, up to seven hours a day, will be focused on learning Tunisian Arabic. Have I mentioned how critical this is? Given that outside of the classroom my encounters in English will be few, proficiency in the local dialect is fundamental. Beyond necessity, Arabic, I'm beginning to understand, is more than a medium of conversation; it is an object of worship, an almost metaphysical force that draws man closer to God. Will God hear me better if I pray in Arabic? For now it is best to concentrate on the language for my survival. Communing blissfully with God may perhaps come later.

Our teachers are Tunisian nationals most of whom are veterans of Peace Corps training. They will be our lifeline. We will be rotated among them throughout the training in order to become acquainted with their divergent accents. I believe however that I have already met *my* teacher. His name is Hichem. In Arabic his name means shy one. He has an infectious giggle and a smile that spreads from his face to his whole body and yes, there is shyness, too. He shares the deep eyes and dark complexion of most Tunisian men as well as the very heavy mustache. He is sweet and affable. Most significant to me is the fact that he is also abundantly patient and exceedingly tolerant with everyone around him. It's clear he's invested in our learning. Under his temperate guidance I am sure to catch on. I can't even remember the names of my French teachers…

Ten weeks is a precious short time in which to gain a level of proficiency in one of the world's most challenging languages. I've already mentioned my failure to learn my father's tongue, a romance language read from left to right, written in the Latin alphabet, whose sounds and shapes are familiar to speakers of English. Arabic is an entirely different animal with an alphabet that appears more artsy than functional, whose sounds are altogether unpronounceable and whose orientation is opposite and therefore seemingly unnatural—it is read from right to left. I am happy to discover there is some logic to the language. Unlike English, if you learn the Arabic alphabet you can spell pretty much anything phonetically. Consonants are written first and vowel identifiers are placed into the word. After three solid hours I know three things: *yibni, wi:n* and *ana:na:s*...the words for "he builds," "where" and "pineapple." Let's see...three words in three hours. Clearly this is going to be a grueling process.

In the afternoon, halfway through the alphabet I reach the point of saturation. I simply cannot not absorb another shape. I immediately direct my frustration at Hichem, whose English I suddenly decide is poor (not true...as though it is his fault I am overloaded). I shut down and behave badly. Only the brain dead, the monolingual brain dead, would be so childish in the face of this kind and patient man who speaks four languages fluently. I am an idiot.

Complete Immersion (the methodology under which I am learning) requires that English not be used in the teaching process, which makes any issue I have with my instructor's English moot. This means for the next ten weeks Tunisian Arabic will be the sole language of instruction, every day, all day long. How does one teach a word like "idea" if it cannot be translated into the language the learner speaks? I've heard "immersion" described as "being thrown in the ocean to learn how to swim." If I don't watch my *bratitude*, there won't be a teacher willing to throw me a lifeline.

It is late in the afternoon, just prior to the close of our review session. I am blank. I am toast. Not Hichem (with that huge smile of his).

"*Hayya* Lora." Let's go. Encouraging me with words like *b:ahi:*, which means "good" and my new favorite *biligeda*, which is an even cooler way to say "good." But toast is toast. I'm a little frustrated. It is way too early for me to be experiencing failure. Deflated and with a pissy attitude, I carry my mood right into dinner.

Speaking of which, I love the food here…perhaps too much. I don't know if you can really call the place where we dine a restaurant. It is just a large room with a few long tables in it, around which classroom-style chairs are placed. There really are no other furnishings or adornments. We call it "the restaurant" and it is where we meet for our meals and have the occasional meeting. Bread is served at every meal. Now there's a word everyone got right away: *xubz*, a word that starts with a throat-clearing and ends with a bzzzzz. Bread. This is not just any bread, but the crusty on the outside, warm and soft on the inside, can't stop eating it for the life of me kind of bread. It arrives at the table, several loaves at a time as if magically. It is our utensil for scooping and sopping and shoveling food. *Xubz* is a sacred addition to the meal. It is never wasted and never thrown away. Leftover pieces are placed outside on the walls that surround the restaurant and on the walls of traditional *dar arby*, Tunisian homes. I haven't figured out what happens to it once it goes on the wall. Maybe those mangy dogs and the random cats, which seem to be everywhere and belong to no one, survive on the leftovers.

I've also been introduced to Tunisia's signature meal: couscous. It is a mountain of tiny granules, made with olive oil and garlicky tomato sauce over which mysterious hunks of meat and vegetables are piled. Tunisia is *no* place for a vegetarian. In an effort to appear absolutely flexible and positively willing to experience the unusual, I outright lied during my interview when asked about my comfort with all things edible. "No issues here." A bold-face lie. I stopped eating meat four years ago out of a desire to be the master of my destiny, but mainly because I just don't enjoy its taste or texture. As in many places in the world, food in Tunisia is the vehicle for hospitality. To reject that which has been hard won, lovingly prepared and generously offered is an insult. I haven't quite figured out how I will negotiate my vegetarianism here.

It bears mentioning that Tunisian food is very spicy; as in burn your innards spicy. Mercifully, the training staff has instructed the cooks to slowly increase the heat as a way of helping us to assimilate. *Harrissa*, a fiery-hot paste made of hot peppers, olive oil, and garlic, is incorporated into almost all of the main dishes. For now it is served separately in little bowls into which those who dare dip bread. Meals turn into contests to see who can ingest the largest dollop. Eventually, harrissa will begin to show up in our food little by little, until we are able to eat without our heads blowing up.

· · ·

The vast Sahara desert is on my doorstep. The Sahara! I couldn't conceive of it until I saw the red billowing wall approaching from the south. It was a sandstorm referred to locally as a *qibli*, otherwise known as a Sirocco wind. A *qibli* can reach hurricane speeds, bringing with it immense amounts of sand. I saw it before I felt it. It was the color of rust. It filled the entire sky. Soon hot winds began whipping my skin in advance of the looming wall. We knew enough to hunker down back at *Hamdullah* House while it deposited a layer of sand over the whole of Hergla. The wind in his hot fury scooped up the Sahara, enmeshed her in his tempest and scattered her throughout. The vast Sahara is now literally on my doorstep and everywhere in between.

The heat is inescapable: over one hundred degrees Fahrenheit (roughly thirty-eight degrees Celsius—there's another conversion I am going to have to make). As a summer girl who loves peak temperatures and the shunning of footwear, I am surprisingly affected by this sweltering, stifling, stink-producing hot. It zaps my energy and requires constant rehydration, not to mention a reevaluation of wardrobe. I never feel clean. My hair stays wet. My inclination is to wear less, not more. The observance of modesty requires that I wear body-concealing clothes: ankle-grazing skirts, loose-fitting, non-revealing tops. As smothered as I feel, I can't help but pity the Tunisian women draped head to toe. Wretched heat.

• • •

Time to admit something...I've become a bit distracted. I didn't join Peace Corps to hook up with someone, especially right out of the gate. Thus, I am genuinely bothered that Sam (the very first trainee I met that very first day of our orientation) has invaded my head. We were the first to arrive in Philadelphia. He showed up with a steamer trunk featuring Goofy and Mickey Mouse, travel gear more befitting a toddler, not an explorer.

"Hey there." He said as he approached me. Green eyed...fresh faced...lavender Polo shirt...jeans...construction boots...a tiny gold loop in his ear and a sweet face bearing an expression—part Boy Scout, part Indiana Jones—that was just a wee bit too eager. I recognized in him immediately a kindred spirit.

"Peace Corps?" I asked.

"Eeyup. You too?" I remember thinking, "my goodness, I hope they're all this yummy!" Sam and I spend our spare time together, studying mostly. I have no business diverting my focus, especially in an atmosphere that doesn't remotely lend itself to romance. I feel a little possessed, a bit out of control, adolescent. How disappointing to allow such a distraction in the first place. Best to get back to the business of becoming a volunteer.

· · ·

It is Saturday, a day off from being spoon-fed Arabic by the steady hands of my patient teachers while confined to a seat, withering in heat that reaches incendiary far too early. At four weeks into our training, we have learned just enough Arabic to be dangerous, possibly to ourselves. So what to do with this first taste of freedom? Oh wouldn't it be fun to take the training wheels off just to see what will happen? To test what smattering of skills we think we have thus far acquired, test them outside of Hergla, outside this tiny hamlet that holds us safe and minimizes our opportunities for failure (or getting lost). Outside in the *real* world? Four of us weigh the option of going to the city of Sousse, a bustling city a short taxi ride away. Strength in numbers assures, mostly, that at least one of us will have a general clue when we get there.

The adventure begins when we try to hail a taxi. One must be very aggressive if one wants to get anywhere. Our trainers told us that no matter what the driver asks for, give him 550 millemes upon arrival (that's about fifty cents for a twenty kilometer trip) and exit the taxi immediately, which we do though it has a distinctive "dine & dash" feel to it. When we arrive in Sousse, it isn't long before we realize not one of us thought to bring a map or the emergency phone numbers we were ardently warned to carry with us at all times, potentially helpful given that we've landed in the third largest city in the country.

Sousse was once a Phoenician port in the ninth century B.C., but is now a summer gathering place crawling with European tourists. It is one of the oldest and longest functioning ports on the Mediterranean. The first thing I notice is the fortress whose simple yet imposing sandstone walls and turrets enclose an ancient city and clearly anchors Sousse—no matter what it is today—rather visibly in the past. Our taxi drops us at the main entrance: "*Place des Martyrs.*" The driver gestures in the direction of the way inside the walls. The entrance is named for those who died when the Allies dropped a bomb on the wall during World War II. This section of wall has not been rebuilt—there will always be a gaping hole here.

Before things become too serious, we discover that we don't need a map to locate a watering hole. It's interesting how the prohibition of a perceived want has a way of honing the senses. Hergla is a dry town. The presence of Islam altogether discourages the consumption of alcohol under any circumstances. Sousse, a city of roughly 150,000, is an exception. International tourists are drawn to this Mediterranean hotspot, lured by the relaxing of Islam's grip and loaded with the kind of obnoxiously huge hotels that cater to them. Once inside the doors of these monstrosities, any observance of cultural norms goes right out the very elaborate Moorish window.

Ancient and modern, holy and unholy, Sousse is successful because it is resilient and considerably flexible. The cocktail lounges may be occupied, but inside the fortress walls is where the real center of Sousse's business and busy-ness dwells. In addition to the two dozen mosques and a litany of historical monuments wtihin, there are the *souqs*. *Souqs* are the traditional market places of the Middle

East where shopping and trading have prospered for millennia. The shopkeepers and craftsmen have had hundreds of years to hone their tactics—they are decidedly aggressive. More than once I am entrapped in tiny shops by no less than three men eager to sell me anything; anything at all. They seize me by the crook of my arm, wave trinkets in my face, bar exit—they hold me hostage! With stipend in hand I relent...I blow my tiny allowance on a pair of flip flops to give my toes, yearning to breathe free, a little respite from the oppressive heat. Two in our foursome buy *darboukas*, authentic hourglass-shaped Tunisian drums. They play them in the cab all the way back to Hergla, while our driver beats rhythmically on the dash. The highlight of my day is a marriage proposal that comes from a man wearing a silky track suit: "I just love the "Amedikan gulls" my prospective husband tells me. Our day of freedom was a resounding success.

CHAPTER 7

A vegetarian and a sheep on borrowed time

An unmistakable "baaaa" manages to abruptly curtail my dream state. In these first few moments I am not sure where I am. I am unaccustomed to waking to the sounds of farm animals. I recognize my foam mat, my sleeping roommates. I remember I am in *Hamdullah* House, in Hergla, in North Africa. I follow the noise out to the balcony. I follow it until I find it tied up in the yard behind Hamdullah House. The family that owns this house lives on the lower level. They lease the rest of the house to us. Usually they ignore us. Not today. They catch me peeking out over the balcony and motion for me to join them. Excited at the prospect of furthering my cultural education, I grab my camera and take the steps down two at a time.

Eid al-Adha, the Festival of Sacrifice, has arrived. To Muslims, *Eid* is Christmas, Easter and Thanksgiving all rolled into one. In other words, it is a celebration of enormous import. The holiday commemorates the end of the *Hajj*, when faithful Muslims make the annual pilgrimage to the holiest of all cities Mecca and a time when millions of sheep meet their untimely demise.

I have brought with me a translation of Islam's irrefutable holy book, the Qur'an. In Arabic, Qur'an means "the recital." The recital is the very voice of God speaking directly in the first person, making Himself known and laying down the law. Mohammed, whose name means "highly praised," arrived in the world around 570 A.D. He was a caravan trader, a man of integrity, a man of compassion, a ready soul and he was the one to whom God chose to reveal Himself. He was God's final prophet. Beginning in 610 A.D., 77,934 eloquent, masterfully-woven Classical Arabic words were delivered directly from God to Mohammed—God's final revelation to humanity revealed to this one man. This revelation became the Qur'an, embraced today by over one billion Muslims who live its core tenets—that's one in five people on earth. Mohammed remains the most revered example of pure Islam.

The importance of this holy book in the life of a Muslim cannot be overstated. The language within it is believed to be perfect and often it is memorized in huge portions. All the answers one needs in all areas of life are contained within. Answers to questions like who is God? How should we pray to God? How should we conduct ourselves in our lives? How should we treat others? What are the rules? The Qur'an answers all these questions, *every* question—explicitly. It is more than doctrine, it is a clear prescription for living that, as religious scholar Huston Smith explains, "joins faith and politics, religion and society, inseparably."

I am going to attempt to read through my entire Qur'an (imperfect because it is a translation). I have never even read a bible cover to cover, but growing up I was fed a steady dose of its parables, stories from history and teachings from the Old and New Testaments, texts that pre-date the arrival of Islam's book. I scan my copy and happen upon several passages that resonate, passages whose chief sticking point is that I must not deny these words from God. Plus, it's made pretty clear that I cannot use the excuse that I am a Catholic because my father is Catholic, his father was Catholic and so on; that I believe what I do because it is also my father's belief. Why? Because God has had it put to paper—information, new, clear, direct—information which trumps all that came before it. It would be illogical to not take into account this new information…and considering the source, do I really have a choice? I will read my Qur'an for my education. Or is it…for my salvation?

In keeping with the Qur'an's instructions regarding the proper way to commemorate *Eid Al-Adha*, the devout slay a sheep in an act that symbolizes Ibraham's (a.k.a. Abraham's) willingness to sacrifice his son, as God commanded. To further venerate Ibraham's obedience, one third of the meat must be given to the poor; one third must be given as gifts; and the remaining third feeds the family. The fluffy alarm clock tied up in the yard is living on borrowed time.

Urban Americans—myself among them—are fairly divorced from the processes that bring food to our tables. We are not habituated to the befriending of animals and then eating them. So what transpires next is indeed a strange experience for me, the vegetarian. The family asks me to photograph them posing with the sheep. I snap away as they change positions, move the sheep to and fro, front and center. The children (the smallest no older than two) take turns petting the animal and taking their places in the pictures. The father even offers to snap a few of me with the animal. Next they light some incense and then summarily slit the sheep's throat releasing an eerie rush of wind. I watch as the blood pools on the cement and then as air is blown into a small hole in the hind quarter, bloating the body and separating the fur from the musculature. Next they cut off the hooves and head, peel back the skin and hang the carcass from a ladder. They pull out the innards and butcher him.

I feel a little queasy having never once seen an animal killed before my eyes. I turn my attention to the children. The smallest standing front and center watches unaffected. When I was their age, I couldn't tolerate being anywhere near my Mom when she prepared chicken from pre-packaged cuts of poultry purchased the grocery store. For some reason, I am able to bear the drama of a life ending before me. Is it the ritual? Is it the holy sacrifice? I'll never forget the whoosh of blood draining from one well-placed cut. Or the body flailing wildly in its last moments. Or me, standing there watching.

CHAPTER 8

July 1989

"Staj"

Allah's 99 names

Our language training continues. Out of necessity, I have developed my own phonetic system to help me with pronunciation. It makes words with throat clearing consonants, like *alaxatir* (which means because) more manageable. I am enjoying the challenge and my enthusiasm, which was temporarily dampened because of the difficulty of the language, is now at an all-time high. Our days are carefully apportioned between language, culture, study and meetings. My roommate, Deadhead goddess from New York, has fallen in love with Hichem. I think it was the ninth or tenth day of classes when she bubbly confessed to me that she was convinced they shared a vibe. I thought she was imagining it. Hichem is sweet to absolutely everyone, but what do I know about fate and its plans for them?

The idea that the female trainees should altogether ignore Tunisian men is pervasive (with the possible exception of the aforementioned roommate who is cautiously conducting her romance on the sly). As a result, we've learned that our male host country nationals—at least those who reside in this tiny village—think we are rude. Duh. I have difficulty accepting that all Tunisian men are a threat and that they have a singular motive: sexual liaison. There's got to be more to this. Perhaps naively I have ignored the warnings and have been reserved, though openly friendly. As a result, there are several of the male persuasion who know me by name and will say hello. My counterparts are not comfortable with this. I detect (unwarranted) fear on their part. I am after all, a product of Detroit and my street sense tells me that maintaining such a high level of defense is nonsense. I'm not being reckless—I just don't want to disappear.

We have started the technical portion of our training. Within our group there are a number of specialties: large and small animal husbandry, agricultural extension, bee keeping, deaf education, special education, university and secondary English (including my area, TEFL, teaching English as a foreign language)—a whole range of disciplines whose imparting are meant to advance the capacities of our hosts. Our training is focused on adapting our skills to the local context. One does not waltz in here and "do as you do in America," so we've been told. Our initial meetings clarify one thing only: I'm in trouble because as I have mentioned, I do not know how to teach in America (which negates the necessity of translating my skills to the Tunisian classroom). I am untested, unproven, unqualified and this weighs heavily on my mind.

Perhaps it is prudent to mention how I was eligible for Peace Corps in the first place, given that possessing a skill is a minimum prerequisite. I graduated from a middle-of-the-pack university with a degree in Journalism and English. At one point I thought I might actually become a teacher. That brainchild evaporated after I spent a semester in a classroom with a bunch of eighth graders. Somehow that brief experience, coupled with my degree (and the fact that I was a ruthless résumé builder in college) put me in the category of teacher and ultimately qualified me for Peace Corps. Teaching, gathering acorns, darning socks; I would have agreed to just about any job if it got me in. So it is with some level of trepidation that I begin this segment of my training. An open mind does not a qualified teacher make.

Last night I took a walk solo, down to an area of the beach the trainees have laid claim to, American Beach we call it. It's well on the outskirts of Hergla, a secluded spot where we can find some measure of discretion. Parading around in bathing suits is not the province of Muslims, especially women, and we have enough attention already. On the few days not dominated by Arabic classes, we gather there to swim in the Mediterranean. I have been stung twice by jellyfish I never saw coming. Both times I thought I was being electrocuted. Now when go swimming, I make sure to swim with a group to diminish my odds of getting zapped.

It was just before ten when I picked my spot and plopped down in the sand so I could gather my thoughts. The moon was full, low over the water and cast a glow that cut a path right to my feet. It was at once reminiscent of that night at Jefferson Beach and of the need to avow decisions. I stayed at the shore's edge for a long time crafting poetry in my mind. Such is the influence of nature with its capacity to inspire. I don't know how long I lingered there, mingling words, hours maybe. Finally, when I turned my eyes toward Hamdullah House, all of the mystical thoughts that roamed freely in my head vanished. What was left was me, reinvigorated and supremely at peace with where I am right now. I am digging in while others are leaving, in rapid succession. At this point six trainees have quit, packed their bags and high-tailed it back to America. The real Peace Corps, not the stuff of fantasy, is not for everyone.

. . .

I turned twenty-three today. I was loitering on our balcony, taking in every hue of blue before me when I heard, "birthday girl... come down here." I was greeted on the porch by two fellow trainees, Sam and Kent. They presented me with a birthday cake, bearing the signature doughnut shape of many things baked here. Household ovens do not exist. So the Palestinian oven, which isn't an oven at all, is a desirable option. It resembles a Bundt pan with a lid and a handy little flame thrower that sets underneath as it cooks. My birthday cake—more cornbread than cake—was laced with a sugary drippy frosting of unknown origin. The fact that the candle could not quite gain footing in the cake hardly mattered. Joy colors everything delicious. As late evening fell, Sam and I went to American Beach drawn by the voluptuous moon, deep orange, hovering low in a black sky. Sam and I...I hesitate to define it. Our conservative surroundings have fostered an intense yet innocent closeness. Fingertip to fingertip, touch has never been more powerful. Tonight on the beach, under the harvest moon he kissed me, just once. The war of wills is over. I surrender. The day was perfect, though it passed without receipt of a birthday card from home.

Sand

Sits in the corner of my room,
where last night
I disrobed.
Crystals
in free fall
came to rest
about my feet...
for a time.
Swept unto themselves
in the fullness of the moon.
Clinging...
Lingering...
Silica skin.
Such things are fleeting.
Sand in my hair,
in my mouth,
pooled in the corner.
In time
a breeze may lift
or careless feet scatter...
free it
from hands that couldn't possibly keep it.

• • •

As part of our indoctrination, after learning just a smattering of Arabic, we've been informed that we will be making journeys to visit second-year volunteers at their sites. I've been placed in a group of five whose destination is Beja, a city two hours west of Tunis and east of the Algerian border. With a handmade map, a few dinars and a backpack, we catch a bus to Sousse (you have to go south to go north). In Sousse, we take a train to Tunis and another to Beja. It is my first opportunity to experience how a typical volunteer lives. Heather, the second year volunteer who agreed to host us without ever having met us, resides in a traditional *dar arby*. Hers lies within the medina, the oldest section of the city. The *dar arby* is an enclosed structure hidden behind high walls. The entry gate gives way to an open-air courtyard around which any number of rooms are situated. Heather's home is very small. She has two enclosed rooms, plus a tiny closet of a kitchen and a separate little enclosure in which dwells her Turkish toilet. As enamored as we are with Heather's unique home, the toilet takes center stage as none of us has prior experience with one. There are two footprints stamped on a cement slab with a hole betwixt. The idea is to squat, aim and hope for the best. Gotta say I am thankful for the wall, which has steadied-my-stance more than once. Yet another skill I will need to master, lest I spend two years soiling shoes. There is an upside, I fancy how sturdy and potentially strapping my quadriceps will become. To "flush" the toilet, a bucket of water is tossed into the hole to wash away its contents. Where they go, I am uncertain. The slight human stink that floats about appears to be universal, given the plumbing. That and the existence of open trash heaps.

Another comment on the trash. It seems plastic bags are a commodity here. When we place our trash in front of Hamdullah House in Hergla, it gets dumped in the street and the bag is confiscated. Things discarded get scattered, get picked through, or can fall into the wrong hands. A few days ago, one of the trainees produced a spent packet of birth control pills during dinner. Apparently, she acquired it from some boys on the street. They had been playing with it. Since the item in question had a name on it, ownership was not in doubt. The placebo pills, which were in the packet when it was discarded, were missing.

To my delight, the aroma of baking brownies reaches my nose and for a moment I am home in Mom's kitchen, with its dark cabinets, red countertops and sunlight filtering thru cafe curtains. In an instant, thousands of miles are subtracted. The soothing sweet scent of chocolate. Ecstasy. Until the braying of a donkey tethered somewhere not too distant snaps me back. I turn my attention to Heather. She is what I hope to become, content, self-reliant and adapted. With the bulk of my training yet to be completed, I am beginning to get rather eager in earnest. I envision my own quaint little Tunisian *dar arby*, cooking comfort food in a Palestinian oven in my little closet of kitchen, with my very own four-inch foam slab for a bed, and yes, my own set of cement footprints. This first foray out is proving motivational.

By some stroke of synchronicity, while I am camped out here in the north with Heather, Sam is at the bottom end of the country in Tozeur visiting Drew, Heather's beau. Turns out, romances are popping up everywhere.

I go to sleep in the open courtyard under the stars. I lay atop a blanket, a densely constructed and heavily weighted expanse of wool. The blanket belongs to Heather. It was expertly woven for her over many weeks by one of her neighbors. For her work, Heather paid her 45 TD (Tunisian dinars; dinars are roughly equivalent to U.S. currency). That sum will help feed the neighbor's large family for some time to come. And Heather has a blanket that will survive us all. I spend my evening sometimes in, mostly out of my sleeping bag. I am restless. At 4:00 a.m., the silence is shattered by the call to prayer bellowing from speakers perched high in the mosque's minaret. It is so ridiculously loud I burst out laughing. Good morning faithful! The houseflies that swarm about me shortly thereafter are not enough to dampen my enthusiasm. I love Beja.

The highlight of our sojourn to Beja is a tour of Bulla Regia, led by Charlie. Charlie is an unassuming elderly American man who lives a very Spartan existence, alone in a very ancient dwelling in the Tunis medina. He spends his days sketching life-sized mosaics in painstaking detail on huge rolls of paper. He is creating a vast historical record of Tunisia's partially excavated treasures. Though he is an aging man, bent, increasingly fragile, he is tireless in his dedication to amassing his library before he passes. How lucky we are to have him guide us today.

Roman ruins can be found all over North Africa. Tunisia is home to some of the least well known and partially excavated sites anywhere. In fact, we have the run of the place—there are no other visitors, which seems odd considering the sheer magnitude and historical import of Bulla Regia. Bulla Regia was an ancient Roman city whose Berber origins pre-date the fourth century. One overarching reason people are absent of the site is the blistering heat. Bulla Regia resides in one of the hottest regions in the north, or anywhere, as far as I am concerned. To escape oppressive temperatures, ancient residents engineered lavish subterranean villas, architecture altogether unique throughout the Roman empire. While at first glance I can't comprehend why anyone would want to dwell in this sun-battered dreary landscape, I clearly understand the need to find shelter from the relentless midday sun. My feet are on fire, despite the newly acquired flip flops. I am well past perspiring—I am steeping. I am so parched my tongue might drop out of my mouth and burst into a puff of dust when it hits the waterless earth. My kingdom, this kingdom, any kingdom for anything that will quench my crushing thirst and pacify my dehydrated body. The struggle to assimilate to Tunisia's heat is ongoing. I really should have been better prepared. But, this is my first Roman ruin. We tour the amphitheater and public baths, but most impressive to me are the intact mosaics, whose true brilliance is revealed when precious water is poured out onto them to clear away the dust and reveal their mastery. Berbers, Romans, Carthaginians and Numidians walked here before us. What a baby America is.

· · ·

Back in Hergla, my work load has increased exponentially of late. I find that I have to budget my time as carefully as I did the semester I took twenty-one credits, worked two jobs and obligated myself into oblivion. Beyond the load, I am undergoing some conflict of interest—same old shit. Do I have any business instigating a romance? Getting entangled? I worked so hard to get here, persisting through an application process that was longer than most. For reasons that have previously been described as indescribable, intuition told me that I needed to pursue my Peace Corps dream, regardless of any obstacles or entrenchments of home. At long last, I find myself living in the present—I am finally here! I celebrate this. But, there are distractions that bubble up, including the fact that I have received not one letter from home. Miss Independent—right. Tired of waiting, I walk over to the PTT (the post office) at 7:00 a.m. to call home. At 7:30 the call is placed for me by the operator. For over an hour I anxiously stare her down, waiting to be waved over, as if she has total control over international communications. Finally, she motions. I sprint from my seat but am told that the line is occupied. I'm not certain what this call would have accomplished, but I had wagered on it, staked my confidence on it. Now, I feel my self-reliance wavering. Damned emotions are muddying-up the place.

Out of a desire to manage these emotions, I still get up early nearly every morning to go running. This morning, as I do each time I go out to run, I am locked and loaded: I carry large rocks at all times. The pack of dogs always about on the fringes of the village has begun to get ever closer and more threatening. One in particular, a white mangy thing, seems to want to confront me. This morning as I near the point of my turnaround, he is standing in the middle of the road, waiting. I stop in my tracks. He is up on his haunches, lips curling, teeth bared. He growls viciously with intent. Then all of a sudden he begins racing in my direction, kicking up dust and rapidly gaining speed. I have just enough time to wind up and hurl the largest of my rocks in his direction. It hits him squarely in the head and he drops…dead. I can't believe it. I was always the very last person picked for teams in gym class. Always. Amazing what pure fear will do to inspire accuracy. I look for the pack, certain they will be next to pounce. They are gone.

CHAPTER 9

August 1989

I work for Who, exactly?

The minaret of Hamouda Pasha Mosque, Tunis

The TEFL trainees have been spirited away to Tunis to welcome five additional trainees to our program and to attend meetings. We call them the "China Five." They were about to inaugurate Peace Corps' entry into China when Tiananmen Square erupted and the government cracked-down on the peaceful gathered there. The Peace Corps program there is indefinitely on hold, another tragedy of these historical events. Martial Law (or their government's version of it) has been declared in China for over two-and-a-half months now. The protests and the unforgettable images, (particularly of one man standing before a tank) have galvanized international support;

millions within and beyond China's borders hope for a more democratic government—for the many citizens who put their lives before safety in the name of securing their voice. The protest has become a silent one while the government hunts down some of the very student leaders that the China Five might have taught. It makes us feel helpless.

Peace Corps Tunisia's Assistant Country Director invites us to his home for a welcome dinner feast. How strange to drink Coke out of a can, to be served hot dogs with ketchup and mustard. Even more strange, me the vegetarian considers eating a hot dog. Clearly this flirt with "home" manifests a craving for it, such as it is.

We visit the Institute Superieur de Langues Vivantes, also known as the Bourguiba School, in Tunis, where three of us will be placed (we do not know which three). The desire for English is growing and the demand for the American accent is particularly difficult to meet. The administrators who welcome us are especially friendly. Regardless of my assignment, I am expected to teach three hours a day, which is considered full-time. Three hours? One of the China Five has a Ph.D. He will be required to teach just one hour a day! As professors (did I hear that right—me, a professor?) we can take language courses at the university for free. We can choose to study either Arabic or French. Peace Corps offers free individual tutoring in Arabic for as long as we wish. I've no obstacles left to Arabic competency so long as I partake of these gifts. This is all very good news. Except, of course, that the administrators think I am a professor.

Following our visit to the Institute, we are taken to the United States Information Service (USIS) office, where the propaganda portion of our tour of the capital takes place. There, people who work for the same government I do, but are charged as the official keepers of the American image in Tunisia, inform us that we must tow the partyline. As such, I am to support the stated goals of USIS and counter attempts to distort U.S. policies and actions. Huh? I am *sure* I am not qualified for this. Turns out my role as an American teacher of English is pivotal, not as it pertains to the teaching of English for the greater good, rather, as it pertains to the dissemination of proper information concerning the United States. With my one-inch-thick folder of documentation, I am now armed as a foot soldier of U.S. policy. The very first page reads: "Since for the vast majority of Tunisians the only instruction about the United States is provided by the English teachers, it is clearly in the interest of the United States Government to insure that these teachers have the training necessary to present a clear, informed view of the United States." I *am* naïve. I know I joined a government agency and agreed in principle to be an ambassador of sorts, but I never expected to be so obviously manipulated in this way.

While filling out the twelve-page Peace Corps application, I considered only momentarily the extent to which I would be an "agent" of my government should my application process be successful. Now, I am part of an aid package to a developing country, pedaling benign influence at a very low cost to the U.S. The legacy of maintaining a "positive" presence is one I must consider in earnest and support if only to countermand moments in our history when U.S. policy has failed and garnered us more enemies than friends. For this reality alone, Peace Corps is relevant. The fact that Peace Corps must be invited into a country helps me to feel that the desire for our presence here is at least mutual. In fact, the United States and Tunisia have shared a long history, one that dates back to 1779, when the two countries signed a Friendship Treaty. Since then, there has been military cooperation, and economic and technical assistance (of which we are a part). So, things have been pretty peachy between us for over two centuries, with the possible exception of the incident four years ago, when Israel bombed the PLO headquarters in Tunis. The U.S., being Israel's closest ally, was held mutually responsible (though President Reagan condemned the attack). Ahhh, but what a sticky wicket is the US/Israel connection.

Well, now that my role has been clarified for me, at least on the U.S. side of the equation, I cannot help but wonder what lies beyond Tunisia's desire to host us. These are just some of the questions I ponder as I volunteer to serve at the pleasure of my country.

At the British Consulate, we are invited to examine teaching resources and investigate the library. Our final stop on the tour includes a visit to the United States Embassy in Tunis, a fortress protected by automatic weapon-wielding Tunisians (although there are U.S. Marines about) high walls, gates and cameras behind whose bulwark one can buy Pop-Tarts, eat a burger or place calls to home, if desired. I skip the tarts and the burger and finally get in touch with Mom and Dad, who are out there facing thorny questions of their own. My attachments to home still serve to keep at least one foot on the other side of the Atlantic. I continue to worry about my parents and the mess that threatens their marriage of twenty-seven years. Their voices are reassuring. They are trying to save the relationship and neither one wants me to be concerned about their chances.

· · ·

I've started practice teaching at the Bourguiba School in Sousse. At the age of five, most Tunisian children enter school and are taught to read and write in Standard Arabic. Tunisian Arabic is learned and spoken at home. From the age of eight, students are taught French.

English is introduced at age ten. I have twenty-one students, age fourteen, who, while fluently bilingual, bear little evidence of having been exposed to English. They are beautiful, energetic, bright and to my enormous relief, appear not to notice what a complete and total neophyte I am (and, bonus, they are forgiving of my monolingual status). Lesson planning is an undertaking with which I seem to be struggling a great deal. For every hour I teach, I spend multiple hours in preparation. I am working without books, without guidance, without a clue. Every day for the three-week duration, there will be two people who sit in the back of the classroom evaluating my dog and pony show. To make matters worse, just days from now, Peace Corps Tunisia's #1 and #2 guys, plus two administrators from the Bourguiba School in Tunis, plus our English Coordinator, are going to be members of my audience.

As if I wasn't already having a jolly good time with all of this, our language exam is taking place next week. Classroom misadventures aside, even more critical is the passing of this test. I will be scored between 0 and 5. I must achieve a 1+ in order to be sworn in as a volunteer, possessing at least a limited working proficiency. Hichem bet me a bottle of Bouka (a horrible liquor made from figs) that I will get between a 3 and 4. My teacher is a most generous speculator; his offer, though, is a lose-lose bet.

CHAPTER 10

The Medina House

Entrance to 173 Rue de la Kasbah

After ten weeks of intense togetherness, our site placements were announced. We are being flung to the far reaches of the country and everywhere in betwixt. The English teachers have been assigned to one of five cities in the country, while the rest of the volunteers will be scattered as far as the oasis towns bordering the Sahara. I will be living in the largest metropolis, Tunis, and teaching at the Institute Superieur de Langues Vivantes, the Bourguiba School. In 1958 the American Cultural Center started teaching evening classes in English at what is now the Tunisia Palace. Over time, the program has grown considerably. Though it is known locally as the Bourguiba School, a name that is a throwback to an earlier time, today's students can pursue advanced degrees in language teaching, interpretation and translation.

I was hoping I would be assigned to the capital with its easy access to resources, to culture, to staples and to my Arabic teacher, Hichem! How serendipitous that Hichem should reside in Tunis, affording me continued access to my ever-patient teacher, as the process of negotiating the acquisition of the lingua franca will be an ongoing one. He will be there studying law and, lucky me, he has already agreed to continue to tutor me. Arabic fluency is crucial for my understanding, for my success. About my Arabic test, I got tripped up by the accent of one of the testers. He sounded to me as if his Arabic had a strong Texan lilt and I cracked up before and during the exam. In any case, Hichem owes me a bottle of Boukha. I think I will make him share it with me!

Finding a place to live is the responsibility of the volunteer. We were given the names of our "Host Country National" directors along with general instructions for locating them...and, just enough Arabic to make our way to our assigned sites. Each person upon arriving must conduct a search, solo, or very quickly begin the process of networking. Sound daunting? Incredibly, there isn't a soul among us who cannot wait to get out there.

Out of our group, I think I am the only one who has already secured housing. The "medina house" in Tunis has been inhabited by Peace Corps volunteers for over ten years. Kristy is its current occupant and she is in need of roommates (and dinars). She's a second-year agricultural volunteer who teaches in Tunis. Her sales pitch was so convincing, I agreed on the spot without having seen the dwelling, without knowing where it is in relation to the Bourguiba Institute, without knowing Kristy. Additionally, there is no real understanding of the economics. We'll split the rent, which should leave me half my monthly stipend. Eager rookie that I am, I have no idea whether or not 250 Tunisian dinars a month is a living wage.

At the first opportunity, Sam comes with me to inspect the medina house. We decide to hitchhike. There is something about the fusion of youth and travel that imparts such an exaggerated sense of security that one who has never before hitchhiked would, without hesitation, throw herself at the mercy of a Third World motorist. We are immediately picked up by an off-duty police officer. He scolds us repeatedly for our foolishness, then drives us ten kilometers out of his way to the train station.

It is almost midnight when we arrive in Tunis and are met by my soon-to-be housemate Kristy and her beau, my fellow trainee Tom (who already knows more about my future home than I do). The hookups between volunteers continue, as more unlikely partners link, like Kristy and Tom. I never saw that one coming. We are the stuff of romance novels; couples improbably paired, or secretly paired, fleetingly devoted, or let's just tell it like it is, codependent. Would Casablanca have been as dramatic without North Africa as its backdrop? One can never underestimate the power of place or circumstance to propel and fuel liaisons.

After a short cab ride, we are dropped at Place de la Victoire, the entrance to the medina. It is marked by *Bab el Bhar*, or the Sea Gate, an enormous archway built of stone. Tunis was once a city inside ramparts, surrounded by a moat and accessible by one of four great gates. Back then, the sea reached all the way to this entry point, *Bab el Bahar*. The sea has receded and in its place, greater Tunis grows and grows. Of the four grand gates, only two remain. The French demolished the ramparts. Today, *Bab el Bahar* serves as the boundary between old and new; each step forward takes us back in time.

Kristy guides us to one of two routes that lead directly into the ancient city. Suddenly, we are in a scene from West Side Story, darkly thematic, part gritty and menacing, part intriguingly romantic. The sound of our footsteps on the silvery-black cobbled streets ricochets against the constricted corridors. It provokes a desire to break into song and dance. This is a very old place, primeval and subterranean, saturated with both secret and memory. Somewhere in this deep, I will make my home!

Into the blackness we go. Any romantic first impressions quickly morph into altogether different ones; Gotham City comes to mind. The route in darkness feels circuitous. The diffused light of random bulbs barely illuminates my cautious footing over the uneven cobblestones. We go deeper into the labyrinth. The pathway is populated with cats picking at scraps from discarded heaps of food and garbage. Running through the center of it all is a three-inch-deep, one-foot-wide channel, part of the early public sewage system, which, not surprisingly, carries undertones of human odor. I begin to wonder where my eagerness has landed me. I look to Kristy, who guides us unwaveringly through the tangle, bearing complete indifference to our less than savory surroundings. We reach the medina house too late to get the big tour. We decide to sleep on the rooftop terrace. I meet my slumber as happy as any one person can possibly be—at the full measure of my dream.

The light of the morning does more than illuminate my surroundings, it casts out any perceptions that I might be living in Gotham City. Not me, I will be living in a UNESCO (United Nations Educational, Scientific and Cultural Organization) World Heritage Site, a place old enough, exceptional enough and cool enough to be considered a world treasure. The medina certainly qualifies as old. It's been around since medieval times...and it hasn't changed very much at that. The dense winding narrows are still filled with foot traffic, accompanied in these modern times by the random moped (and the occasional idiot driver—going where I don't know—always stuck backing out).

Built from the center outward, the very heart of the medina is the Zitouna Mosque, meaning "from the olive tree"—and all roads lead to it. Founded in 732, it is still the very hub of life. The *souqs* that encircle the mosque abut right up against the holy site so that it nearly becomes invisible except for the minaret which reaches to the sky and can be easily seen from the medina house terrace, along with a host of minarets from other mosques nearby. Only the noblest of trades are located within proximity to Zitouna, jewelers, sellers of silks, perfume and books. Tanners, blacksmiths, fruit and spice vendors, extend farther out from the holy ground.

In stark contrast to the shadowy underworld that is evening, the medina teems with life during the day. Among its features, the medina is home to over 700 monuments. There are palaces, mosques, mausoleums, *madrasas* (Qur'anic schools) and fountains. It is a center of commerce, bustling with shoppers and with vendors plying their trades. In an area that measures roughly 1,600 by 900 yards, there are also some fifteen thousand residences nearly invisible from the street into which over 100,000 people disappear every night. It is a city within a city, a sensory overload of sights, sounds, smells and non-stop activity—that is, until darkness.

The quickest way to the medina house is not the way we arrived last night. It is far easier to enter the old quarter from the west, the opposite end, at Place du Gouvernement, otherwise known as The Kasbah. The Kasbah is built on the highest geographical point in the medina. From its upper reaches, smooth cobblestones lead to a narrow corridor that descends past stately colonnades and black and white striped Moorish arches and windows adorning what was once the guest palace of the eighteenth century Husseinid Beys. The Beys were Tunisia's royalty, the local monarchs in power until as recently as three decades ago. Today the palace houses the Prime Minister's Office. My street, Rue de la Kasbah, begins a few steps beyond the Prime Minister's stark white portico, and travels past two impressively dressed and armed guards standing sentry, past the walls of various government ministries, also former mansions belonging to the upper class. The view ahead is dominated by the minaret of Hamuda Pasha Mosque. From this vantage, it appears as though the minaret sits on top of the medina house. But throughways are not straight ways and a second later the view changes dramatically—the minaret vanishes. The sky begins to disappear, replaced by bulwark looming overhead. The sky reappears. Food vendors, a man with a sewing machine, a guy fixing radios, another selling shoes, operate businesses out of *hannutes*, shops the size of closets. The commerce here is random. Foot traffic is steady.

It takes five minutes to walk from the taxi drop off at Place du Gouvernement to the medina house, recognizable by a set of double brown doors with a brass hand of Fatima door knocker (a traditional symbol of protection that is literally the shape of a hand), otherwise, easy to miss. Clearly Kristy opted for the more dramatic route through the medina when she brought me for the first time by way of *Bab al Bahar*. That long and dark journey shall be my commute to school...hmmm. Inside the doors, the way is up, two flights of marble stairs. The stairs are bordered on both sides by brightly covered hand-painted tiles. The tiles lead to home...sweet home.

I love my "new" medieval digs. There is electricity, running water *and* (I am so excited I can hardly stand it) a European toilet with a pull-chain! The kitchen is the most rustic area in the house with nothing more in it than a tiled countertop and an unusual sink. The sink is a smooth stone well, just three inches deep, with a tiny spigot that sticks out two feet up the wall. The fill in the sink is too high, so water cannot completely drain. There is a half-size refrigerator that looks as though it hasn't much life remaining. The floors throughout the house are marble tile, which will keep the house cool in summer and an icebox in winter. The walls soar to eighteen feet. The portion below the chair rail is covered with striking blue and yellow ceramic tiles running the whole length of the house, to match our stairwell. There are several very tall unscreened windows with working shutter doors (albeit missing half their teeth) providing views to the foot traffic far below, ears to the chatter of life, unfettered access to open air, and ample daylight. Every room sports the ubiquitous bare light bulb dangling from a wire. An unexpected bonus, and my favorite feature, is the roof terrace, accessed by a narrow stairway, painted cobalt blue and tucked against a wall in the kitchen, a secret pathway. Terraces are the flat roof-tops, practical spaces used for drying clothes, certain cereals and animal parts. And, of course, for sleeping on sweltering evenings. Our home, being located on highest ground, provides a spectacular 360 degree view of the whole of the medina, with its cubist architecture, awash in random angles and interpenetrating planes, structure after structure, merging into one another. The views extend to the suburbs, the Gulf of Tunis, Zitouna Mosque, and in the distance the monolith that is to be Arab League's headquarters currently under construction. This will be my space, here, at the top of everything. The breathing room.

The medina house is furnished (albeit sparsely)—a benefit of seeing so many volunteers over the years. Once I buy my four inch foam for a bed, I will have the luxury of elevating it onto a metal frame, kindly provided. Well appointed, we have all the necessities required for daily living in Tunis, including a Palestinian oven, a range of Turkish coffee makers, a mismatched collection of Tunisian ceramic ware and a selection of American fly swatters. Pretty much perfect. Except that the very tall walls are filthy to the brim and could do with smothering of paint. Plus, there will need to be a purging of a whole mess of accumulated whatnot. In my delight, I will defer consideration of the logistics required to accomplish both the painting and the purging until later. My spontaneous decision to live in the medina house was both accidental and fortuitous.

Marché Central (Central Market) is the largest in Tunisia and twenty minutes from my doorstep. It is an epicurean delight boasting a vast array of fresh food: fruits, veggies, legumes, nuts, spices, cheeses, fish of every conceivable variety and butcheries where you can select your dinner still in its living state and have it butchered before your eyes (I won't be doing that). Speaking of eyes, you can buy those too, sheep eyes, all lined up on the counter waiting to be scooped up...yummy. Acquisition of food will not be an issue.

Acquisition of other things is another matter entirely. Gastrointestinal maladies are so commonplace among trainees and volunteers that tummy talk is unfortunately a regular part of dialogue. Today it is the province of the men, Sam and Tom, our fairly constant companions at the medina house.

I remember the first time I saw Tom. He was wearing a t-shirt that had an enormous honeycomb graphic on it.

"You wouldn't happen to be a beekeeper, perchance?" I asked him.

"Very astute." He replied—clearly not a man to suffer fools. The next thing I couldn't help but notice was the massive swathe of curls encasing his head and serious eyes behind his round wire-rimmed glasses. Tom *is* a serious guy, one perpetually in deep thought, contemplating world events and big ideas. His demeanor was at first off-putting, but he has grown on me. Of great interest to me is the fact that he was a writer and a journalist stateside. As a kindred spirit, I see that his sober disposition informs his work, fuels his creativity, but also means his head is often elsewhere. Thankfully, such things are tempered with his kindness and too, such things mask deep emotions. I have to say I don't get what he sees in Kristy, who to me is a cold fish. But, who can explain the how and why of romance under these circumstances?

So, getting back to the issue of the day, our earlier exploration of the Central Market yielded one important find, *hindi*, otherwise known as Barbary fig or prickly pear, touted by our medical officer as the miracle cure for Sam and Tom's very specific ailment. We bought a bunch, sliced off the spiny skins (discarded those, ouch) chopped the fruit and fed it to our infirm.

It is afternoon in the medina house. Kristy is locked away in her room with her patient. Mine has been sacked out all day. Up on the terrace, I've been devouring David Lamb's book, *The Arabs*, unaware that our toilet paper reserves are dangerously near depletion. Suddenly, Sam appears to rally! Hindi *is* a miracle!

"Kristy wants us to go on a mission." He tells me. Thus, we are deployed, tasked with securing as many rolls as we can find. Toilet paper is available in Tunisia, but not widely used. Our search takes us all the way out of the medina, into several pharmacies, until at last we find a tiny little store that has a few precious rolls located high up on a shelf behind the counter. The store owner obtains a ladder to get the rolls down. Then, he dusts them.

CHAPTER 11

September 1989

al Hamdullah

al Hamdullah: a blessing from Michael Wilger, Peace Corps Volunteer & artist

W e have left the idyllic fishing village in our wake, returning the hamlet to the few who keep it. With our training
complete, we set our sights on matters of great import, hot baths,
air conditioning, proper beds with proper bedding, courtesy of the
Hotel National in Tunis. Eight of us depart in advance for a scheduled interview with Tunisian journalists. En route we are instructed
to represent Peace Corps as an "apolitical" organization. We are
informed that while representative of America, we are not to speak
for the American people as a whole (somewhat in conflict with earlier coaching). We all gather back in the offices of the USIS in a
room with a dozen or so journalists. Their inquiries at first are just
what is expected, not very probative, general human interest stuff...

safe: "What do you think of Tunisia?" "How will you survive without fast food?" And, "Will you attempt to blend into Tunisian culture or isolate yourselves?" But then, a question is directed at me:

"What are your qualifications and experience?" Yikes! I tell them I studied journalism and English in college. I watch eyebrows go up; go up *not* in an "ahhhh that's interesting" kind of way, but in an "ahhhh, that's suspicious kind of way." About the media here, everything—Tunisian TV, newspapers and radio—runs under the watchful eye of the government. Although Tunisia's constitution extols free speech, in theory, there isn't a whole lot of free speech that is actually allowed. The heavy hand of censorship ensures that nothing subversive, nothing remotely critical of the government reaches the masses. Speaking your mind, be it in the media or on the street, just might land you in prison.

One journalist at the front of the pack fires a second question my direction.

"Tell us what you think about Salman Rushdie's book." He is trying to provoke a debate. Mr. Rushdie is the author of *The Satanic Verses*. It is strictly banned in Tunisia because it is considered blasphemous and because it is believed that the book mocks the Islamic faith. When it came out last year, it so offended the Muslim world that it earned the author—and everyone involved in the book including its publishers—a death sentence from none other than the late Ayatollah Ruhollah Khomeini. I keep my mouth shut; think it better to appear ignorant…think it best to not mention that a copy of the book is currently circulating among the trainees. The interview ends abruptly.

• • •

Our official Swearing-in ceremony and the conferring of the title of "volunteer," is hosted at the home of the Assistant Ambassador to the United States. Officials, dignitaries and us (numbering far fewer due to several more bailing out over the past ten weeks) swarm into the stunning villa where hors d'oeuvres and an open bar are almost too much for us to bear. It might have been prudent to withhold our access to booze a wee bit longer until after the official ceremony was completed. Prohibition breeds overconsumption: by the time we are called upon to recite the Oath of Duty, we are sufficiently marinated.

"Repeat after me, I state your name…"

"I state your name…"

Hugs. Kisses. More cocktails.

The party, sans the ambassador-types, relocates to the medina house. The entire slush fund—profits collected from all of the soda consumed during training—was entrusted to me earlier in the week so that I could gather necessities for our soiree. By necessities, I mean alcohol, primarily. Islam forbids its consumption, so purchasing it is no small matter of logistics. In the few places where it is available, it is invisible: not to be found on store shelves, or in coolers, behind counters, or high up on shelves…it is nowhere, well nowhere *inside* the store. It gets sold clandestinely out of the back of the store—though never on Fridays, the holiest day of the week. It all feels a bit like bootlegging. For those inclined to drink, along with the logistical challenges, there are considerable monetary ones. The selection is severely limited, if not outrageously pricey, on average four times the going rate at home—out of range for us, even after ten weeks of feeding our piggy bank. I blew the whole wad on Boukka. As for my recipe, I culled expertise from our seasoned volunteers who have had plenty of time to figure out how to make that crap palatable. The result: a Boukka-Kool Aid fusion featuring an enormous array of fruit, no ice...a tolerable, if not potent swill, if you will.

We gather to decompress (the Boukka helps), to celebrate, to share the waning hours of our togetherness. For when night gives way to morning, we the happy, sloppy lot, will greet our first day as Volunteers, then move forward on our own. After ten weeks of preparation, the time has come to fly solo to sites as far flung as the Island of Jerba, or a desert oasis town, or holy city, or capital. The dream begins in earnest for each of us, brimming as we are with the promise of the coming two years.

* * *

In furtherance of my celebration weekend, I depart from the weeks of cultural immersion, to return, albeit briefly, to the very heart of America...or so it seems. The American Cooperative School in Tunis, which serves Tunis's English speaking expatriate community, hosts students from over sixty countries. It is protected by armed guards who grant access to those with specific passports. Beyond the gate lies a baseball diamond, one of perhaps three in the whole of the country. This is where I spend my day. If you can ignore the presence of the military and the high perimeter fencing, you might just come to believe you've landed in America. There are hot dogs, Coke, root beer, Dr. Pepper—garbage truly—until they become absent in your life and are thus accorded an automatic upgrade. Unbeknownst to me until now, I learn that Peace Corps has an ad hoc baseball team. They are set to play a team made up of Japanese volunteers in service to Tunisia, a group not unlike us. Guess who grew up in a culture that revered baseball? Guess who didn't? It's the New York Yankees vs. the Bad News Bears: atrocious mismatch. The Japanese *athletes* spend more time on the field struggling to compose themselves than making plays. Error after error sends them into fits of laughter, from which there is no return. The laughter ripples through the Japanese team, to the American team, to the spectators. Very little in the way of actual play takes place. Peace Corps wins 28-2 and the Japanese couldn't have been happier. Never have I had so much fun watching competitive sport. After ten weeks of immersion, it is nice to come up for air—and deep belly laughter.

• • •

The weekend concludes with a day trip to Carthage in the company of Sam, Jack and Molly. Jack and Molly are married volunteers from Ohio, both in their early twenties and pretty much my most favoritest people in-country. They have been here for a year, but look and act as though they have lived here for a decade. One might even say they swagger. You know the type, laid-back, reliably cool, the ones always having the most fun. They are my optimists. It bears mentioning that there is a lot of complaining among the ranks. A fair number of volunteers endlessly grumble about their dissatisfaction with all things Tunisian and cannot or will not make a happy transition to life in this country. They make for miserable company. Jack and Molly, on the other hand, fly far above the fray, plainly on the joy ride of their lifetimes.

Molly and I connected immediately, like magnets, during the few hours she visited our training in Hergla. I am drawn in because of all the things I've mentioned and more, but particularly by her appetite for this country. "You have to come to Beja" she keeps saying. Though I have only been a volunteer for a few hours now, only just been granted full freedom. "I love Beja...I love the *souq* there... I love the people there...I love my students." On and on she gushes. Molly is savoring her moment. She is my reminder to do the same. In an environment where not everyone is rising to the occasion, I think it best to align myself with those wearing rose colored glasses, like Molly.

Just a short tram ride away from my new home in the medina is Carthage, the once magnificent ancient city. In 1835 Grenville Temple wrote in his *Excursions in the Mediterranean* "All vestiges of the splendor and magnificence of the mighty city had indeed past away...I beheld nothing more than a few scattered and shapeless masses of masonry..." I have the same reaction. I might not know much about Tunisia, but Carthage is legendary and my awareness of it preceded my arrival here. I imagined I would find something Parthenon-like. Instead of grandeur, I find randomness, a pillar here, a cornice there, concrete bodies without heads, chunks of history sprinkled against the backdrop of what is now a well-heeled Tunis suburb. It was not what I expected.

Like a lot of ancient cities that have seen better days, Pompeii and Troy come to mind, catastrophe left them ruined, then time buried them under, where they'll stay. That is, until the diligent few deem them precious enough to keep them. But, they have to find them first. Eighty-three percent of Tunisia's great ancient cities lie buried six to ten feet under. Efforts are underway to unearth them. University of Michigan students are on-site, digging. Eager young things, getting down and dirty with history (how's that for a nice little connect with home)! In 1921, a large discovery of children's remains was made here. Rumor has it that the Phoenicians, in residence 2,700 years ago, sacrificed children to their gods on a fairly regular basis. Well, if ever there was a reason to sack a place...surely this. Eventually, the Romans did, several times during what are known as the Punic Wars. Speaking of ancient wars, the Punic Wars didn't officially end until four years ago, when Rome and Carthage finally got around to signing a treaty—two thousand years *after* hostilities ended. So anyway, instead of spending our day in the past contemplating history, instead of actually observing many of its relics, we find ourselves in a coffee shop ordering up a hookah.

The smoking of *shisha*—honey-soaked tobacco—out of elaborate water pipes is a favored activity, a cherished social habit, mostly the domain of men and in touristy places, tourists. It is definitely something that needs doing at least once. This café, despite its location in one of the more swanky corridors in Tunis, is like every other, austere, furnished with spindly tables and chairs, few matching, with the requisite embossed posters on the walls. When it comes to décor, options are fairly limited. Tacky plastic flowers, a portrait of President Ben Ali and framed posters containing words only are standard.

In Islam, both God and his Prophet Mohammed may not be imaged or depicted in any way. Period! So, instead of say being able to look into the unmitigated, loving and long-suffering eyes of Jesus for example, as he looks out at us from the dramatic painting that is the Sacred Heart of Jesus (an image most Catholics know well) or seeing the him hanging on a cross (a representation that is recognizable to virtually everyone in the world), Islam has no face, no body. Islamic décor is relegated to magnificent architecture or words, either phrases from the Qur'an or one of Allah's 99 names. But not just words, exquisitely arranged Arabic Script, in sweeping shiny gold against a black velvety background. *Allah* and every variant that can be used to describe him, is everywhere, in cafes, in homes, in the post office, on dashboards in cabs. Allah is everywhere...but no one knows what he looks like.

Oh, and speaking of taboos, another Muslim author is in trouble, this time it's a Tunisian. Youssef Seddick is being denounced all the way to Kuwait for drawing a comic strip depicting the Qur'an. It was his attempt to make the holy book more accessible to young readers. But, this is a no-no. He is being called a heretic. Islam is serious business.

Our waiter brings us our hookah. It is elaborate and I'll admit, intimidating. He sets it next to the table. It stands about three feet tall, has a series of brass chambers and a cobalt blue glass base. The *shisha* is a rich brown clump sitting at the very top. Sam and I both lean in at the same time to get a closer look. There are two hoses extending from the pipe—the waiter promptly hands those past my nose to the guys (of course). He leaves and returns carrying a chunk of smoldering coal in a pair of tongs. He plants it atop the tobacco and leaves us. Jack attempts to hand his tube to me, to be polite.

"Ummmmm." I hesitate. Sam is already at it. His cheeks suck in as the smoke pulls through the water and the water rumbles in the glass chamber. Molly and I cannot contain our amusement. Watching the rapidly changing expressions on Sam's face, we burst out laughing at the same time. We spend the next hour taking long drags of sweet smoke into our lungs and listening to Jack and Molly hatch a plan to buy a boat…on a Peace Corps allowance. Then we go to the marina to find one.

CHAPTER 12

Settling into the dream

The view outside the medina house door

It occurs to me…ever have I been future-oriented, living for tomorrow, until now. I am awake. There is nowhere else I would rather be than in the fullness of this moment, actualizing a dream that has become my life. No measure of gratitude is sufficient; to "the big Guy" (Dad's reference for God), to Mom for a lifetime of nudging (she started giving me luggage when I was twelve years old), to any in my path who influenced this one. I am just so happy to be here. Contentment aside, I cannot help but wonder about my parents in the midst of their own revisionist drama. Two summers ago my sibs and I threw Dad and Mom a twenty-fifth anniversary party. We all assumed theirs was a forever marriage, that a quarter century is the kind of investment you work hard not to fuck up, that you try with great effort to fix if you do. Now that their four kids are out and about, it's just the two of them, struggling to see if what's left can be salvaged. It could go either way, as letters—particularly Dad's—reveal. I received one yesterday from him. In it he wrote "You know Boo (Dad's name for me) as I write this letter I don't really want to talk about what has transpired over the last few months. It's tough to put into a letter. Yet, if you were here, I would have a very difficult time telling you face-to-face. I need you Boo. Even from this great distance I need your love and affection."

Dad and I have always had an intensely emotional connection. It troubles me that I deserted my parents. Troubles me enough to feel a stab of guilt whenever I think of them. I abandoned Mom, though she is clearly with me. Her strength shows up in me when each day brings the unexpected, when nothing is simply done, when I stand alone—when I meet all of it, head on. She would have me nowhere else; knowing so sustains me. I remain unshakable and utterly optimistic.

Not true for everyone: we lost another volunteer this week—he ET'd, early terminated. This brings to nine the total of volunteers from our group who have bailed. One left because she couldn't endure being away from her stateside beau. Another departed (and I am speculating on this) because her religious practices sparked controversy, like the day she chopped off the head of her pet chicken, named after a trainee with whom she had conflict. I was there when she shrieked his name to the heavens and brought the cleaver down on the fowl—right in the presence of the man she disdained so much. In view of this, I think she was asked to go. Mostly, I suspect some folks are having difficulty making the adjustment to Tunisia's culture, having trouble finding ways to cope with the fact that all of our familiar cues are gone. It's not the physical challenges that make living here difficult.

Although…budgeting is proving to be a challenge. My monthly living stipend is 220 Tunisian dinars (TD) each month, out of which I pay my share of the rent, 83TD. We inherited a 77TD electricity bill from the slackers who lived here before us, as well as a 20TD water bill. Additionally, we have maintenance issues to the tune of 70TD. With 34TD left in my pocket, fiscal restraints have required us to put on hold having our heat fixed, which means there is no heat for cooking or warming the medina house. It is October and the long days of living in my perma-sweat have given way to cooler temps; my house—awash in marble and tile—is an icebox. These days, my mummy sleeping bag rarely leaves my body. In fact, I have developed the ability to walk rather efficiently in it, like an upright caterpillar.

Painting the medina house has been an exercise in setting and resetting expectations. The small wad of dinars I was issued for the purchase of move-in supplies was spent on paint, 120 TD, and the renting of the longest ladder I could find. Maneuvering it through the narrow medina streets was pure comedy. Even more hilarious, now that I've dragged this thing through the whole of the medina, up two flights of stairs and commenced to painting, I cannot come within four feet of the ceiling. So I paint as high up as I dare, leaving the last four feet dingy gray. Sam sketched a huge tree on the wall in my bedroom, to which he will eventually add color. I created flowers and grasses that grow out of the top of the tile.

Another exercise in futility is the pursuit of exercise. I have identified a space where I can run without hindrance, but it involves a twenty minute walk to the train, followed by a thirty minute ride to Sidi Olympique where there is a track. In the beginning, I had to be out the door by 5:00 am in order to beat the heat. For the public journey, I wear a skirt over sweatpants. For the run, I hide the skirt in a tree. The train is always packed on the return. I am self-conscious about my sweaty ripe body amid the masses, but it is the price I (and everyone in my proximity) must pay. As a time saver, I did once try to run inside my house. For thirty minutes, I ran from one end to the other. Just once. As a post-run treat, I buy "chicken milk" from a vendor outside my door. It is a thick blended concoction of milk, raw eggs, honey and strawberries. It is the closest thing to a milkshake that I've found, pure comfort. So, exercise challenges, my significant budget issues, any paint deficiencies and malfunctions of my dwelling notwithstanding, I love my home sweet home. I love my sweet life. Al Hamdullah—Thank God!

While I am on the subject of sweet, I should mention Sam, who is the nearest and dearest to me here. What a struggle this relationship has been, a very private struggle. We lack definition. We exist in a state of torturous limbo. Well, torture for me, limbo for him. I have to continually temper my behavior and bury all the big stuff I am feeling. And, while I believe I am experiencing a once-in-a-lifetime longing, I am mortified that I have gotten so sidetracked. Falling in love was never part of my Peace Corps dream.

CHAPTER 13

October 1989

Who will teach the teacher?

```
UNIVERSITE de Tunis
INSTITUT BOURGUIBA DES LANGUES
        VIVANTES


              ATTESTATION


      Le Directeur de l'Institut Bourguiba des Langues Vivantes
certifie que M.Mme.LORA PARISIEN
Né (e) le 7/08/1966        à Michigan  U.S.A.
de Nationalité Américaine
Exerce les fonctions de Professeur d'Anglais


      Cette attestation est délivrée à l'intéressé(e) sur sa
demande pour servir et valoir ce que de droit.
                              3- OCT. 1989
```

A departmental meeting at the Institut Bourguiba des Langues
Viviantes marks the first order of business and the commence-
ment of my teaching appointment. I am anxious to receive my
assignment. Plus, it is an opportunity for the school's three new
Peace Corps teachers to meet the entire language staff. Our supe-
riors at Peace Corps emphatically stressed the need to be punc-
tual, especially for meetings. Dutifully, we arrive fifteen minutes
early and gather ourselves around the large conference table until

the appointed hour comes…and goes. Could we have gotten our information wrong? One hour passes. We remain parked at the table, occupying ourselves with reading, letter writing and the general shuffling of paperwork. One by one, our new colleagues casually stroll in, among them some Germans, a few English, several French and a good number of Tunisians. The chatter of conversation fills the room as another half hour elapses without the appearance of the boss of the applesauce.

I can wait no longer; I have to inquire. "What time is the meeting?"

Finally, some two hours after the appointed time, the boss lady saunters in, pauses at the head of the table and, in a breathy, come-hither voice says, "Let's go and get some coffee, shall we?" On cue, the group exits en masse down two flights of stairs, out the front doors of the Institute and across the very busy Avenue de Liberté to a coffee shop. Confused, I pick up my backpack and fall in behind the group. I can feel myself becoming agitated. This is unacceptable. Unprofessional. Classes are scheduled to begin in one week and I am woefully unprepared and getting restless (plus, there is the presumption that I am an English professor, which has me a weensy bit stressed). I came here with an agenda. I need to know what levels I will be teaching. I need to know about textbooks and teaching materials. I need information. I need someone to hold my hand. NOW! But, none of these things are going to happen, because it is social hour!

I don't quite know what to do with myself; I am too uptight to make happy talk. I order a Coke. It arrives in a six-ounce, old-school glass bottle with Arabic script on the classic logo instead of English. The bottle is so worn that very little of the shiny surface remains. Because bottles are recycled over and over again, they are rustic and smooth to the touch. I sit alone, drinking, pondering the proliferation of Coca-Cola to every nook and cranny on the planet. I am antsy. My American self wants to get down to business. There is work to be done, chop chop. This "meeting" is supposed to launch my professional duties here in Tunisia and lay the groundwork for the next nine months. Instead, we waste three hours—three hours that might have been critically productive. I return home empty-handed and pissed.

This is my teachable moment. Well, it could be, if only I had the presence of mind to notice. But no, I unequivocally do not have the grace to catch myself in the midst of a critical incident because I am irrationally impatient, observably inconvenienced and I don't for the life of me understand why I am the only one who is. Sometimes I am too wrapped in my Americanness to notice the clues and cues that inform the way things work around here. If I don't get out of my own way, I will leave as ignorant as the day I arrived. From this afternoon's conundrum, I can extrapolate two things only: my notion of time is about to get an overhaul; all other perceptions will need to be on high alert.

In the U.S., time is a fixed commodity. It punctuates the day, provides structure, has clear starting and end points. It is logical and we are literally slaves to it. Not so in Tunisia, where time is fluid. To suggest a meeting time is just that, a suggestion. Tunisians, I'm learning (albeit slowly) are very comfortable with the idea that time flows easily and that they are not acutely subject to it. The real force to be reckoned with is fate. When you live in a society where speech is peppered with words like *n'shallah*, which means "God willing," the concept of time takes a back seat to the very will of God. But, that's another matter, with ramifications all its own.

• • •

Turns out, the whole point of the meeting was *meeting*. Shame on me for wanting to charge into business without first trying to relate to the people I will be working with. I was impersonal and unsocial. Plus, they probably think I am rude. Yup. That about sums me up: bad-mannered American. Way to change minds and hearts, Lora. I left the coffee shop discouraged that nothing was achieved. Because this was my singular point of view, I also missed the opportunity to connect…with anyone.

• • •

It has been a week dedicated to busywork and getting the lay of the land, both of which have been undertaken while camped out in the staff room at the Institute. I've been closely observing the comings and goings of colleagues, noticing the ease with which they move through their day, practiced, in the know. Then there's me, of so little know. I couldn't even administer the placement exam with authority. I caught a student, inches from me, cheating, twice. I mailed out reporting instructions to countless students, yet still do not have specifics on my own schedule. This morning I waited over an hour for a meeting that lasted less than five minutes. I find it difficult interacting with the department head, whose casual nature makes me want to clench my teeth, or worse, snap my fingers in her face. There is absolutely nothing that ignites any urgency around here. Clearly my deference to time is not mellowing one iota and the relationship building is still taking a back seat to my need to be productive.

• • •

Things are not going swimmingly. The language department is inefficient and disorganized, swamped by muddle. Here's what I know: I am to teach three classes, three different levels, for a grand total of twelve hours a week. Twelve hours a week! So what's the problem? There are no books. There are no teaching materials. There is no guidance in the absence of both. Adding to this vacuum, I have been designated the first-year coordinator for the department, making me solely accountable for the procurement of teaching materials. Furthermore, I've been asked to create a workbook to supplement said nonexistent text. It appears my ineffectual social graces manifested this.

Teaching has officially begun, but not without a last-minute rearranging of classes, in keeping with the organizational challenges of the Institute. Now I am teaching one "false start" first-year class, made up of students who failed their first year of English, one second-year English class, and one fourth-year. I remain overwhelmingly clueless, though I won't for the life of me admit this to anyone. I can barely manage a rollcall. With names like Abdelrazziek, Souqeina, and Dthouha, butchering my students' names does not endear me to them. Mohammad I can pronounce. Luckily, there are several of them in each of my classes. Each section has thirty-two students ranging from age eighteen to forty-five (the bulk of them older than me) mixed evenly, men to women.

For most in attendance, this is *the* single opportunity to mix with the opposite gender. Merrymaking gets underway once the amusement of rollcall has concluded and doesn't end until the bell rings. In the throes of social opportunity, most of the students are not so much interested in acquiring language as communing with the opposite sex. The department head, who has already paid my classroom several visits, offered me the most aggressive professional advice I have ever received: "Be a bitch." This, she asserts, is the only way I will be able to wrest control of my classroom. I am fairly certain being bitchy is not part of my Peace Corps mandate.

Arabic classes, also underway at the Institute, are taught at lightning speed. Most of the students, many from Europe and some from the Soviet Republic, share roughly the same level of proficiency. We are not allowed to take notes. This will be a challenge for me, as I have been completely reliant on the phonetic system I created for my learning. Our instructor insists we "listen." I need to work on listening.

It appears I have a safety problem. My schedule, which materialized hours before I was to report to my first class, requires me to work evenings. My commute to the Institute is a thirty-five-minute walk along the darkened streets of the medina, westward through the city, at an hour that finds most women safely sequestered indoors. Out of concern for my security, the director of the English department asked me to move closer to the Institute. Walking in the capital at night isn't such a problem for me, as I am accustomed to moving in a manner that does not convey frailty, a credit to my Detroit upbringing. But, as the streets give way to the shadowy and ominous labyrinth of the medina, my veneer of security evaporates. From the entry point at Avenue Habib Bourguiba, it's a fifteen-minute journey through the very heart of the maze to reach my door. I travel on nearly empty streets, vacant with the exception of the homeless, who under cover of darkness drag their dilapidated refrigerator-sized cardboard boxes from where I don't know and crawl into them for the night. There are five boxes along my route. For the first few nights I dashed past them, wide-eyed and paranoid. Then, last night

I offered *"t'spalahir,"* which means "good night," to one of the boxes. "Good night daughter" came the strong reply. Now the box people are my sentries. I am no longer afraid. I will not give up my home.

• • •

One unexpected discovery: the United States is not the center of the universe. It took leaving my country to realize I have ingested a lifetime of baldly one-sided information. Tuning in to international sources of information on my shortwave radio, reading foreign newspapers and having conversations with Europeans and Africans has wakened me to the fact that as an average American, I've been comfortable operating as if my country is the hub of the world, with no real understanding of humankind beyond the borders. The American dream is a beautiful thing, truly unique in the world. But, I have never been conscious of the fact that we are but a fraction of the planet's residents and there are a lot more of them then there are of us, with stories as compelling as my own. I am small and embarrassed, and feel even more ignorant, if that's possible.

CHAPTER 14

Tunis

Art by Paul Domick
(arrived on a letter from home)

I t is easier to move without notice at night. Daylight brings exposure. Stares, comments, a non-stop barrage of encroachment.
Though I share the hair color of 99 percent of the population, I stick
out, glaringly obvious among homogenous locals. My skin is ghostly
pale. My eyes are light. My clothes, though exceedingly modest
with skirts to the ankle and shapeless skin concealing t-shirts, are
foreign. I am a magnet for any roving eye, someone to be hissed
at, solicited, even followed. The streets I walk are saturated with
provokers. My armor is on; my stare fixed. I waver not from my
course. I snub all of them. The dissent in me grows, as does hard-

ness and resentment. The truth is I am deflated. Relentless petitions and uninvited attention chip away at my armor and along with it my good intentions. What happens if I end up hating, not loving, Tunisian nationals? I've taken to wearing headphones which do a supreme job of filtering. Though, I have to wonder about my blatant cultural insensitivity given my clear attempt to tune out the masses. My best friend sent me away with the music of the B-52's, incongruous, yet comforting. "Roam if you want to. Roam around the world. Roam if you want to, without wings, without wheels." The levity dampens the din and jumpstarts my humor. For if I don't find a way to laugh at my isolation, I might just implode.

Solicitations notwithstanding, Tunis is a great walking city abounding with infinite sights and curiosities, most of which are accessible by foot and affordable; perfect for the cash-strapped me. While there is an abundance of vehicles congesting the streets, there are massive numbers of pedestrians, quite unlike the ghost town that is the Motor City. An enormous source of joy for me is the open flower market in the center of Avenue Habib Bourguiba, where the freshest calla lilies can be had for pocket change and daily the rainbow of blossoms in stands, one after the other, greet me like the promise of spring. There is an abundance of patisseries, featuring dozens of delicacies immaculately displayed under glass. Why, I wonder, are they always more appealing to the eyes than to the taste buds? This hasn't stopped me from sampling, though. I have discovered French restaurants, a superb Syrian restaurant and a Chinese restaurant in particular where, desperate to shake up my weary palette, I sporadically blow my finite resources on authentic veggie fried rice. More affordable and practically unadorned, are the numerous "jej joints," tiny Tunisian eateries whose principle offering is rotisserie chicken and French fries served without fanfare, but always substantial, for about a buck. And of course, the coffee shops, per-petually crowded with men only, in chairs and tables spilled out onto the sidewalk, forcing the pedestrian to nearly step into the street to pass. Drinking coffee and tea, smoking cigarettes, smoking *shi-sha*—this is *the* national pastime for many men all over the country. With staggering unemployment, the coffee shops house the labor market, socializing, lingering and ogling women passersby. Recently in my wanderings, I spied a Tunisian man, cupping a cigarette in one hand while daintily sipping his tea from a shot glass. I noticed him because he was wearing a Detroit Red Wings hockey jersey. I'd wager an entire month's stipend that this Tunisian has no idea what a Red Wing is, or possibly even hockey.

In a city of just under one million, Tunis has an abundance of beggars, on sidewalks, perched in doorways, at entrances to mosques, on my stoop. A great many have severe deformities, missing arms and legs. I will never acquire a comfort with them. Resembling Christianity in its notion of charity, Islam requires that alms be given to the needy. The difference however, is that Islam obligates the faithful to help and to provide that help without pity. *Zakat*, char-ity, is one of the Five Pillars of Islam. The Five Pillars regulate what Muslims should do in their personal lives. The others are *Shahada*, the profession of faith as heard in the call to prayer, *Salat*, prayer five times a day, *Sawm*, fasting during the holy month of Ramadan and *Haj*, a pilgrimage at least once in a lifetime to Mecca.

Altruism and compassion are more than gifts to the needy, they are gifts to Allah. The guy on my stoop recites verses from the Qur'an—most of them do—and confers blessings at the drop of a coin. I see many of the same people every day, in their customary places. A blind man, with eyes frosty white, travels the length of the medina daily, hand extending, stick tapping, announcing holy passages as he goes. He trudges, a slow-moving monolith, as the crowd struggles to accommodate and wiggle around him. How does the guy, whose legs are missing just below the hip, manage to get to his spot on Tunis' busiest boulevard day after day? Where does he come from? Does someone drop him off? I give as often as I can, out of benevolence and yes, out of pity. Yesterday, there was a tap on my shoulder. I turned around and found myself staring into the face of a woman who had no eyes, just holes where her eyes should have been. Damn right I gave her money.

Among Tunis's offerings is the Bardo Museum, which boasts the world's largest collection of fully intact Roman mosaics and Phoenician, Christian and Arab historical collections. Resembling oriental carpets, mosaics, each one deeply significant, adorned with symbolic figures and motifs that have been used within the cultures for thousands of years, grace floors and walls, covering completely the expanse of the museum. Their geometry is precise and meticulously enshrined, one more amazing than the next. There are art galleries and, for distractions far less cerebral, the cinema. Last weekend Sam and I went to a Chinese film, dubbed into French. It featured a female Chuck Norris-type. The sound system was so poor, even the French was unintelligible. Yet, we watched the entire film and laughed hysterically throughout, though never when anyone else was. I was the only woman in the theater, not uncommon.

• • •

Letters from home today stir up painful emotions. In my melancholy, I decide to stay in bed, finding solace in a Snickers bar, a rare and pricey find. In through my barred and chicken-wired window wafts the clamor of Tunis: the constant hammering and chiseling of brass tinkers producing plates and platters for tourists, the wailing of children. Arabic voices float through the air and random mopeds whir by far below. The cacophony is disturbingly foreign, forcing my withdrawal from it, pushing me into myself, paralyzing me. I stay in my room, insulated, safe from intrusion, except for the clamor. My intellect is well aware of the fact that I control whether my days here are happy or sad ones. After three months of conjuring mostly happy ones, I am in quicksand, done struggling against the strange and unfamiliar. The exotic is no longer alluring—it is repulsive and I want to exorcise it from my awareness. Into the hollow, cutting through my pensive meditation is the clock, beckoning me back to my responsibilities. I manage a few sit-ups, cut my hair with a pair of craft scissors and dress for school. My mood morphs from depression to hostility knowing I have a meeting, an appointment to which I shall arrive promptly, for which I shall inevitably sit alone waiting for it to begin…late. The honeymoon is over.

CHAPTER 15

Weekend explorations further afield

The Genoese fort at Tabarka

This weekend is the Tunisian holiday *Eid Mouled*, which celebrates the birth of the Prophet Mohammed. In observance of the holiday, schools all over the country are closed. I take the opportunity to exit the capital.

My favorite mode of travel is louage. Owning transportation is beyond the grasp of most people. Yet, Tunisia boasts a well-developed highway system which connects to places far and beyond. The louage, a communal overland taxi, is the affordable way to go virtually anywhere, including Libya or Algeria. The taxi is usually a beat-up Peugeot station wagon. It travels back and forth to destinations all over the country, without fixed schedules or guarantees.

The louage station is not a station at all, but the designated spot in a town where people gather to wait until a vehicle bearing the name of their destination arrives (the name appears in Arabic on a small placard atop the vehicle—thus, knowing how to read Arabic is rather helpful). When a louage rolls in, it's game on, an all-out scramble to secure one of five coveted seats. It gets messy, because most of the time there are more bodies than seats. Sometimes, the scramble begins even before your car arrives. It goes like this: Stay alert. Be ready to hustle. When your louage approaches, the best strategy is often to run like hell alongside it. If you can, grab a door handle and hold on until the car comes to a complete stop. Open the door. Do not let go of the handle—it's your anchor. Jockey for position if necessary and wait (this can be trying—stay focused) for the arriving passengers to exit. As soon as there's a clearing, rush inside. Timing is everything and claiming a seat can often mean throwing (or being thrown) an elbow or hip. When all the seats are occupied, the louage turns right around and departs.

On the flip side of scrambling for a louage is waiting for one. If you are the only passenger bound for your destination, you will sit in your seat in the vehicle until four more people show up. If you are unlucky enough to be the last passenger to board, you will be relegated to the jump seat, in the third row, a terribly cramped space that sits awkwardly about six inches higher than the mid row, where your skull will graze the ceiling for the duration of your travel.

Regardless of the seat, traveling by louage means I can go whenever and wherever I want, for very few dinars. One of the drawbacks of voyage-by-louage is the likelihood that the driver and four other passengers will light up en route. If someone whips out a cigarette, he will naturally extend the courtesy to all present. Since most Tunisian men share the habit, a smoke fest almost always ensues. For some reason I cannot fathom (nor have found the gumption to ask), smoking does not automatically elicit the opening of windows. This can be tricky.

Another enjoyable facet of the experience is the entertainment: Arabic music played at such a high decibel it no longer resembles music. It is screech and clamor blasted through tiny speakers. Think nails on a chalkboard…all the way to the end of the road. My ears, unlike Tunisian ones, cannot adapt to the deficiencies of Tunisian electronics or the abuse of them. With the exception of Qur'anic recitations which get broadcasted on Fridays, most music is enjoyed this way. I'm okay with the droning of the Qur'an. It is more meditative than grating, more emotive than invasive.

Finally, driving in Tunisia can be an all out free-for-all, where lines on the road and speed limits are only suggestions and passing on the shoulder—EITHER SHOULDER—when traffic is oncoming, is common. I should also mention seatbelts and airbags are non-existent, no trappings of federally mandated safety here.

These considerations aside, I go by louage almost exclusively. It provides me with enormous mobility, the nature of which I never experienced in America. The Motor City, from whence I hail, with its glut of vehicles and almost complete absence of public transportation, is no place for someone who doesn't own wheels. It took moving to North Africa to get my first real taste of the kind of freedom that comes from being able to go at a whim. And go I do, as often as I can.

Tunis has two main louage stations, one for locations north; one for locations south. I wait for an hour in the rain at the Bab Saddoun, the north louage station, for a ride bound for Mateur, Sam's site. Sam has been assigned to a small city north of Tunis. Being relatively close, we have been able to maintain fairly regular contact. Mostly it is he who travels to Tunis. Today I am to going to him for the first time. But, I can't find a louage to Mateur. I grab one headed for the next closest city, Menzil Jamil, and make my way to Mateur from there. Remember my comment about straight ways not being thruways? It's true of many things. In a country where nothing is easily done, I am starting to relax around the idea that the way forward sometimes requires running round in circles. Eventually I will land where I need to be.

In Mateur, I haven't taken two steps out of the station when a man latches onto me and insists he escort me. In two more steps, he is inquiring of my status. I tell him I am engaged, a sure-fire way to incite disinterest. I move in what I think to be the general direction of Sam's dwelling. The stranger, unfazed, stubbornly gloms onto me. It isn't long before he begins to lob zingers at me, words that start with "z" and reference specific body parts. I am having trouble locating the landmarks Sam has drawn on his map. I forge ahead while my "guide" offers everything…except direction. Finally, I locate Sam's house and rap on his metal door, eager for sanctuary behind his walls. When his door opens, I am stunned. Sam is transformed. The all-American visage has vanished. The once youthful face of this clean-cut Midwestern boy is now covered in scruffy beard. His hair is stuffed beneath a Tunisian knit cap. His clothing is disheveled and faded. He looks like he has been toiling…for months. Suddenly I remember the interloper. He is gone. Sam slams the door shut. Within his walls, out of range of all the eyes of Mateur and the whole of the world, we hug with desperation and release, clinging as though we have been parted for an eternity, rather than just a few weeks. Maybe this intensity is due to our real affection for one another. Though I think there is something else at play here. Feelings are amplified and improbable alliances are formed in this foreign environment. We crave the familiar; we seek a kind of comfort that will provide safe refuge. When I hide in you, I forget temporarily that I am too far out of my element. Sam may be my sanctuary. Whatever it is, this moment of clinging is one of the most authentic and blissfully mutual expressions of affection I have ever shared with someone.

We spend all of ten minutes in Mateur, long enough for Sam to grab his backpack and for us to make the five minute walk to the bus station.

Here's why I try never to travel by bus. First, there are never any queues, anywhere in this country. There are only swarms, which move in one heaving mass. Buses are always overcrowded, *kif hoka sardina,* (like a sardine can) a driver once happily joked as he directed more people into the bus than I thought physically possible, a common practice. Bodies are crammed three to a seat, with more bodies standing in the aisle, on the steps at the front entrance and rear exit of the bus and seated up on the front dash perilously close to the steering wheel, sometimes with a passenger's legs straddling the gear shift. Once in a while, the doors might stay open to provide a measure of give to the crowd. Before reaching a police check point, the driver yells to the passengers to squeeze back in so that he can quickly close the doors until such a point as the police are safely in the rearview. Again, for some reason I cannot not fathom, windows stay securely shut. The oppressive heat and intense odor of too many bodies having consumed too much garlic permeates the quickly depleted oxygen and inevitably, someone throws up right on the floor, often triggering a chain reaction. And *still,* the windows stay up. My insides pitch and my head spins long after I have placed my feet on solid earth. Avoiding travel by bus is fundamental.

Today, we have no choice. We stand in the aisle near the front, which at least affords a decent view. The fertile uplands between

Mateur and Beja coil through the foothills of the Atlas Mountains, a range that extends eastward thirteen hundred miles and culminates in the snowcapped peaks of Morocco. The bus heaves and hurls through dips and turns making my knees buckle like I am skiing moguls. I begin to crave air, to wish for the return of my land legs, to need stillness. We ramble on, finally reaching Beja. Our plan is to visit Jack and Molly. They, inconveniently, are not in residence. Without benefit of telephones, it is not always possible to cement itineraries. So, minds must remain open and flexible. Rigidity guarantees perpetual frustration—for this is not a place that bends to the will. Quite the opposite. Giving in has become a way of life for me. And strangely, it extends further the freedom I have eagerly wrested here. If I cannot dress as I wish, speak as I would, or operate as I must, I will hone my gypsy skills and sate my wanderlust. Tunisia, with all of its restrictions and missed connections, is in fact blissfully free for our exploration.

We make the impromptu decision to head to Tabarka, a picturesque town located on the Mediterranean near the Algerian border. Back on the dreaded bus, the two-hour ride northwest progressively undulates, plunges and tosses us as we dig deeper into the mountains. Despite having secured a seat, I become seriously nauseous. Did I mention this intrepid traveler has a significant issue with motion sickness? Obsessively, I monitor the kilometer markers which indicate we are not making any progress: Tabarka 30 km. Breathe. Breathe. Next sign: Tabarka 30 km. Five queasy minutes later, Tabarka 30 km. What is happening! The road, spectacular in its beauty, is one huge set of switchbacks; we are endlessly trapped. I can feel myself turning green. At the very moment I am sure I will lose my lunch, we are deposited in the incredible port city. Ham-freaking-dullah!

Tabarka is distinctively festive with its European bent—everyone appears to be on vacation, which is perhaps so. *Eid Mouled* has brought them here in droves. During the summer months and holidays, Tunisians are drawn to this region because of the temperate climate. Also, the architecture is distinctive to the northwest. Red-tiled roofs pop out of the verdant mountains. The tiles, first utilized by the Romans, may have been recycled by the Andalusian Moors in the sixteenth century. Along with being tiled, the roofs are pitched, a feature unique to this region. The design was influenced by the French who took note of the fact that once in a blue moon snow falls here. In neighboring Aïn Draham, residents and shopkeepers like to talk about their snow. Everyone seems to have a copy of *the postcard*, which is essentially a photograph. It was taken ten years ago after a light dusting materialized and painted the ubiquitously green landscape white—proof, they say, that this area is some kind of tundra. Snow, they say, is testament to the region's specialness. This is the upper northwest, where snow falls on enchanted oak cork forests, where wild boar roam and where tourists come to shoot them. You won't find Tunisians hunting boar, even for sport. The consumption of any member of the swine family is strictly forbidden by Islam. But tourists don't care about local taboos. Sadly, tourists also support the harvesting of coral from the surrounding sea.

No matter where I go in Tunisia, I am reminded that its past is long and eventful. I walk through the remnants of ancient empires or societies that have risen or fallen or both, of cultures that lived and died over thousands of years…all I can do is wonder. Try as I might to feel some kind of connection to a Punic tomb, or a Roman cistern, or a Genoese fortress, I cannot conceive of the people who belonged to these artifacts, so I feel nothing. My irreverence comes from being ignorant. I chastise myself for knowing so little about the world.

After bunking in a cheap local hotel overnight, we get our first inclination to investigate the Genoese fortress that sits atop the hill overlooking the sea. The fact that it is uninhabited makes it curiously enticing. Standard modis operandai (read youthful naiveté) dictates that we explore first and (maybe) ask later. How does it go? It is easier to ask for forgiveness afterward than to ask for permission beforehand? Foolhardy? Reckless? Whatever it is, it propels us into doing before thinking and leads to things like taking taxis to the PLO headquarters in Tunis...more on that escapade later.

The fortress is not a developed tourist site. It is intended be admired from afar. The fact that it has no obvious way to approach it makes it all the more seductive. We follow the beach around and proceed to climb. Part of the enchantment of exploring Tunisia's sites is that others are rarely present. Time and again, we have the run of the place—even in the zones *touristique*, sanctioned tourist areas—no one visits except for us...at least that's how we find it. The day is warm and the sun is high. As we ascend, we pause every so often to take in an expanding view of the Mediterranean, the rolling forest, the picturesque town, the colorfully painted fishing boats bobbing in the harbor far below. We summit and claim the garrison for our own. We celebrate our victory by nibbling tart mealy quince, something I never ate at home, but have taken a liking to here. As we linger there pondering the realm, taking in the fullness of our kingdom, I fantasize that I have been assigned to Tabarka instead of the teeming capital with its confining concrete, diesel engines and stagnant breezes—I never feel very regal there. Nor do I dare fill my lungs the way Tabarka begs me do. I take in luxurious breaths, deep and clear, as if in breathing I may absorb enough nature to sustain me long after I depart.

CHAPTER 16

Daniel

I welcome the arrival of a new roommate. Daniel is a scholar-
ship student from the University of Minnesota who has come to
Tunis to study Classical Arabic at the Bourguiba Institute. I don't
know how Kristy found him; he just appeared one day and promptly
moved into the mix. Along with being very clever, very pleasant
and very amusing, his presence helps defray costs for Kristy and me.
Regarding Kristy, I don't really know her at all. Our personalities,
while not in conflict, are not harmonious either. Therefore, we make
little effort to cultivate familiarity. This is absolutely okay. Our comings and goings are entirely separate. We share living space, not our

lives. Daniel, on the on the other hand, will be more than a room-mate. Our friendship is certain.

Daniel del Castillo (a name worthy of note) has become my guardian angel, walking me home every night after school. At the close of class, he is there, at the foot of the steps outside the Institute, freckled nose and face beaming with his most endearing smile, Daniel the genteel. We have thirty minutes of concrete and cobblestone to travel together on the way home to the medina, but never enough time to exhaust our conversation. He calls me by my middle name, which I don't use.

"So tell me, Lora Lee, how were your students this evening?"

"I give up. I think I am going to take a white flag into class with me tomorrow night. But, I don't know if that'll translate. How do you say 'I give up' in *l'Arabia fusha* (classical Arabic)? Daniel begins to dig into his bag for his dictionary. He searches for the translation for me, for himself too, since he didn't know. He is not the kind of person who leaves questions unanswered. That's a good kind of tenacity. He'll probably dig up a hanky when we get home so that I can have it at the ready tomorrow night. But, by then I will have forgotten our conversation, my frustration. The troubles I carry out of the classroom cannot persist in the presence of Daniel. He has a way of vanquishing them.

There are many many things to like about Daniel, but it is his smile I love best, because of its "I dare you" quality and because I see my brother in it. It is generously offered with ease. He is insatiably curious and has the tendency to ask non-stop questions of anyone in his proximity. He wants to know everything about everything and everyone. Like I said, the man doesn't fatigue.

Daniel's curiosity conducts him to areas less traveled, like the deep reaches of the medina. Already, he's happened upon a source for coal, chalkier, in jagged shards, nothing like the uniform briquettes of home. His discovery has provided us new options for cooking and lent to the spending of a great deal of time on our rooftop terrace utilizing our makeshift barbeque, and consuming horrid wine. Daniel has led me to the herb vendors, who sell enormous scraggy lengths of brush, thatched and dried in quantities far larger than we could ever need. He has led me to the fabric dyers with arms permanently stained indigo up past their elbows, the result of stirring deeply hued potions in huge cauldron-like vessels, day after day. Daniel's fearless explorations continue to unearth surprises. Tonight we are in the medina. The night is pitch black, exceedingly quiet and for a moment I begin to feel my nerves seize in my gut. But I soon set aside the temporary consideration of my safety, because I am with Daniel.

"Follow me." He says as he veers in a direction opposite home.

"Where are we going?"

"I have a surprise for you. Trust me." He says with a smile.

"Are you sure you know the way? Because I am already lost."

"Trust me, Lora Lee."

"Don't I always?"

I follow him through the dim, in and out of passageways until I see men loitering in the shadows, others emerging from darkened doorways still zipping their pants.

"Where are we?" I whisper.

"Dear lady, we are in the red light district." He informs me.

"Tunis has a red light district?" I assumed nothing that seedy could exist here.

"Well of course it has."

For those that cannot abide the overwhelming restrictions that are required by Islam, there is this strange sanctuary tucked into the deepness. Men lurk in the dark, hungry, needy, they take no notice of us. We are in their underworld. Such glaring contradictions under the cover of night reveal that people are people, universally primal at our core. The medina is infinitely fascinating, complex and gritty. I thank Daniel for every nook and cranny he reveals, even the ones less savory.

When Daniel is not studying or leading me astray, he is making connections and ingratiating himself to high level diplomats in Tunis. He is bound and determined to schmooze an invitation to an embassy dinner, with the end goal of rubbing elbows with members of the Foreign Service. Herein lies his ultimate goal, to join the Department of State. He has already taken the practice test numerous times. I have no doubt he will someday craft an international career. His energy is too boundless to not realize his dream—I know one when I see one. Our time here will be precious short, so I savor that I have him almost to myself and know already ours is the stuff of lifelong friendship.

• • •

It is 9:30 on a Tuesday evening. Arabic class at the Institute has just ended and Daniel and I are joining two others from my class for coffee. Tigran is from Armenia. Serik is from Nevinnomyssk, a small city in southern Russia. The only common language among us (except for Daniel and me) is the smattering of Arabic we have each acquired thus far. Despite the language conundrum, we manage gracefully and have a lively time.

We discuss our jobs, the relative challenges of living in Tunisia, cognac and marijuana. Tigran endured two years in the military during which he lived alone in a cabin in Siberia. There really *are* people who get sent to Siberia! One morning he woke up to discover that he couldn't open his door. He yelled to a comrade whose cabin was over one hundred meters away. "What is happening?" He screamed over and over until finally he heard the muffled voice of his comrade trapped in his own cabin. They were completely buried under snow. It took over ten hours to dig them out, once they were discovered. He says the two years in frigid Siberia prepared him for any climate. He is very tolerant of the cold now. Yes, but how are you handling the inferno that is Tunis? I wonder. He enthusiastically invites us to visit him in his homeland, drink cognac, "ensemble," dance, play cards and sing by the sea. When in my life have I ever gotten such an invitation?

Walking home, Daniel and I reflect on our evening.

"So tell me Lora Lee, how did you enjoy your evening?" He asks in his highly refined manner.

"I have to admit, the depth of what I don't know is staggering."

"What do you mean?" He asks. I explain how the evening reminded me once again how very little is my knowledge of the world and how very many are my indoctrinated beliefs and my monochromatic relationships. My self-focus knows no limit. It is humbling.

"Aren't we in the process of remedying that?" he asks.

"Indeed, we are. Thank you." Daniel gives me a pass. Daniel and I are both astonished by the simplicity, the naturalness, the fellowship of our evening. An unlikely assortment in an unlikely place.

Oftentimes, the people I meet put me face-to-face with hard truths, not only about myself, but about my country. Among the many criticisms that have been lodged in my direction is the widely-held belief that most Americans are monolingual and disinclined to do anything to about it. Another biggy is the criticism that most

Americans cannot—nor do we attempt to—understand Islam. Here's another, it is also widely accepted that many Americans live like the characters in the T.V. series "Dallas" (dubbed and beamed into many homes here). Just when I am about to take exception with the notion that we are all being chauffeured around in white limousines, I have to acknowledge the fact most of us own cars—and park them in homes of their own. Garages are a wholly foreign concept in Tunisia.

When I compare the relative luxuries I have enjoyed all my life to the relative lack that persists elsewhere, I feel self-conscious. I have to accept responsibility for my part in all of it, even if partially it was an accident of birth. That I should be reared in the most materialistic country on earth is a fact I consider every day. I am a product of my culture and am now having to answer for it. Why do so many Americans believe we are the world's moral authority? How can we champion morality when we have so little knowledge of or concern for anyone who doesn't look or sound like us? Why do we fear the unknown?

. . .

We aren't the only ones that are afraid. I am visiting my friend and colleague Wahid in the modern apartment he shares with his roommate, Muncef, whom I meeting for the first time. Muncef is ardently anti-American. Meeting me is a jolt to his system. Upon discovering an *Americania* (American woman) in his kitchen, Muncef goes into a tirade, spewing promises to kill all Americans and all of America's spoiled children, the Israelis.

"Me too?" I inquire.

"Of course. I will kill every American I meet—shoot you right in the face." A death threat. I look to Wahid, hoping he might referee. I know Tunisians to be passionate, prone to raising voices when the subject matter moves them, but this is making me a tad uncomfortable. Wahid is indifferent to his roommate's rising anger. Is he accustomed to Muncef's outbursts and therefore able to casually dismiss them? Or, does he in some way support his viewpoint? I know better than to debate Muncef, seething the way he is, dangerously angry. I wait for my moment and then make a hasty departure. I don't believe for one second that I shall meet Muncef again under any circumstances, though I still feel the impact of his rage. Bearing that much hate, that level of contempt, must be a terrible burden.

The altercation with Muncef excepted, I am lucky to be here. Living overseas, as each encounter here demonstrates, may potentially create in me a true citizen of the world. Borders blur. Blinders come off. Perspective is blown wide open. I am marinating in the smells and tastes and the moments as they come, until I am saturated. I will never be the same person again.

CHAPTER 17

I digress

Me with my some of my students
at the Institut Bourguiba Des Langues Vivantes

Teaching confounds me. I feel a weight of responsibility because the students pay to attend my classes. It takes me an eternity to figure out what to teach, as textbooks are still not forthcoming. I burn two to three hours for every hour I teach, crafting lackluster and uninspiring lesson plans. I take some comfort in the fact that I am not alone in my feelings of inadequacy, feelings which have swept through the ranks of the Peace Corps English teaching contingent (with the exception of the China Five who all arrived far more credentialed than the rest of us). We rookies are experiencing a great deal of anxiety about our considerable lack of teaching expertise. It doesn't help that the English department remains woefully disorganized, with too many questions unanswered, our inquiries dismissed. I acknowledge that it is not anyone's job to teach me mine. I take some comfort in a divested administration that doesn't appear to be overly concerned with my performance, thereby providing wiggle room for my shortcomings as a teacher, while I do what I must to get it together. Truth is I am operating in a vacuum and no one really knows what's going on in my classroom. Bald truth is I am struggling, stressing and losing ground. I endeavor to do better, which means competency must be acquired on-the-job, at my students' expense. The Catholic in me feels very guilty about this.

• • •

Problems of my heart are triggering problems for my head. My relationship with Sam is still so damned mystifying. When he's with me, everything falls away—there is no more blessed a place in which to find myself. But he can be indifferent, inconsistent in the granting of his affection. Dare I say, he's even a bit cruel. Yesterday, I did him the favor of picking up his "friend" at the airport. She flew all the way from Ohio to see him. Next, I helped her make her way to his site, provided explicit instruction, accompanied her to the *louage* station, made sure she secured a seat in a car. This "friend" turned out to be a blond bombshell. Perky young thing was a bit too eager to see her "Sammy." I made few inquiries—convinced myself that it is indeed just a friendship, because the truth is really too difficult to stomach.

This is painful, wallowing in misery and bliss, but it is what I do. This is my construct. I have co-created it, put my insides on the rack and stretched them to the point of calamity. If I allow this to continue, I deserve the outcome. I make my home here, pitiful as

it is, in this glass house on the brink of shattering, of being obliterated. It will be painful and ugly. I will be cut to pieces. I want
affinity; I get distance. I want connection; I get separateness. I want
reciprocation; I get sucked dry. This is how I have come to define
love and the terms on which I have accepted it. All I ever do is
want. The universe in its great wisdom provides me with exactly
what I want: more of the same. When giving up might have saved
me, I gave in. There is no peace in this weak heart, nor a brain in
this head.

"The mind is its own place, and in itself can make a heaven of
hell, and a hell of heaven" --- Milton.

Hear, hear, Milton. Don't I know it.

Moon and Misery

Once upon a moon eclipse
The shadow of the earth
Falls
Slowly.

For some time
I have been howling
At the moon,
Like a thing wild.
The need to draw my pack to me is primal.

I love the moon when it is full of itself.
I love the moon when it is full
…waxing or waning.

But,
the day comes.
Bringing with it
Brutal
truth.

What to make then,
Of this eclipse?
This play of shadow and light?
This...omen?

Bliss
and its collaborator
Misery
Cannot inhabit the same space
Indeed, they never have.

• • •

While I am feeling so chipper, let me make mention of my discontent with all things Tunisian. No amount of cross-cultural training could have prepared me for what awaits me once I step out my door. I am bombarded by a barrage of discontented faces. I am hassled, followed, verbally assaulted everyday. My mood determines whether I graciously absorb the onslaught or become tremendously vocal. It is often said by Tunisia's corps of volunteers "It is not the physical challenge of living here that is difficult; it is the mental and emotional challenge." Where is the Peace Corps I joined? The one that makes possible the bridging of gaps and the promoting of cultural understanding? There are sixty-five other countries where volunteers serve; perhaps they are making inroads in those places. I am not fulfilling my mission here; I suck at my job and I dislike the people here. I am losing my conviction.

I am in the throes of culture shock. That black hole of mis-understanding, of funk and confusion. Now that the honeymoon is over, I am coming to grips with the fact that the context in which I find myself bears no resemblance to anything I know... except for perhaps Elizabeth Kübler-Ross's Five Stages of Grief. I definitely recognize those...interesting that I can identify with the first four:

1. Denial. "This isn't happening to me." The ecstasy of the honeymoon stage, I have already acknowledged, is over.
2. Anger. "Why is this happening to me?" Demonstrated at present by my propensity to seethe when walking in public and lob judgments at every Tunisian in my path.
3. Bargaining. "If ..." If I work really hard on my Arabic, noth-ing bad will happen; confusion will cease.
4. Depression. "What's the point?" I am definitely suffering from a "why bother" kind of attitude.
5. Acceptance. No, not there. Not yet.

These stages were originally applied to people dying from a ter-minal illness. Later, they were expanded to include anyone with catastrophic personal loss. I daresay they might just be applicable to the Peace Corps Volunteer in the early months of the tour. I sum up the loss this way. All my stuff, my practices and habits, my cues and values, everything that defines my world, that helps me make sense of it and navigate through it have been eliminated and replaced by things foreign, things different, things that have no translation. Disorienting, with a capital "D."

Let's start with the language, which I have already described as replete with unfamiliar sounds and constructions and punctuated with religious uttering. I am dedicated to attaining proficiency. But, there are so many missteps along the way. It can be frustrating maneuvering through the simplest interactions, especially when it comes to the legal stuff. I recognize that the language is *the* primary tool in my arsenal. Without it, I will no doubt continue to reside in this fog of misunderstanding. Thankfully, Tunisians welcome any attempt at their mother tongue. I have yet to witness one person become annoyed by my feeble skills. In fact, being able to call up words like *sa:mahni min fadhlik*, which means excuse me, is a phrase which universally elicits help from anyone and assures me I am not without lifelines. This will take time. Perhaps one day, I won't have to rely so much on the benevolence of strangers to find my way.

Another source of dissonance is the music, which I have already mentioned with regard to how it gets blasted beyond recognition. When it isn't, the only thing my Western ear can discern is that every chord is purposely performed between the notes, which I interpret as "out of tune." As a former music student and one who was eager to embrace this aspect of culture, it is both perplexing and disappointing that the music is too "foreign" for me to enjoy.

And the mother of all road blocks: Islam. Because I am not a Muslim, I will always be an outsider, a "them," an infidel (a nonbeliever). And when I walk the streets, or engage in conversation, be it with a taxi driver or just about anyone here, it will always be open season on me for inappropriate questions. "Why aren't you a Muslim?" "Do you really believe that Jesus is the son of God?" "Do you know that Mohammed is the last prophet of God and that Islam is the *only* truth?" "Why don't you marry a Muslim?"

Perhaps the most exasperating reality of living in this "religious" culture is the sleazy nature of the verbal attacks, the harassment that shows up in stable supply, everywhere I go. I don't get it.

In the face of overt assaults on my Catholic upbringing, my previously shaky religious footing has newfound stability. All of a sudden, I cling to my religion as though my sanity and my life depend on it; on God. To have my faith slammed on a daily basis only strengthens my resolve and Catholicism's new hold on me. I cannot ignore Islam. Its dominance in my new world is unquestionable. I will have to find the grace to listen to countless Tunisians—as their duty requires—explain Islam to me, again and again and again. Never ever is the same courtesy extended to me.

Disillusioned, but determined, there is an education to be gained here. I figure the second tool (apart from Arabic) I need to remember to employ in a hurry is an open mind, easy to suggest, quite another matter to conjure. As for a sense of humor, which no doubt would serve me very well, I am just not there yet.

It frustrates me that I do not see myself returning to the U.S. with warmth in my heart for Tunisians, and go ahead, lump in all Arabs as well. I wanted of my Peace Corps experience to embrace my hosts here, not learn to abhor them. Before my arrival, I knew there had to be more to Arabs than the stereotypical view that the vast majority of them were either fanatical terrorists or camel herders. I had heard this from members of my own tribe, who professed it as though they had direct knowledge. Even so, I dismissed such proclamations as harsh; I would find out for myself. Now, my day-to-day experiences are reinforcing the negative and causing me a fair amount of distress. At the grassroots level where I live, I feel myself hardening, closing. How can I possibly be effective if I am disillusioned and angry? How will I, with my "mandate," advance the status and capabilities of my Tunisian hosts (albeit as a foot soldier)? How am I to bridge that huge gaping cultural hole which has become a gaping black hole into which all compassion and understanding are being sucked?

We have already lost a fair number of volunteers to early termination. Many of them were placed in assignments where their talents and knowledge were either stifled or wasted. Left to languish, tired of writing endless letters home and having read every book in their collection times over, they bailed. Some simply could not create their way out of the ambiguous situations in which they found themselves, like our volunteer who showed up every day at the agricultural office where he was assigned, only to park behind a desk with nothing to do. Or the special education volunteers (yes, more than one quit) who take exception to the way children with special needs are discarded in this culture. I wonder how many quit because they just couldn't spend another day swimming against the tide. I wonder if anyone else just gave up on the Arabs, as I feel wont to do. Margaret Mead said, "Never doubt that a small group of thoughtful, committed citizens can change the world. Indeed, it's the only thing that ever has." Exasperations aside, I can go on another day, if only to give effort to finding a way to eclipse my growing self-doubt.

• • •

Geez-Louise, am I relieved last week is over. I have heard Peace Corps described as a wavelike experience. I am pleased to be emerging from this latest near-drowning slump. Here it is, the underlying issue, the very crux of my woes: I have allowed myself to dwell in a one-sided love affair (how convenient it has been to blame the Arabs for my disillusionment). Sam is painfully random. I've been looking to God for answers, begging for intercession (an act gener-ally reserved for the desperate and forlorn), oblivious to the fact that the truth is smack dab in front of me. My pitiful state has led me to correspond with a priest whose address I found at the Peace Corps office. I dumped the whole of my desperation into these letters, in a vain effort to lean on someone inside my faith. Here's what I cannot reconcile: this is wholly within my intellect to manage; my will just won't show up. Knowing full well I am responsible for my own hap-piness, and conversely, unhappiness, I just cannot break myself free, even as my grief grows exponentially.

And that's all I'll say about that, for now.

It is no surprise I find myself, for the first time, desiring home. Desiring frustrations within a context I can understand and control. Succumbing to stress, I am being bombarded by a flurry of migraines so intense, I cannot bring myself to teach. At my medical officer's prompting, I find myself at the mercy of a Belgian doctor who is subjecting me to the first of several rounds of acupuncture. She spends an hour lecturing me on the history and miraculous benefits of this ancient Eastern practice. Next Madame Doctor proceeds to stick fourteen needles into various parts of my body, eight alone into my head. She leaves them protruding from my parts and exits the room. Every so often she returns to twist them, causing me distinct queasiness.

"Open your mind. Relax. Allow the released endorphins to do their thing to ease your dis-ease." She counsels me.

I leave her office with a packet of needles I am supposed to take to the American Embassy for safekeeping in between visits. I tuck them into my backpack and go directly to school. When I arrive in my classroom I am met at the door by Abdelrazzeik.

"Bonjour Miss. Ça va?"

"Ça va. How are you today?"

"Better than you, I think. You have blood on your head." He tells me.

I drop my backpack on my desk and head to the restroom. Sure enough. There is a thin line of dried blood running from the center of my forehead to the bridge of my nose. Nice. There will be ten treatments in all. Maybe Madam Doctor should just extract my heart from my chest and I could forgo the probable fruitlessness of being a human pincushion. Maybe with my heart out of the way, I could begin to wrap my head around the fact that I chose to be here—with all of its attendant challenges and frustrations. This is my journey. This is what I wanted and I created it. If I fail at this, I will fail at everything hence. There is an Arabic expression, *n'shallah labass*, which means "God-willing all will be well." Tunisians rely fully on God and fate to do their bidding. My American wiring is willing in part to concede to God's wisdom, but I must take responsibility for making a hell of this heaven.

CHAPTER 18

Hassle at the castle (does the queen know her subjects think she's a hussy?)

View from medina house rooftop terrace with Hotel Africa in background

When you live in a house that's several hundred years old, things can go wrong. After six weeks of concerted effort, we finally have gas in the Medina House. Apparently the gas lines were blocked and it was no small matter of inquiry and exertion to remedy the situation. Then, almost at the exact moment we obtain the facility to cook, to take hot baths, to hand wash our clothes in hot water, a new obstacle appears: our house floods. The source of the flood is the leaking bathtub. This is not just some innocent little puddle, this is inches of water, flowing into the middle of the house, where Daniel sleeps, into our dining area, down the stairs and into the two shops located directly under us. Substantial. The bidet, which we refer to as the foot wash, has started to moan obnoxiously whenever the sink is used. As a result, anything related to water has been rendered unusable. No bathing for us.

Two men arrive and proceed to excavate the tile floor and gut the eight-inch cement pediment which supports the tub. It is a colossal mess. The feverish digging eventually reveals the source of the flood: three dime-sized holes, minute, yet clearly enough to render disaster and mayhem. Tomorrow is Friday. Work will cease so that the holy day can be observed. Of course there will be no work over the weekend. Thus, the mess will remain until further notice. And of course, our landlord has informed us that this disaster is our responsibility. This house is Humpty Dumpty.

To add to the joy of my week, I am now an illegal alien in Tunisia. My visitor's visa, which covered my first three months in country, has expired. Beyond the fact that I could get arrested if I cannot produce the appropriate card when stopped at a checkpoint (which happens to foreigners fairly regularly here), even more problematic is the chaos that would ensue if I were to have a medical emergency (one greater than having long needles stuck in me). Should I require immediate medical attention outside of Tunisia, the American Embassy would have to step in and the quickest possible departure would be three days in the making—three days being the most expeditious scenario. So, the illegal alien had better keep herself out of detection and harm's way.

Hassle is a word synonymous with daily living here. For weeks I have been scrambling to assemble all of the legal documents for my *Carte de Sejour*, the magic credential that articulates and legitimizes my status here. I have crisscrossed greater Tunis to chase down the following: two applications (one in French and one in Arabic); a housing contract—with the legal stamp on it; an attestation from the Bourguiba Institute—with the legal stamp on it; an attestation from the Peace Corps—with the legal stamp on it; and four mug shots. A forty-minute trek over to the office of the Special Police leads to five separate visits to my landlord, a man who cannot comprehend a word of my Arabic. Four times I visit him in his shadowy underworld of an office tucked away deep in the medina. Four times I stand before him in that dark dusty space pleading my case, beseeching him to bestow upon the housing contract the legal stamp. Each time he sits motionless and emotionless in his red fez and formal caftan. Each time I leave empty-handed and frustrated. It takes five attempts. At the last, a son-in-law emerges to speak on behalf of my landlord. *"Mush mushkul."* No problem, he tells me and grants my request. With the official stamped contract finally in my possession, I slog back to the Special Police only to discover that the office has been moved and is now located just three minutes from the medina house. The pursuit will have to continue on another day. I have had my fill.

Aziz is a gentle elderly man who everyday sets up shop just feet from my stoop. He sells individual cigarettes. They are displayed, propped just so, in a beat up Lucite box that he sets on a fold-up chair. He sits on a wooden crate turned sideways. He is an unchanging fixture, as permanent as the stone archway that rises against his back. He is always dressed in the same blue peasant coat and red *chechia*, a round and peakless felt hat, part beret, part pillbox. Every day he bids me a hello just friendly enough to put his singular tooth on display. Today, as I approach my door, he waves me over. He has company, another man who strongly resembles him, identical, except for the beat up tweed blazer and a full set of teeth.

"Shnuwwa hwalik? Laba:ss? Labass inti? Shnuwwa hwalik?" Standard greetings in Arabic. Here's an aspect of this culture I love:

the greeting. It's long. It's a mouthful (makes me feel fluent). It doesn't feel transactional: when you spend five minutes just saying hello, it's hard not to make a connection with someone.

"*Nqaddimlik xuya,* Muncef." Aziz introduces his brother (you don't say), Muncef. To Muncef he explains. "This is our American...what's her name? She lives here."

"*Ismi* Lora." I offer. (What's her name?)

"There are a whole bunch of Americans living up there. They are always coming and going. Every day I watch them coming and going and coming and going." Aziz enlightens Muncef.

"Americans." Muncef says, shaking his head as if he himself has issues with the traffic in and out of the medina house.

"I have to ask myself, what are they doing up there? Always coming and going." Aziz says to Muncef. How long, I wonder, has this question been burning in his mind? How can it be that he doesn't know we are volunteers? Volunteers have been here for nearly a decade! Only now, when he has an ally, does he find the gumption to probe. This is my moment to put to rest for him his sordid speculation. So, I set about to explain myself, only *Filoq asSilm*, Arabic for Peace Corps, does not translate...at all. I try to explain all the good works being done around the country, but the light bulb never comes on.

"*Ana ustada.*" I am a teacher. I announce. "I teach English."

"*Ustada?*" Aziz asks in disbelief.

"*Nam.*" Yes. "At the Bourguiba School."

"*Fi* Bourguiba School? Ah ba ba ba ba ba ba." He says, vigorously gesturing to the heavens. I love when Tunisians do that—so demonstrative! The light bulb is ON! "*Ustada!*" Aziz reaches out for me with both of his weathered bony hands and grabs me jubilantly.

"*Ustada. Bahi. Bahi yessir!*" Good. Very good, he says. "*Ustada!*" He repeats to his brother.

"Ahhhhhhh. *Bahi,*" Muncef agrees.

So glad we got that cleared up. Perhaps Aziz can rest, now that he knows we aren't running a brothel upstairs.

Suddenly the scent of garlic reaches my nose. It is coming from the open doorway behind Aziz. Farid and Habib, also brothers, run a brisk business out of a tiny space directly below the medina house. They sell what can best be described as Tunisian fast food. *Casse-croûte,* which means snack in French, are sandwiches, entire loaves of French bread, sliced right up the middle, stuffed with potatoes or fries, tuna, egg, cheese and harrissa, a hearty meal on the go! Now I understand why the sandwich makers have maintained an obviously defensive distance from me. And I thought they were shy. What do *they* think is going on overhead? Well, beyond the obvious, the appearance of a waterfall where none should be—our flood. I sheepishly peer inside their *hannute.*

"*Salaam wa leykum.*" Standard greetings. I inquire as to the well-being of business, given the natural disaster and offer my sincerest apologies. Habib, wearing an immaculate white lab coat over badly worn blue jeans, begins to throw together my sandwich, while his brother fries an egg for it.

"*Rabi yarf. Rabi yarf.*" He says in a breathy and conciliatory tone. "God knows" he tells me. Habib turns the whole matter over to God, absolving me of culpability. I take the opportunity to formally introduce myself to the brothers. I make sure to repeat several times the magic word: *Ustada!* I get nods of approval.

CHAPTER 19

Besma

Sam and I are walking through the medina toward my house when a young woman steps ahead of us suddenly turns on her heel and faces us.

"*Vous parlez en Anglais?*" She inquires in French whether we speak English. In Tunis, a city colonized by France, it is assumed any foreign resident or visitor speaks French. I have been shocked to discover that for the first time—ever—I can easily comprehend

French (though I am not at all comfy speaking it). I attribute this new understanding to an accent that is profoundly different from that of my French Canadian heritage. Somehow, the French I hear on these streets makes total sense. Lucky for me, because French is the language of administration in Tunisia, which means official business, including that at the Bourguiba School, is most often conducted in French—and not the Canadian variety. Plus, I have a mixed bag of words that I can call upon in a pinch when I am at a loss for Arabic.

In any case, as for this young woman's inquiry, we inform her (in Arabic) that we are Americans. Her face lights up.

"I am Besma. You have to come over for couscous. You have to meet my family." Before I know what is happening, she has me by the crook of the arm and is whisking me, with Sam in tow, down a random corridor, into and out of light, into and out of small spaces compacted with people, through bleak deserted passageways, all the while pulling me forward and chirping happily at her find. I cannot tell you how many of my relationships are being born in just this way—spontaneously—initiated by insistent Tunisians issuing on-the-spot invitations to meals in their homes. Learning Arabic is the one tool that opens doors, entertains the incredulous and elicits more invitations than any in my arsenal—even though my language skills are dubious. I am the circus monkey amusing a wide-eyed, good-humored and seriously indulgent audience. The attempt is in fact my ace in the hole—so genuinely appreciated, doors magically open, whether I am ready or not.

Besma leads us out of the maze of winding medina streets across a busy thoroughfare to another section I have not yet explored, such is the complexity of the old city. She stops in front of a bright blue door made of planked palm wood. It is intricately decorated with crescent and star motifs made of studded nails. She rapidly taps the hand of Fatima door knocker against its metal nub.

"*Shkun?*" A muffled voice bellows from the other side of the door. "Who is it?"

"Me." Besma responds. The door opens just wide enough to reveal the wizened eyes of a woman concealed beneath a white *saf sari*. Besma pushes her way in and introduces us to her mother, then, rather unceremoniously, asks her to feed us. And, just like that, the woman disappears into the house. Besma guides us past the traditional courtyard to a sitting room. She is visibly excited and talking a mile a minute. We are excited too, though working hard to conceal the fact that we are both beset by the kind of tummy issues that seem to continuously plague our not-fully-acclimated constitutions. Her mother soon returns with a tray of food. She sets it before us and orders: "*Kul! Kul!*" (Eat! Eat!)

The notion of hospitality is so over the top here, that a Tunisian would rather give you a wrong answer than not give you one. In other words, generosity of spirit is demonstrated in many ways, though not always understood. Kindness is the heavily sugared tea that flows bountifully here. It is the forsaking of business; nothing is so pressing that cannot be set aside for a few moments so that food or drink can be shared. When the food appears as if from nowhere, you can bet is the very finest that your host has to offer and she would rather go without—even forsaking her children—than deny you the greatness of her heart, her hospitality. It opens doors. Today at the whim of a young lady, it materializes in seconds, for complete strangers.

Our maladies allow us to stay only long enough to hastily accept the hospitality given us before necessity dictates we make a speedy departure for the haven of my western toilet, the only fixture in the medina house currently working.

Sweet Besma. She is unlike any Tunisian I have met. Her appearance in my life could not have come at a better time. Just when I was beginning to believe I would find no love for my host country nationals, she pops up. Already, she has proven that many of my hasty assumptions are dead wrong. Her friendship is the critical connection I needed to make; I don't have to wallow on the fringes of the culture, a tourist without a guide. Though, I couldn't have known that out of her impromptu gesture would be born a unique alliance, one that would initiate my entry into unknown, sometimes dark, territory.

Besma is beauty personified. Her look is very exotic. She has the rich olive-toned skin shared by many here, with eyes so dark as to appear black and full lips that demand attention. She is tall and thin, which she hates. She is forever layering herself—even in the wretched heat—to add bulk to her tiny frame. She insists skinny women are not attractive. She is beyond exuberant. Each time we meet, she covers my face in kisses, grabs my arms into her own and steals me away as if she has a great secret to share. She is just two years younger than me, though in many ways more school girl, immature perhaps, if not altogether sheltered. Certainly this is due in large measure to the fact that even in this European-influenced city, men and women are sexually segregated, as Islam requires. Thus, her interaction with the opposite sex has been limited to her older, ultra religious brother.

Besma is wildly free, insatiably curious and wholly charitable. In our meanderings through the crowded alleyways of our jam-packed neighborhood, never once has she passed someone in need on the street and not dipped into her pocket. "*Zakat.*" She explains, charity, a requirement of Islam. She is probably the least devout Muslim I've met, but the one teaching me the most. I don't know of a single possession that Besma calls her own, except perhaps for the pocket change she so easily gives away. Besma's benevolence—as demonstration of her pure heart, or aspect of her religion, or both—humbles me. I savor these times the most, when we wander aimlessly, content to purely be together, arm in arm. Out on the streets, our only agenda perhaps is to seek respite from Besma's more serious siblings.

Besma's joyous personality starkly contrasts with the other members of her family. I can't help but wonder how someone so progressive could have come from them. They are all excruciatingly devout. I have only seen the father once or twice, in the shadows. He will not allow himself to be in the same room with me. Her brother I see even less—he is the flash I catch out of the corner of my eye. Studying to be an imam, he takes his preparation to the extreme, refusing to come anywhere near me. The two sisters, one older, one younger than Besma, both felt the early pangs of Islam and adopted the veil at a young age. They are rather demonstrative in their prayer-making. They also make quite a stink about my not being a Muslim. They taunt me, boasting that their hair is far more luxurious than mine, but dare not remove their veils to prove it to my infidel eyes. If it were not so serious, it might be laughable.

Though the holy book of Islam, the Qur'an, does not specifically dictate that women veil, wholly or partially, most married Tunisian women and some younger ones choose to wear the *saf sari* in deference to Allah, in deference to custom and discretion, and a few in deference to extremism and its perversion of Islam.

In Beyond the Veil, Fatima Merniss writes: "The Islamic Veil originated in eighteenth century Samaria. It was worn by Samarian women to symbolize a woman's freedom—that she should not be assaulted because she is shielded by the veil. Without the veil, she is tempting the man to think about sex. With the veil she saves him from the opportunity to have bad thoughts."

I didn't understand at first how a veil could offer freedom. I viewed the wearing of it as compulsory, as a sign of submission to men, with God factoring nowhere in the equation. But I learned that, in some Islamic places (and places not Islamic), women have a choice of whether or not to veil. So, to me, having the choice conveys something else entirely. If veiling is not a religious requirement and their men aren't making them do it (in several areas of the Islamic world, compulsory veiling is enforced by men) why do women veil at all? More often, it is local custom that dictates what a woman wears in public. The individual makes a conscious choice to seclude and protect herself from the prying eyes of men, because she is chaste, because she is married, because it is her tradition, or because it's just easier to throw a veil over her house clothes for a run to the corner *hannute*, than to change into something more modest. Veiled women are not to be bothered. I can certainly appreciate this, as I garner my fair share of unwanted attention on the street. Sometimes, it would be nice just to be invisible. That is exactly what a *saf sari* does. For good or for worse, it makes a woman invisible.

In the case of Besma's sisters, to veil at a young age was indeed a conscious, serious choice. That they would berate Besma or me is both juvenile and misrepresentative. This is the context in which my wildflower friend has somehow flourished. Besma, in utter contrast to the members of her household, does not veil, does not pray five times a day, does not fit the Muslim profile in the least and clearly, does not fit in this family. Her failure to observe the outward displays of faith causes tension, communicates that Besma rejects the presence of Allah in her life. Not true, but she will not conform to prove it. She is tolerated, though not understood. Constantly she is pressured to yield to the will of their faith; to fall in line and be a good Muslim. How ironic that she epitomizes a loving graciousness few can match. Islam is first and foremost about submission, which for Besma is quite impossible. She cannot, nor will she, stifle the fullness of her *joie de vivre*, her zest for life. It is who she is. "There is a difference," she says, "between giving in to God and giving myself over to God. My soul is a free agent. God knows me and knows my soul."

Though I spend a great deal of time visiting her at home, she always manages to find a reason to visit me in mine. She is enthralled with my American friends and deeply envies our freedom to freely mingle, males with females, without ever attaching anything sexual to it. It is an environment so unlike the joyless vacuum of hers. Each time she crosses the threshold of the medina house, her confinement behind her, she exclaims "*J'aime la liberté!*" I love liberty. How many times have I heard her express it…when she is jubilant, when she is exasperated, when she is hopeful. Indeed, it is what she craves. It is what she puts herself in jeopardy to experience. Her visits to the medina house are not altogether sanctioned. When we're not there, we're stealing away to the beach at Carthage or Korbous, well out of sight of her family, where Besma, in the shorts she's borrowed, is a starlet on holiday, buoyant, blossoming.

One day, she had me tagging along to the middle of nowhere town of El Haouaria on the mountainous tip of Cap Bon, on the north coast. She had arranged to meet two of her friends there, two of her male friends. We spent the afternoon in the craggy cliffs overlooking the beach where below us Tunisian women, in full dress, swam, while their men splashed about in proper bathing suits. Nothing untoward transpired between Besma and the very handsome friend she clearly favored, just innocent conversation in a location remote enough to free her to be the energetic spirit she is. She goes to great effort to put distance between home and her social life. In many ways, our sneaking around is reminiscent of my high school days, saying one thing to parents, doing something else entirely. I am complicit. I will not deny her. She in turn, has not denied me the cherished gift of her friendship, the sweetness of her heart, her unwavering patience as I peck my way to Arabic fluency and the sincere pleasure of being in the presence of her brand of unbridled joy.

CHAPTER 20

Be careful what you wish for

Another rendering by
Peace Corps volunteer Michael Wilger

A t Besma's invitation, I am spending the night at her home. As she has become my sole prospect for fully engaging with Tunisians—something I am both duty-bound to do and quite wont to do—I seize the opportunity. Unlike my cohorts throughout the country, living in Tunis with Americans doesn't exactly equate to cultural immersion. Wanting more out of my experience here, I am thrilled to spend a night with Tunisians.

The ladies of Besma's house decided before my arrival that I should be henna-ed. Henna is derived from the dried and ground leaves of one of the loosestrife family of plants, indigenous to the Middle East. It is customarily used to dye hair, leather and, in some parts of the world, skin. The use of henna has its origins in Sufism, as a way to provide protection against the evil eye. And, while remnants of that belief system remain embedded, it is primarily a women's art, a celebrated and intimate ritual which often accompanies marriage and circumcision ceremonies. That henna is being offered to me, an outsider, is an honor I am happy to accept.

The process of henna application is long and laborious. Water is added to the dried henna until it can be worked with the hands, malleable, but not quite dough. Over several hours, it is carefully applied to the hands and feet in a pattern specific to the given region. Tunis' design incorporates the tail of a fish, which symbolizes fertility (they told me this after the deed was done). The hands and feet are then carefully wrapped in cotton and strips of cloth and placed in cotton bags or ornately designed oversized mittens. The henna must not be disturbed for a period of time—usually overnight—so that the color can penetrate the skin. In the morning, the wraps are removed and the dried henna is scraped off leaving a burnt orange tattoo. As the marriage celebration takes place over several days, henna is applied consecutive nights until the design becomes nearly black. I am pleased to experience this celebrated custom and eager to wear a badge of assimilation and acceptance.

Here we are, one little happy group (as happy as this group gets), the five of assembled in the main living room. I am enjoying the royal treatment, propped up on pillows, nibbling on dates and chugging Coca-Cola (pronounced "Kooka-Koola" here) as first my feet, then my hands are attended to. I enjoy the way the henna feels, slimy and cool, as it is being meticulously applied to my skin. I watch, a little grossed out, as Besma's mother, Laila, rolls tiny pieces of henna on her tongue in order to form the correct shape. Over time, henna accumulates on the edges her lips and creates dark deposits at the corners of her mouth. She places each piece skillfully onto my skin and pats it down with the tip of her finger. I behold the form of a fish taking shape on the palm of my hand. When she is satisfied with her work, she gingerly pulls bags onto my hands and onto my feet. A few knots at the wrists and ankles ensure that the bags will stay in place well enough to contain any henna that chips away during the evening.

Besma retires to another room leaving me with the sisters. They ceremoniously cover me with blankets, carefully place my hands atop my chest and instruct me to maintain this position throughout the night.

"Do not disturb the henna!" they warn.

Two hours after lights out, I feel a twinge deep in the recesses of my bladder. I recall the several bottles of Kooka-Koola I shamelessly chugged a few hours earlier. What to do? I decide to ignore as best I can these urges and I close my eyes in the hopes of drifting off to sleep. Not a chance. Discomfort intensifying, my mind swiftly becomes fixated on relief…and my options. Should I wake up the sisters sleeping nearby? Ask them to remove the bags, at least from my hands, so I can crawl on my knees to the Turkish Toilet? But then, I think, any movement this early on will surely destroy the work that was hours in the toiling before it has time to set. Perhaps I can enlist their help? They are both fairly sturdy girls, perchance they can carry me to the toilet and suspend me over the hole whilst I pee? I decide to wait it out in the dark, knowing the call to prayer will sound around 5:30 a.m. Certainly my devout hosts will rise to pray. Enough time will have elapsed by then; the henna should be sufficiently set. The moments tick by excruciatingly slow, while my anxiety and bladder swells. I grit my teeth, slow my breathing, imagine a dry lake bed. When the muezzin's voice finally shatters the silence, I think I might cry for joy. Only, no one wakes up! I wait to hear rustling about me. Nothing. No movement. I want to cry in earnest. I can wait not one second longer. I crawl on my knees and elbows, out of the room, across the courtyard in the dark toward the little closet of a restroom. With the greatest economy I can muster, I place my feet carefully on either side of the hole. I can feel henna pieces starting to peel away from the skin on my feet. With my forearms, I maneuver my skirt up to my mouth and clench a wad of it between my teeth. I repeat this move several times until I feel I have enough clearance. I tug at my underwear with my wrists, but can't get it to budge. Finally, one inch at a time, I feel progress. Yes! I have never been so happy to pee. Then I realize there is no toilet paper, just a bucket of water on stand-by. Desperate times these…I stand there, in that dark little closet of a restroom, with my undies down to my knees, with bags tied about my hands and feet and my skirt still wadded up between my teeth and wait until I drip dry. It takes many more moments to gather myself together. I slowly open the door and look to see if the coast is clear. I crawl back to the room, on elbows and knees, where the girls are still soundly asleep—devout my ass! I feel enormous relief wash over me, first for obvious reasons and relief that no one has woken up and discovered my nocturnal quest. In the morning, the ladies are very disappointed at the unveiling of their masterpiece. In place of fish tails, I have rust-colored blobs. They berate me for being a restless sleeper. This is the stuff of cultural immersion.

CHAPTER 21

The art of being a good guest

Sweet tea with pine nuts atop

Today I woke up with a severe backache. The source of my pain presented itself within the hour: *kurshee tisjree*, literally translated, runny tummy...again! When I first arrived here, I couldn't help but take note of the frequency with which conversations among our second-year volunteers seemed to revolve around gastrointestinal issues, particularly during mealtime. Night after night, discussions inevitably degenerated in that direction. I felt sorry for them. They have been out of the U.S. too long, I thought. They've gone and lost their manners. How sad. What I soon realized is that intestinal maladies are not the exception; they are part and parcel of daily life here. More often than not, our foreign countenances are at war with any number of triggers, be them amoebic or parasitic in nature. Since, more often than not, we are under attack, adaptation requires us to learn to function with them, inevitably leading to dialogue on the topic. Today is just another one of *those* days. Thus, physically weakened but not out of the game, I manage to teach four hours this evening, in between runs to the restroom. I even keep my promise to dine at the home of two of my students, Salim and Nadia. Daniel, ever my faithful, accompanies me.

It is our second visit to this household. Mother, Donyes, is waiting at the top of the stairs when we arrive. She is only about four feet tall, but has the hearty voice of one much bigger and a graciousness (so typical of Tunisians) that overwhelms me. She eagerly ushers us into the formal dining room where an enormous plate of couscous with every conceivable vegetable piled on top awaits us. There is a radish salad, bowls of olives, many loaves of bread and little condiment bowls of *harrissa* spread out on the table. We are directed to sit while Donyes heaps food onto my plate. I take a great deal of time chewing, moving the couscous around so as to appear as though I am eating more than I actually am. I am nervous, given my fragile state, concerned my innards will not abide spicy food. As soon as I make a dent in the colossal heap on my plate, Donyes is there ladling on more. She refills my glass at each sip, wipes my mouth with a napkin and fusses like a mother attending to a small child. Desserts follow, the typical look prettier-than-they-taste layered cakes purchased from the local patisserie. Then, the onset of grumbling from deep within my gut sounds alarm. I know I have only seconds. My gut begins to churn. I spring from the table and head to where I think the bathroom is. Only, it isn't there and I am quite certain I am going to vomit instead. What a dilemma. Do I have a choice? Or, will nature choose for me? Neither. I pass out.

I come to, aware only of the cold marble tile pressing against my cheek and sweat accumulating at my hairline. I sit up in the middle of the hallway floor and bury my head between my knees. In my grogginess I know that I am not being a very good guest and I am definitely not getting another invitation to dinner. I recover and make my way back to the dining room where Daniel is busy reading the Qur'an with Salim (score points for Daniel—he'll get another invite). Donyes has only the slightest look of inquiry on her face when I reenter the evening in progress. She disappears into another room and returns with an exquisitely decorated bottle.

"*Zem-Zem!*" She says gleefully. I see recognition on Daniel's face—he knows what it is. I require explanation. "I've been hiding this for over a year. I am saving it for Salim's *baccheloreate!*" The *baccheloreate* is the crucial exam that will determine whether or not Salim can go onto college. In the bottle, there is maybe a half cup of liquid. Donyes pours half of it into two glasses for Daniel and me. We drink it...tastes like water.

"*Bishfay!*" The family says together, a blessing upon the drinkers.

"*Yishfik.*" The drinkers respond.

On the way home, Daniel is a bit in shock.

"Do you know know what *Zem Zem* is?" he asks me.

"Well, I gathered it was water from Mecca. So, it's special."

"It is very special. It is very sacred. *Zem-Zem* is mentioned in the Qur'an. *Zem-Zem* is very holy water drawn from a spring in the middle of a desert in Saudi Arabia. The spring is supposed to have been found by Ibraham. People from all over the Islamic world travel to Saudi Arabia to collect this holy water. Its medicinal properties are claimed to be miraculous. We should consider it an enormous honor to be given even a small taste—especially considering we are not Muslims."

"I have never heard of *Zem-Zem* before. Did you find it a little awkward that Donyes' two children were not given a single drop?" I asked.

"Yes I did! All the more reason to appreciate the gesture."

I have tasted the holiest nectar in all of Islam. I will try to savor the privilege. Secretly, I hope it will heal my insides.

CHAPTER 22

November 1989

More hassle at the castle

A work in progress

I am snoozing in my bed in my room at the medina house, cocooned in my sleeping bag, when I feel a slight thump on my chest. I open my eyes to discover a three-inch-thick piece of plaster that would have landed on my sternum if not for the fluff of down that encases me. I examine it, fairly weighty this little chunk, and allow my eyes to wander upwards. I discover cracks in the ceiling, extending from one side of the room to the other. When did those appear? I shed my bag and march the piece of plaster over to the den where my landlord spends his days. I hate going there. It is dark and confined. The only light coming in must fight its way through filthy windows and seep through cracks between the folds of the deeply faded, heavy damask curtains, which are, of course, closed. The only thing in the space is a large formal desk, a desk with nothing on it. Behind the desk is my landlord, in his perfectly pressed finely woven caftan, sitting there taking audiences, indifferent to petitions, handing off the dirty work to his intermediaries, like some kind of Tunisian Godfather.

"My house is sick again." I blurt out. "This fell from the ceiling… from over the bed where I sleep." I said, shaking the shard before his eyes. "You're going to have to fix this." I put the shard down on his big empty desk and wait for his response. I get the blank stare. Okay, I know my Arabic is sketchy, but this man plays games with me. Can it be that he won't listen to me because I am not a Muslim, or because I am female, or both? I don't know what combination of factors prevents him from comprehending me. Nevertheless, this much should be clear: sick house + shard of concrete = consideration. I take a deep breath, select my words carefully and offer them slowly: "You have to fix my broken house. It is dangerous." Nothing. I get nothing. I turn on my heel and make my dramatic departure.

Two days later. The medina house is inundated with guests: Peace Corps Volunteers reporting to Tunis for their scheduled gamma globulin shots and meetings with the Peace Corps staff. I wake up earlier than usual so that I can make a run to the *schnake* guy around the corner. *Schnake* are the most delicious pastries I have ever had. They are honey-kissed croissant-like deliciousness, often still warm and gooey when I get them home. My guy sells them fresh every morning, for milimes (pennies). This morning, I clear him of his inventory, have my empty pitcher filled with fresh squeezed blood-orange juice by my juice guy and return home eager to serve the bounty to my guests. When I open the door to the house, I find my visitors clustered at the threshold of my bedroom, mouths agape, eyes wide and there is silence. Around them a thick chalky cloud hovers in the air. Upon seeing me, they part, revealing the source of the cloud emanating from my room. The ceiling has caved in. This time, concrete, several feet wide, and several inches thick, has in one enormous mass, fallen to the floor AND onto my bed, where just moments ago I had been sleeping. Hundreds of pounds of cement lie in a heap the size of small car in my room. I grab the hugest chunk I can carry and march it right over to my landlord. I find him still sitting at his throne when I enter. This time I don't bother with Arabic.

"I almost died!" I scream. I rant for a minute, dump the concrete where I stand—its impact is TREMENDOUS—and exit.

Fifteen minutes later, my landlord shows up at the medina house with a broom and a dustpan. Wearing his perfect silken robes and jewel red fez, he shuffles around the pile saying nothing, making no eye contact, obviously humbled. He doesn't make a dent in the mess. I don't move to help him (obviously not humbled). His lack of action up to this point could have killed me. The United States is just beginning to recognize that it has to invest in an infrastructure that is on the decline after less than three hundred years in the making. Our bridges are falling down. Our foundations need shoring up. Our roads are forever crumbling. My medina house has its origins in the eighth century. As thrilling as it is to live within a World Heritage Site, it does not come without risk.

CHAPTER 23

Do you take this man? Of course you do!

It is very late in the evening. There is a knock at my door. It is rapid and continuous.

"*Shkun?*" Who is it? I yell.

"Besma." Comes the reply. "*Izrib! Izrib!*" Hurry up. I open the door. "You must come over to my house right now, please."

"What's wrong?"

"My mother wants to see you and dinner is waiting." Although it is late, I've become accustomed to spontaneous invitations to meals at the Tounsi household. I change out of my medina house clothes, shorts and a T-shirt and into my street clothes, an ankle-length skirt and loose, flowing shirt. We step out into the night. As many times as I have been to Besma's, the trek there has not yet become second nature. The circuitous route through complicated narrow streets is especially intricate in darkness. With arms intertwined and Besma's guidance, we walk hurriedly toward her neighborhood. She knocks on her door in the same manner as she had on mine, with urgency. On the other side of the door, her mother's voice cries out,

"*Shkun?*"

"*Besma wa Noora.*" Noora, pronounced very nasally, is my Tunisian name. The door opens and I am flooded with kisses by Besma's mother, Laila. She seems especially excited to see me. She holds my hand and escorts me through the courtyard into the family living area.

When I enter the tiny chamber that serves as the dining room, recreation area and bedroom, the people waiting there, perhaps nine in all, stand up to welcome me. As an arriving guest, I am obligated to go around to each and plant the customary four kisses—two per cheek—to everyone present. They are all on their feet in line a little too quickly, a little too eager to see me. I recognize almost everyone in the room as family. The only person not positioned to greet me is an older gentleman, who has not moved from his seat. He stares at me. He seems amused. When the elaborate greetings are at last completed, Laila pulls me to the couch but does not release my fingers from her tight grip. I am seated facing the stranger. The room is suddenly very quiet.

The stranger addresses me. His English excellent, though his accent very heavy. He introduces himself as Uncle Mohammed. He is finely dressed in a suit with a tie. But even his chic wardrobe cannot conceal the fact that he is bloated, that he long ago succumbed to the ravages of middle age. He tells me his abbreviated life story, explains that he is educated—that he "took" a degree in dentistry, that he is financially secure. He promises me frequent vacations in Europe and a yearly trip to America to see my family. He explains that he saw a photo of me, one that I had given to Besma. In it I am wearing the very fou fou bridesmaid's dress my best friend's mother picked out for her daughter's very fou fou wedding at the Detroit Golf Club. In it, I am pure fluff and stuff. Uncle Mohammed leans in across the void, looks into my eyes and proclaims,

"I knew the very second I saw you that you should be my wife. Do you accept?"

I am dumbfounded. Around the room everyone is perched on the edges of their chairs. Except for Mohammed and me, no one in the room can understand English, but they know what is going on, so they are anxiously awaiting my reaction. I shoot Besma a "what-have-you-done-to-me" look. I turn to Laila, who has now deprived my fingers of blood flow for nearly five minutes. She is frantically nodding her head yes, yes, yes! I look back at Mohammed, self-assured, clearly prepared to receive my favorable reply.

"How old are you?" I ask.

"Forty-six." He replies.

"Wow."

"It's a wonderful opportunity for you." He informs me. "Really, the chance of a lifetime."

Laila chimes in.

"You will be in our family. I am so happy." She is already congratulating me.

"*Besma, najjim nitkallim mayik?*" (Can I speak with you?) I ask her. Besma follows me into the courtyard. "Really, Besma, he is only four years younger than my Dad. He is too old for me—way too old. Could you marry someone twice your age?"

"No! Never." She cracks up, scrunches her nose as if she just got a whiff of something distasteful. "I'm sorry. Everyone thinks it is such a perfect arrangement. You're all alone here." Actually, the word she uses is *miski:na,* which means pathetic or wretched. "Don't worry. I thought you might not want to." Great. How am I going to gracefully decline without offending this family? In their eyes, it is as though Mohammed has handed me the keys to a brand-new Ferrari and said "Here: take it. It's yours. No strings." Who would say no to such an offer?

We return, the room hushes. I sit across from Mohammed. Everyone readies for celebration.

"I am sorry I cannot accept your gracious offer. My family wants me to marry a man from my neighborhood. We have known his family since I was a child." It is a blatant lie. "He is waiting for my return. I am here because there is so much yet to learn. I want to be ready for marriage and right now I am not. I am too young. But when I am ready, it will have to be him I marry."

"I understand." He concedes. "Thank you." He says nothing more, gets up and exits the room, then exits the house. Laila looks like she is going to cry. The room collapses in defeat. Later, Besma clarifies "my reasons," which are accepted without question. Marriage, and with it my status, is mentioned nevermore.

CHAPTER 24

Two roads...diverged

Today there is an enormous protest underway outside the Institute. Students are marching in observance of the second anniversary of the Intifada, the Palestinian uprising. I walk past the crowds and I can see several of my students in the mix. They wave "hello" to me. One, Nejma, comes over to speak with me.

"Teacher will you join us?"

"I'm sorry Nejma, I cannot be involved in this. It is against the rules for me. Please understand."

"Yes, I understand," she says. "But our cause is just."

"I know." I tell her. "I'm sorry. I could be sent back to America if I were to walk with you."

"I understand." She turns and leaves me. I walk into the school and up to my classroom where just one of my fourth-year students is waiting.

"So Rached, you are not joining the protest outside?" I ask him.

"No. It is not possible for me. My mother is Israeli. My father is Tunisian. My father and I are Muslim, but my mother is not."

"It must be difficult for you," I offer.

"Only on days like today."

"I pass the synagogue everyday on my way to school. It's guarded by men with very large guns. It's a bit scary. I suppose it's difficult for your Mom to practice her faith."

"We used to live in Jerba (an island in southern Tunisia) where there are many Jews. It was easier there." Rached explains. "But my father took a job here and now it is not the same."

"Well, how would you like to have a private lesson? We can work on anything you want to…what do you think?"

"I think this will be good," he says. He asks to review the Robert Frost poem, *The Road Not Taken*, I presented the previous week. In lieu of textbooks, I have had to be creative.

"I am the man in this poem," he tells me.

"I am too!" I laugh. Just then, we hear commotion outside. Students are running into the school. The police have arrived. "Stay here." I tell him. I go out to the front doors to see students being hauled away in police vans. Everything is over in minutes. The peaceful demonstration is done. Tunisians are passionate about the Palestinian crisis. They identify with their Arab brothers who they say have had their homeland unjustly usurped, leaving them homeless. The Tunisian government however, does not allow the public the right of assembly, no matter the cause. Such is the way of the authoritarian rule here. I thank my lucky stars I knew well enough to not get involved, though I wonder about Nejma and the rest of my students.

CHAPTER 25

Legal at last and other stuff to celebrate!

My student card

After three months in flux, I finally have my *Carte de Sejour* in hand (not be confused with my student card, above). It isn't that I've been residing illegally, per se; the issue is that I cannot legally leave the country if I need to. Like all the other visits to the Medina Special Police to secure the card, this last one is fraught with pomp and ceremony. The officer presiding over my status has me sit beside his desk while he peruses my paperwork for a good twenty minutes...again. I watch his eyebrows rise, then lower, rise and lower; this is a man deep in concentration.

Just when I think I am about to be denied yet again, he reaches into his desk and pulls out an elaborate wire structure, which contains a massive collection of official stamps. Stamp. Ink. Stamp. Passport. Stamp. Ink. Stamp. Pad. Stamp. Ink. Stamp. Document. Eight different stamps, each with a pounding of authority. Then he disappears into a huge filing cabinet and emerges with three more official stamps. Again with the pounding. I can't help but laugh.

"Congratulations!," he says. "Are you happy?" Damn right I am. "I am going to keep this forever!" I tell him. A thing so hard won is not easily surrendered. I probably will keep it forever.

· · ·

Speaking of things legal and not so legal, my students involved in last week's demonstration managed to get away before the police arrested them. Many however, did not and were arrested. I have no idea what became of them.

· · ·

The holiday season is here, well, not visibly here, but it is that "time" of year elsewhere. Thanksgiving, our distinctively American holiday, obviously not observed here, was last week. In Tunis, our Associate Peace Corps Director (APCD) graciously opened his lovely villa to the Tunis volunteers for a Thanksgiving feast, complete with a turkey, cranberry sauce, veggies, biscuits, yams, mashed potatoes and gravy, pumpkin pie and cocktails. Most of the fixin's were acquired at the commissary at the American Embassy. The commissary is a slice of home where deprived expatriates can meet their need for quality American goods, items that cannot be acquired in Tunisian *supermarchés*, things like Jiffy peanut butter and sliced Wonder bread. Any holder of an American passport may patronize the commissary, any-one that is, except Peace Corps Volunteers. Why the injustice? It is believed that, in order to connect more fully with the people we serve, Peace Corps Volunteers must live at their level, forgoing the luxuries afforded our Peace Corps directors. Dining at our APCD's home, while very comforting indeed, underscored our exceptionally ascetic lifestyle. In his well-appointed kitchen, the staff who had prepared the meal cleaned up after us. The luxurious furnishings and collection of artifacts from around the world made his home more museum than dwelling. It was exotically posh and considerably more comfy than the medina house. Feeling envious over access to American junk food, among other things, I reminded myself that I had signed up for this. It was Thanksgiving, after all, so I had better start cultivating my attitude of gratitude.

On the heels of Thanksgiving is the other holiday not remotely acknowledged here: Christmas. Here's something I didn't know. Islam and Catholicism have a great deal in common, like the belief in one God, in the angels created by God, in the prophets through whom God's revelations were shown to man, in the Day of Judgment, in God's complete authority over all human destiny during life and after death. That's a major chunk of doctrine held in common. Here is where Islam and Catholicism part company. It has to do with God's final message to man, God's final prophet: Jesus vs: Mohammed. In Islam, Jesus holds a position of status, as the son of Miriam (as the fruit of a virgin birth), as a prophet, as a messenger, but *not* as the son of God. I have had countless conversations with Muslims who've all but laughed in my face that I might believe that God had a living son on earth. That God could ever be a man. At the very least, it is unfathomable to them how I could have come to believe any of it.

WHY DO I BELIEVE WHAT I DO? Gotta ask. Is it an accident of birth? Geography? Education? Conviction? Doctrine? Everywhere I go, I encounter Muslims who test my faith (such as it is) and engage me in conversations about Islam. I am honest about who I am, telling them I am mostly what my parents taught me to be, which, as I read in my Qur'an, is not a viable excuse. And when the passion rises, as it sometimes does, it is easily quelled with a well-placed *"bishshwayya bishshwayya"* which means "little by little" or "slowly." It's my way of letting them know that I am giving Islam consideration, that it's taking me time. Even the most fervent crusader will flash a smile of joy and release me to my own free will if I concede an interest or curiosity in Islam.

Absent, therefore, is Christmas and the hoopla that accompanies it. How strange it is to be completely divorced from the holiday frenzy, from the weeks and weeks of ramp up, from the rush and bustle that typifies the world's largest consumer society's uber holiday. There is none of it. Nary a tannenbaum or tinsel to be found. No fa la la. Zilch. It's true that the meaning of Christmas in the U.S. has become diluted because it is overrun with commercialization and materialism. But, given the void I currently find myself in, I'd choose a bloated and overdone Christmas over nothing. Absent from my culture, I wonder how I shall observe the holiday this year, speculate whether my mind will veer toward joy or directly to longing, or... straight to the box that Mom and Dad sent. It overflows with glad tidings from home, Frosted Flakes (who needs the commissary anyway?), deodorant, copies of the *Detroit Free Press*, fudge from Mackinac Island and Christmas music. More importantly, news on the home front seems promising. Dad and Mom are still hard at work putting forth the difficult effort required of reconciling. Letters that contain both of their signatures sustain my hope. These gifts have arrived with perfect timing, providing some semblance of a holiday and reason enough to celebrate. Dad wrote: "I hope that regardless of your surroundings you do somehow have a Merry Christmas...I will miss singing Silent Night with you in church." *N'shallah labass* Dad and Mom (God willing all will be well) *et Joyeaux Noel!*

• • •

I am at the chalkboard in my classroom, just beginning to plug away at yet another shaky lesson, when all of a sudden, blackness. I stand there for a moment, wonder how long the unexpected power outage will disrupt us...wonder about the existence of a back-up generator...wonder about protocol. I fumble my way toward my desk to wait. Then I hear a stampede. As my eyes adjust, I can see throngs of students working their way down the stairwell. So much for contingencies.

"Well," I say to my students, "Looks like we're done here." From the middle of the room, I hear a student's voice.

"Teacher, tell us about your Christmas." I see the flash of a match being lit. Tarik, the student most prone to forgetting his notebook and writing implements, the student most likely to arrive to class empty-handed, has a candle on him. He puts the flame to one end and drips wax onto his desk. He then places the candle into the wax and lights the wick.

"Yes mademoiselle, tell us." Voices in unison. I look to the stairs. Students continue exiting en masse, but everyone in my room is still seated.

"Okay." I agree. By the light of one candle, I take a seat on my desk and share my story of Christmas. I describe how we transform our homes with lights and decorations, how we chop down an evergreen tree, bathe it in ornaments and place presents below it, spending weeks in preparation and eager anticipation. I explain my family's tradition of going to midnight mass and returning to open gifts and our meal before dawn. I try to convey the origins of Christmas, religious and secular, though for the life of me I cannot not explain what in our history prompted the tradition of cutting down a perfectly viable tree and bringing it indoors, only to let it die sometime shortly after. That is a stumper. For the first time, my students are rapt with attention. Their questions are thoughtful, respectful, curious. It is magical. I have a community that wants to share Christmas with me. We leave the building well after everyone else has gone. At long last, I feel like a teacher.

CHAPTER 26

December 1989

Worth it...if you can get there from here

Drive-up butcher

The day is perfect, sunny, cloudless, seventy-five degrees in late December. I meet Sam in Mateur, his site. We find a *louage* that takes us half way to our destination, Lake Ichkeul, a privately-owned nature reserve, home to scores of wildlife and unique in that it is part fresh and part saltwater lake. We hitch the rest of the way. We are picked up by a *nakarifi*, an open truck. There are already several men seated in the bed of the truck when we climb in. We proceed along a deeply rutted one lane dirt road, ascending steeply to Mt. Ichkeul from its base. In the distance, a tour bus advances in our direction. I give little thought to the fact that the road is not wide enough to accommodate two vehicles, or, that to our left is a sheer drop off and to our right a wall of earth. As the bus approaches, it does not slow one bit. Nor does it attempt to share what little of the road there is. In a swift defensive move, our driver opts to veer left. We bounce violently over the terrain and come to an abrupt halt perilously perched over the vertical drop off. At the rear, enormous boulders block the tires. The vehicle is seriously and profoundly stuck. The only direction we can move is forward, an option we will not survive. Our driver nonchalantly grabs a lead pipe out of the bed of the truck and starts excavating with it, as though this kind of thing happens with all regularity. Sam steps in to relieve him, using the pipe to burrow until eventually, the boulders are freed, a process which takes over an hour (Sam finds it all rather amusing). We push the *nakarifi* onto the road, climb back in and arrive at our destination (as far as our driver is willing to go) all of three minutes later. We offer him money, which he graciously refuses. Then he leaves us, alone in one of Tunisia's great wildernesses.

We hike beyond village or remnant of development, until we find a good place to observe our surroundings. The sky is overrun, the landscape in motion, teeming with hundreds of thousands of birds: wigeon, marbled and green-winged teal, pintail, coots, graylag geese, storks. Our timing could not be more perfect, for this is North Africa's go-to destination for the winged, pushed southward at the onset of European winter. Some make their home here, others refuel then journey to points elsewhere beyond the Sahara. When looking upon this cacophony, one gets a very clear picture of what is exactly meant by migration. Thousands in flight and thousands more weaving in and out of reed and sedge, nesting, feeding, preening, sunning. It's Daytona Beach at spring break, frenzied, overpopulated, everyone on top of one another. The summer months will find a considerably calmer, less inhabited space. Marsh dwells in the lowland, while wild olive trees dominate the mountain. Wildflowers and exotic plants flesh out a cascading landscape below us. In AD 1240, the Hafsid Dynasty managed this region as a hunting preserve. The panorama, I imagine, must have looked exactly as it does now. It was only years ago that UNESCO designated Lake Ichkeul a World Heritage Site, recognizing its importance as a critical habitat for a diverse population of flora and fauna. It is hoped that this status will help protect for all time what is a wonderland of biodiversity and the last freshwater lake in a chain of lakes that once extended across the whole of North Africa.

Following a picnic of fresh bread, gouda cheese, quince and tomatoes, and a day of lingering amid the wildness, eventually it is time to make the ten mile trek back, this time on foot. Less hike and more amble, the winding path lends itself more to loitering or pondering than travel. For me, a perfect moment in time, one saturated in serenity, bathed in the bliss and momentarily free from attachment to any particular outcome. For one who has ever dwelt in expectation, been manacled by her past, I am delighted to find myself....here...right now.

Wilderness eventually gives way to isolated compounds, whose bordering walls and homes are constructed entirely out of boulders (there appears to be no shortage of those around here). Dwellings support roofs of thatch, bound with twine and twig, the architecture of ancients, aided in places by the introduction of more modern materials, huge sheets of plastic stretched to cover gaping holes. There are animals roaming freely everywhere, cows, sheep, dogs. In the distance I hear strange cries I cannot recognize. Moments later, a small boy passes us. In his arms he cradles two newborn lambs. Some twenty feet behind him, the boy's mother follows, her arms wearing the fresh blood of the recent birth. She warmly greets us, but never takes her eyes off her son. All of a sudden, my bliss, my moment in the present vaporizes. *This* is the Peace Corps I fantasized about, the one I *still* fantasize about. I want to live right here on this mountain with these people. Uncomplicated, but not effortless, unadorned but not deprived. Here among the girls drawing water into jugs. With the man whose sheep loiter in the ravine, who despite the hissing and pebble throwing of their master, do not stir from their grassy find. With the women casting laundry over walls for drying. With the boys playing soccer, who have a small hollow in the side of the mountain as their goal. I imagine my life here. I imagine it peaceful, captivatingly serene. I wish it could be and mourn that it is not so. Despite this...craving...the day is the very definition of sublime and I am deeply grateful for it...in any measure.

CHAPTER 27

Nourdeen

The entrance to the Tunis medina

Zipping through the hordes of foot traffic that clog the narrow confines of the medina streets, the day is set aside to accomplish errands, banking, marketing and the mailing of Christmas presents—I have my wheels on. Some of the shopkeepers along my route now know me. They raise their eyebrows, nod their heads in greeting, or call out *"ca va?"* While many others continue to lump me into the category of European tourist and relentlessly beckon in French, English, German, hoping to lure me into their shops. I am hustling as usual, cruising through the masses at a high rate of speed, dodging dawdling tourists, efficiently swerving around obstacles, making great time when into my path steps a man, causing me to stop dead in my tracks. Our eyes lock. He has a look of recognition on his face as though he has been waiting for me.

"*Shbi:k?*" I reach for my Arabic word du jour, (what's your problem?) I maneuver around him and resume my tempo.

"You must be American." I hear him say from behind me. "You are always in such a great rush."

"Good observation." I chuckle, thinking his English quite good.

"Why did you laugh at me just now?" he asks.

I pick up my pace, having no interest in entertaining yet another bold Tunisian. He falls right in step. A strong wave of perfume, like a massive cloud, overtakes my airspace. Tunisian fragrances are generously applied and seem not to be gender specific. The result is men who smell overly flowery and women who smell like my dad. I don't know what's worse, the aroma of garlic excreting from pores or the stench of someone saturated in perfume, not that these things are mutually exclusive.

"I like the American accent," he offers. Despite my indifference and my pace, he persists. As long as I can continue on my merry way, he can follow me all over Tunis, which he seems inclined to do. He is annoying, though non-threatening. He pursues me all of the way out of the medina, out onto Avenue Habib Bourguiba, past the vendors selling their wares from makeshift stalls. On any given day I might find razor blades there, or chocolate bars, nylons, hair accessories, bootlegged cassettes, the inventory is constantly changing. I feel a tug on my arm, then my body being diverted to a vendor at one of the stalls. On top of a cardboard box, a man has two structures displayed. I can vaguely make out that they are birds, constructed entirely from shells, with glitter and pipe cleaners all covered with a thick coating of shellac—the height of tackiness.

"How much?" My escort inquires of the vendor.

"What are you doing?" I ask him.

"Buying you a present. Which one do you prefer?"

"Neither, thank you. I don't like them."

"But these are his art."

"I respect that—but, they don't appeal to me. Please don't. They're kind of hideous." I say as gingerly as I can. The "art" is reminiscent of the work of a child, of things found and haphazardly glued and stuck together, the kind of assemblage that gets presented proudly to a mother (who then has the obligation of displaying it, openly). I have a strong desire not to own one of the masterpieces and no such obligation, to be sure. Because I will not help him with his dilemma, he selects and purchases one. We continue walking.

"Why? Why would you buy such an ugly thing?"

"What's the matter? You don't like it?"

"It's UGLY." I am laughing now.

"Oh, you like the other one better. I'll go get the other one." He turns around and heads back in the direction of the "artist."

"No! No to both."

"A gift for you. I feel compelled."

He follows me into the PTT (the post office). I offload my Christmas presents onto the counter not altogether confident they will find their way safely to America, while the generous one patiently waits. He accompanies me to the bank and then to Central Market where he offers advice on selecting the best indigenous delicacies Tunis has to offer, all the while toting the art. This is curious behavior for a Tunisian.

I am the owner of a hideous shell bird sculpture, which I never touch because it oozes black shit onto my hands. I do not love it, but I have warmed to it somewhat—not enough to take it back across the pond with me, however. Along with my bird, I have a new friend. His name is Nourdeen.

From the terrace of the medina house, I can see the whole of the metropolis of Tunis. Lake Tunis appears to be miles away, but my outing today proves otherwise. I am dining at the home of Nourdeen and his family. They live in Sidi Hela, a twenty-minute walk from the medina house. So abundant are the ancient communities crammed into Tunis's complex tapestry, I would never have discovered this neighborhood if not for our chance meeting (well, chance on my part, stalking on his).

Nourdeen's residence is characteristic of the homes I have thus far visited in and around Tunis, very sparsely furnished, modest, and impressively private given that the homes in this section are heaped one upon the other. We sit on the floor, on a mattress, around a low table. Nourdeen informs me that he has instructed his mother to prepare food less spicy than is typically consumed in his household, not a bad idea given that my taste buds, while adapting, are not yet fully acclimated to the intense heat of Tunisian fare. Before us, Nourdeen's mother quietly sets bowls heaped high with food, *salata mechouia* (a salad of grilled sweet peppers, tomatoes and onions mixed with olive oil and lemon, topped with tuna fish and hard-boiled eggs), *marqa* (a slow-cooked stew with meat, tomatoes and olives) and *xubz tabouna* (traditional bread) to serve as our "utensil" for scooping and sopping. Next, Nourdeen begins instruction on the proper way to sit while eating, taking care to emphasize the position of his torso as he leans back from the table.

"The Great Prophet Mohammed, Allah bless his soul, consumed his food this way because the digestive system functions best when it is not made to operate in a completely vertical position, not at ninety degrees." He explains. To make his point, he provides clarifications in English, Arabic *and* French. Yes. Yes…upright, but not vertical. He even demonstrates several times "the lean." When he is satisfied with his explanation, he stares soberly at me for a few awkward moments. Then, when he is certain his message has sunk in, he launches into a lengthy dissertation on Islam.

"It is very important that I tell you Islam is for everyone. It is in everything," he explains. "Muslims greatly desire to spread this love of God. They are obligated to share their message, not to covet it. If they do not share the news and teachings of Islam, they will have to answer to God later." I can feel my defenses mounting. Here we go again. With so few non-Muslims about and such a high priority placed on spreading the word, particularly to non-believers, I am a party to this conversation more than not. And, sometimes it's tiresome, though, I never allow it to be provocative, as nothing good could come of going there. However, I have to ask myself, why is it always assumed I have no God? Or, that mine is unequivocally not the same as theirs?

"If you want to go to heaven," Nourdeen further clarifies, "you must die a Muslim." Replace the word "Muslim" with "Christian," and I could be talking to an Evangelical—not that I am doing any of the talking. Either way, I don't want to discuss heaven right now or debate my slim chances of getting in. I just want to eat.

How many times am I going to be on the receiving end of this lecture? So many people talking *at* me. Different person, same trajectory every day: Why aren't you a Muslim? Ad infinitum. To be honest, to be perfectly honest, most of the inquiries are peaceful, made by those with honest intentions, who easily disengage instead of push. Maybe I *am* being intolerant. I listen intently, but I don't hear very much. I think I am being objective as I make my comparisons, but I end up taking refuge in my own programming: you have your tribe; I have mine.

While Nourdeen hammers on, I put on my "I am listening face" and begin to consider my bias. Am I truly the open-minded person I believe myself to be? Would a tolerant person adopt, as I did, an I-would-NEVER-convert-to-Islam stance at the very first confrontation with it? It is inconceivable, inherently alien, the whole notion that I could ever be Muslim. I never imagine it. Never. My belly is an open void, awaiting fulfillment; my mind and heart are seriously clogged. One thing's for sure, Nourdeen's passion has caught me, caught me hiding behind my beliefs. But, there's no hiding from Islam here. No way.

Nourdeen's mother joins us, not to eat. Moms don't eat, I discovered, at least I have not yet witnessed one that does. She watches me, listens intently to our one-sided conversation taking place in English, not that she can understand one word of it. The only time she interjects is to remind me to eat with my right hand. The left hand is reserved for restroom hygiene—we'll leave it at that. Mine has no business being at the table. When it pops into the mix one too many times, she suggests I sit on it.

I am taught how to sit. I am taught how to eat, meat first, then vegetables, for digestive reasons. I am informed about Islam and prompted to memorize Arabic quotations from the Qur'an. I get the overwhelming feeling I am being groomed. Nourdeen's father is perhaps the only neutral party in the room. When I have the rare opportunity to interject a word in Arabic, he bubbles with enthusiasm. He doesn't want to convert me. He says he is happy to have a guest. He rubs jasmine oil on my hands, gives me thick sweet tea served in a shot glass with fresh mint leaves floating on top. Then he feeds the chickens—in the house. He sprinkles sunflower seeds over the kitchen floor.

"*Kul. Kul.*" He urges them to eat.

Nourdeen's mother invites me back so that she can teach me how to make couscous and henna my hands and feet, so that Nourdeen can tell me more about Allah and Mohammed.

Nourdeen likes that I "understand" him. He says he feels he knows me. Considering I generally say a whole lotta nuthin', I don't know how that could be. Altogether, the afternoon is pleasant, if not informative. I have to wonder whether it is friendship or conversion that is being cultivated, or God forbid, another marriage set-up. In any case, my attempts to learn about my host country nationals end up teaching me a great deal more about myself.

CHAPTER 28

I hate Matuer

Street view

I am sitting on a standard issue, four-inch mattress in Mateur at Sam's, sleeping bag draped over my legs, hot water bottle pressing against my lower back. Six days ago, I strained something and still I am really sore. I went to the pharmacy this morning in search of relief in the form of a hot water bottle. Because I did not know its name in Arabic, I spent twenty minutes attempting to describe the item I needed, first to the pharmacist, then to his shop keeping assistants and finally to the accumulating shoppers at large.

"A bottle for hot water, for soreness." I struggled. The pharmacist brought me glass bottles of various sizes. "No." He produced an assortment of plastic bottles. People gathered in behind me, offering guesses. Everyone got in on the action; it became a big game show featuring me, the beleaguered contestant and the race to figure out the mystery item. I tried to no avail to elaborate on my description: "A bottle for hot water, to put on my aching back." Someone handed me a glass of water. Finally, a woman tapped me on the shoulder.

"A water bottle for soreness?" Haven't I been saying exactly that?

"Yes! A water bottle for soreness." She turned to the pharmacist, said something I never caught, and voila! Cheers all around. I am the proud owner of a bright blue hot water bottle. Nothing here is easily done.

Mateur is the strangest town I have visited in Tunisia. It feels evil. At night it gets especially dark here, due to the fact that hardly any area of the town has benefit of electric lighting, and partly I think, because it is just a sinister place. People are not as welcoming as in other locales I have ventured. It was here where I was molested in broad daylight by an old man. I was standing right next to Sam in the *souq*. We were buying tangerines when a hand ventured underneath my skirt, right up to my nether regions and dug in. I gasped but could not speak. I was paralyzed, bewildered. I was unable to act. All I could do was to point to the old man, who ran away and disappeared into a crowd on the street. Sam tried to help me in my panic, spinning around wildly in search of the man, ready to pounce. Nothing could be done. Sam is the only reason I come here. I hate Mateur.

CHAPTER 29

I love Kebili

The Sahara

For eight hours my knees jam into the seat in front of me. For eight hours passengers throw up into the center aisle of the bus. For eight hours we dwell in stench and darkness in the sweltering, oppressive foul cloud. It is worth it. This is our voyage to the deep south, to the oasis towns of Kebili and Douz.

Sam, Daniel and I arrive in Kebili at 5:00 a.m., still night. The unanticipated freezing cold is oxygen to deprived lungs—I devour it greedily...I loathe the bus. We step into a *hannute*, the only space at this hour that has its steel door rolled up. The proprietor wears a faded burgundy fez and a well-worn union suit. He works unhurried but efficiently at his singular craft. He specializes in one thing, serving up Tunisia's version of a beignet, bambaloni, sweet donuty cakes. He digs into a huge tub of dough, the consistency of vanilla milkshake—more runny than dense—and pulls out a small wad. He flattens it with a quick twist of his wrist, pops a hole through the center and tosses it into a large drum of hot oil. It sizzles quickly to a crispy brown crunch. He fishes it out and sprinkles sugar over top, then serves it in a section of paper. Hot. Sweet. And, portable. We use one hand to hold our chewy goodness, the other is free to consult our crudely-drawn map. Incredibly, this critical piece of paper with its hand-drawn landmarks and essential details like "turn left at the community spigot" or "right after the mosque" is many times unwarranted. Nine times out of ten we need simply ask: *"Ween dar Ameri-kania?"* Where is the American's house? And anyone or everyone within earshot will point us in the right direction, or give escort. This time is no exception; we are led right to Beth's, my roommate from Hergla. One bonus of living in the capital, I am one of the few volunteers in-country who has any degree of anonymity where I live. Ahhhh, the fishbowl.

Our hostess, Beth, is exceptional. She is a special education volunteer who, after earning her law degree from a prestigious university in the United States, decided to volunteer to go to a developing country instead of going on to earn big bucks. She is here, living on a couple hundred dinars a month, making a difference in this tiny oasis village on the edge of the Sahara. I have to say, I admire those of my brethren who left either budding careers or careers in progress. I left people, but not a "life." So Beth has my admiration for her choice. She opens her door and guides us directly to a collection of mats on the floor. We go right to sleep.

Our starting point for exploration is Old Kebili, once the original site of the town, but now abandoned, save two families and an old mosque which is still lovingly maintained. All of the remaining stone structures are dilapidated and crumbling like ruins. From the minaret, there is a steady stream of the Qur'an being broadcast, a haunting drone blanketing the day, calling. "Come to prayer. Come to the Mosque." It is Friday. Friday is to Muslims what Sunday is to Catholics, the day of obligation. I know obligation. In my childhood, going to mass on Sunday was required. Period. In adolescence, not only attendance was mandated, but proof of attendance in the form of a document. That *and* knowing the name of presiding priest. I watched my brother get booted out of the house after he failed to report an appearance by the Archbishop one Sunday. I know the pull of obligation. For Muslims, especially men, Friday has the added weight of heaven's angels on lookout…and they're taking names! According to one of Mohammed's constant companions, Abu Huraira, (a man who was one of the Prophet's Narrators in Chief responsible for translating the leader's instructions to the faithful) the Prophet said, "On every Friday the angels take their stand at every gate of the mosques to write the names of the people chronologically (i.e. according to the time of their arrival for the Friday prayer) and when the Imam sits (on the pulpit) they fold up their scrolls and get ready to listen to the sermon." I thought I had it tough…Allah has spies!

On and on, reverberating off walls, in and out of spaces, there is one compelling voice, supplicating, prodding and ultimately comforting…seeping into my cell tissue. I am no longer resisting it. The voice follows us wherever we go, our companion. It serenades us as we meander through date groves, weave through rows upon rows of palms dripping with abundant fruit.

The annual date crop yield is a commodity that brings Tunisia roughly fifty million dinars per year. Dates are Kebili's life-source, a staple in the diet, *the* income generator. There are over one hundred varieties of dates known to man. The region in and around Kebili offers the very special Deglet Nour, Queen of Dates, sickeningly sweet, even for me, a certified sugarholic. It has a caramel taste and a long life. It is featured in nationally famous delights, including the very popular *makroud*, small semolina cakes stuffed with dates, hazelnuts, or almonds, cut into diagonal fingerlings, deep fried in oil and drizzled with honey or sugar syrup—mini lead bricks.

Dates occupy a holy place in Islam, as they traditionally break the fast at Ramadan. I can count the number of dates I have consumed on one hand. Arabs eat pounds of them every year. We found them in heaping piles, one after the other, soon to be delivered to a grocer near you. Hard to imagine that a place that delivers such sweetness to the world once exported only slaves.

The slave trade existed in Tunisia until the mid nineteenth century. Kebili used to be one of Tunisia's important slave markets. I live very close to the other one, in the medina in Tunis. Many of the residents in this oasis are Haratin, descendents of slaves. You can see it in their faces, distinguishable by their distinctive differences and skin, dark as night. Kebili is proof that history, even the most heartrending, can be overcome. This place, once an abyss of sorrow and misery, has over time transformed. Expressions are softer. Hands are open. Countenances are happy. Even the palette has blossomed. Instead of bleak ivory *saf saris*, women celebrate and wear color. Passing men in the street is practically pleasant. The children greet with a jubilant *bonjour*, as they did in Herlga. I have missed that. I love Kebili.

With my Arabic improving, my cultural sensitivity honing and confidence rising, I can participate more fully in my surroundings. I cease to be a tourist for larger stretches at a time. I will never be invisible in this country, as is possible back in the States on any given day. I am the elephant in the room, the circus clown, the new puppy, the naive child. I will never be fully assimilated here. But, when I do blend in however temporary, it is very fine indeed.

From Kebili, I get my first sight of the spectacular Sahara. I love the way it is pronounced here: SaH Hra, with a breathy "h" and a rolled "r." The Sahara has an unexpected beauty. It is a glistening white sea whose sugary waves ripple all the way to the horizon. The sand is so soft and fine, I have to rip off my sandals to sift it betwixt my toes, to burrow into it, to feel its warmth on the surface and its coolness deeper and deeper. We scale to the top of the dunes then launch ourselves, several meters at a stretch. We bounce all the way to the bottom of a hollow. We are children let loose at recess; we run and chase and play with abandon.

Further into the Sahara lies Douz, the site of the International Camel Festival, the impetus for our journey. The festival both celebrates and preserves desert culture and has been an important annual event since 1910. Many have come from Algeria, from Libya, and from Tunisia's desert oases. A perimeter of enormous Berber tents has been erected by desert clans. It surrounds what is now the stadium, a sandy expanse of space wherein riders complete astonishing feats of skill while brandishing scimitars and dromedaries or Arabian horses race. Both beast and man are ornately dressed, richly clad in textiles woven of silk that catch the light. They flaunt, with great pageantry, their talents. One man saunters about with six oil jugs balancing on his head. Jubilant dancers thrust their hips to the sounds of drums, *shabbaba*, *rababa* and *mizwits*. There is an extravagant enactment of a Bedouin wedding. And, my favorite aspect, a poetry competition. Though I cannot understand the poetry, I appreciate its inclusion and note its importance in the festivities. The contest keeps alive the Bedouin's principal medium of communication. The Tunisian flag is prominent, as is the twenty foot tall likeness of President Zine Abdine Ben Ali, affixed to a truck which circulates around the field of play. Every time I see his image, plastered as it is throughout the land, I see a vampire, black eyes, black eyebrows in the shape of crescents, his widow peak hairline and tuxedo-ish suit. I don't have to see the fangs to know they're there.

I watch the events for a long while then wander. I join old women making bread in clay ovens, while their men, loosely swathed in layers of wool, from *kuffiya* (head wrap) to sandal, drink tea. Desert people. Nomadic. I study their trappings, tools and gear, the whole of what they own, endlessly conveyed from place to place. They carry only what serves them. So, clearly, material prosperity or acquisition isn't the driver, necessity is. I am strongly drawn to the textiles, hand wrought, dyed, woven, crafted by women's hands, from silk and wool, even fine metal. Textiles are not only utilitarian, functional and durable, but beautiful, saturated with deep color, emphasized with bold geometric designs. There are blankets draped over camels, over saddles, around bridal domes and there are enormous woolen sacks thrown over the backs of dromedaries. I covet them all.

People, and animals that nearly outnumber them, arrive in droves. Tribes of men atop camels fall in behind others, leading packs of greyhound companions called *sloughis*, desert hunting dogs. The men are a union of stark flowing white robes, broken only by the appearance of a red accent, a fez or handkerchief, or a rifle slung over the shoulder. I can't take my eyes away.

I see my first white camels. Rare and pricey, a white camel can fetch over 2,000 Tunisian dinars. Camels, white or otherwise, are extraordinary creatures built for endurance and survival. Their importance in the desert is not disputed. Camels were vital as early as the third century, when they helped create opportunity for regular contact across the Sahara, which lead to the establishment of trade routes and the supporting of economies and dynasties. They are the muscle of the desert man. They provide milk. They can live for decades. They are also worth riding, at least once. How could I come this far and not succumb to the touristy-est of all ventures?

We spend two-and-a-half dinars for our camel journey into the dessert. Thank Allah we have help…help climbing aboard, help getting the animal first to kneel on all fours, then help prodding them to "upsy daisy." The enormous saddle is positioned over the hump; my legs spread so wide to accommodate it, I think I might split in half. The saddle has a wood stalk for grasping, a very prudent addition. Anyone without a death grip on the stalk will be flung into a sand dune, when the beast stands up, front legs first then rear.

We are tethered, my camel to Beth's, Beth's to Daniel's and Daniel's to Sam's. It is not the coolest way to experience a camel ride, but it is practical as the Sahara is a vast domain. Given the way my body is pitching and hurling, there is no concealing how ridiculous I look. I immediately set aside my need to appear as if I do this all the time.

We travel until sand is the whole of our landscape, 360 degrees, an ocean of silica and sky. We stop, disembark and set our eyes set on a herd of camels in the distance arriving from Libya. Several hundred camels and one lone white one, two men tending them all. If I could take and bottle a moment, surely this.

CHAPTER 30

January 1990

Things out of my control

The Sahara and President Ben Ali on display, background

It is the turning of the decade and I am feeling reflective, thinking about the world, feeling rather overwhelmed with recent
events. Though strangely, as my shortwave radio dispenses news of
the globe—one jolt after another—I am safely distant. Last year
alone, a peaceful revolution of young people was bloodied by the old
in China. East Berliners danced on top of the wall that imprisoned
a half a nation. Communism tumbled like dominoes. Things to
celebrate, things to mourn—things out of my control. Things I can
hardly contemplate, operating am I so steadfastly out of range of all
of it.

In my own backyard, Islamic fundamentalism is on the rise. The movement here is not as ominously fanatical as in other places, but similarities abound. Islamists, as they are known here, would settle Tunisia under *Sharia*, Islamic law. Marrying church and state, or rather Mosque and state, is troublesome, especially for those in power. As a political force, the Islamists in Tunisia have been organizing and struggling to be recognized as a legitimate legal party for over twenty years. But they haven't gained traction because President Ben Ali (and President Bourguiba before him) won't allow it.

The biggest fear is fundamentalism's threat to progress. Islamists, in general, support rigid adherence to Sharia law and possess little tolerance for ambiguity in the interpretation of it, citing the Qur'an's authority. Its proponents want to establish new policies and radically reverse others, compulsory veiling for example, and the re-legalization of polygamy. About polygamy, it is widely known throughout the Islamic world that the prophet Mohammed had five wives, as allowed by the Qur'an. The Qur'an "explains" that a man may have more than one wife *if* he can treat them all equally. Either you admit it is universally impossible, unrealistic, unachievable (the Prophet Mohammed excepted) that a man can treat wives equally, or you don't. Tunisia's very first president, Habib Bourguiba did not. He was a true social reformer. He made Tunisia the first and only Islamic country to ban polygamy in 1956.

Tunisia's current president Zine (the beautiful) Ben Ali, deposed Bourguiba in November of 1987, declaring him too senile to rule, but kept the ban in place. He inherited Bourguiba's battle to restrain the growing Islamist movement. He continues to refuse to recognize the legitimacy of the fundamentalists as a political party, claiming that a single party cannot be Islam's only keeper. Everyone is responsible for Islam.

For the vast majority of Muslims, Islam is about peaceful submission to God and there ain't anything political about it. But, there
is this force unwavering in its attitude that even at its most benefi-
cent undermines, weakens and destabilizes. At its most radical, it
militarizes, terrorizes and murders. As much as this government
would like it to go away, it won't.

The fundamentalists are gaining footholds in conservative pockets of the country, with even greater success in neighboring Algeria.
They meet in secret. Or, they meet at the universities where they
have long focused their efforts on spreading their political ideology
to impressionable young people. As a result, the police presence on
campuses is growing. The police presence serves to fuel passions;
students have begun to strike in protest.

In their zeal to express their faith and to articulate their political support for fundamentalism, more and more young women are
veiling. In casual polls of my female students who veil, I have found
that nearly half do so for political reasons. It confuses me why any
woman would want to return to the rule of the Middle Ages, to be
marginalized, to be a second-class citizen. But, it's not that simple.
As I mentioned earlier, as in the case of Besma's sisters, veiling can
be driven by faith, but realistically, social and economic concerns
are perhaps even greater motivations. The reality is that economic
opportunity is severely limited—especially for women. For too
many, the only route to security is marriage. The appearance of piety
(veiling, for example) makes a woman a more attractive candidate
for marriage, implies she will be faithful to her husband and that she
will raise her children steadfast in the faith.

As for those women politicized, they aspire to a society that is
just, under the rule of Islamic law. They envision a society where
stricter adherence to the Sharia will bring equality and an end to

corruption and nepotism. Unfortunately, the fundamentalist men in charge end up exerting most of their energy restricting the rights of women, not focused on those elements that would interpret the law for the benefit of all. Islam doesn't prevent women from seeking education, from earning, from equal protection under the law, from practicing their faith, or from participation in the political process… men do.

For their part, young men sport beards, symbolically and openly displaying their convictions, sometimes making them targets. Last week, the police came during the night without notice and quietly removed the student leaders—*took* them away. I heard that they were taken to southern Tunisia and conscripted into a year of military service. Over five hundred student protesters were arrested. Police used dogs, tear gas and hot water to quell the dissent. The students, some caught feeding on the atmosphere of radicalism, others voicing protest, continue to provoke.

Fundamentalists manipulate Islam to their own end. The government—sometimes ruthlessly—wrestles to protect power, to compel peace, to stem the rising tide, refusing to allow the chaos that festers in neighboring Algeria to contaminate the populace here. Politics and religion; one seems impossible without the other.

CHAPTER 31

Things in my control

View from medina house rooftop terrace
of the Arab League (in the background)

It's a little after 5 a.m. and call to prayer is blasting for the third time in thirty minutes. I was already awake. Stress manifests itself differently in everyone. Mine has appeared in the form of sleeplessness. I am in the clutches of insomnia, struggling for weeks now to get more than two hours of sleep at a stretch. In my room, Sam's partially finished tree on the wall needs red and orange. Directly overhead is a fresh 12 by 9 foot dark gray section of concrete clinging somehow to the ceiling. Here's hoping it stays put. Smack dab in the middle of the slab, Hedi, the guy my landlord dispatched to fix the cave-in, painted a white crescent moon and star—symbols from the Tunisian flag, symbols of Islam. The east wall is being consumed by a mold monster, mangling my expensive new paint job. It spreads like a virulent form of cancer, rapidly invading other areas of the medina house. In the adjacent room, I can hear John, a visiting PCV, snoring. His voluminous rattles fill the spaces and echo through the chambers of the house. He's been here almost two years; he sleeps just fine.

If I cannot dream in a sleep state, I can work on one not altogether based in reality. I have decided to return to the U.S. in August to attend my brother Dan's wedding to Melissa—an interesting decision given my budget constraints. Thinking about a return visit home is too much a stimulant. So, I lay in bed noting my distractions, flirting with fantasy, ignoring other niggling considerations.

Like...I should budget (right, thinking about money is going to lull me to sleep). My stipend is depleted well before month's end. When I arrived in-country, I already had a finely-honed scarcity mentality, albeit one that was acquired in a kingdom of plenty. Negotiating want is a relentless aspect of my culture. I am like most Americans; my wants are rarely subject to my needs. In the material world, Americans have the most stuff and are eternally in the process of acquiring even more. I didn't get it until now. Less *is* more. Short of a little tummy grumbling, other perceived voids have been filled. I scrape together meals from remnants of food in my bare bulb-illuminated sparse dwelling. I haven't a dooroo in my pocket. Yet, I am content. It is stunning to realize I have little and hardly want for anything. This may be the greatest lesson I learn here.

And, while I am at it, I have a few more things to work on:

I will cultivate patience (with a particular nod to bureaucracy). I know most things get done eventually.

My understanding of my hosts requires further consideration and active digging. Somewhere, buried under behaviors, demonstrated by conduct, expressed in speech, are the core values. What is said, what is done—even the incomprehensible—sheds light. Why are men unapologetically aggressive? Why is *n'shallah* (God willing) such a dominant expression in the national lexicon? Why do people universally find it pitiable that I am alone here? Why is it perfectly okay for a man to grab my butt, but not okay for him to grab the tush of a Tunisian gal?

It is also time to improve my comprehension of Arab/Israeli history and relations and the U.S.'s past and current policy therein. As my Arabic improves, so too do the opportunities to weigh in on the many conversations that purport Israel to be America's spoiled child, conversations that call out the U.S. for its role in the injustices toward the Palestinians—a most prominent issue in the collective Arab memory—conversations that put me in the position of having to answer for it all.

I must see my volunteer commitment through, not bail. Volunteers, multiple volunteers, continue to leave. I do not want to be one of them.

Above all else, I ought to let my head do the driving for a while.

These things are in my control. Call them resolutions, declarations. The meanderings of my restless mind are in fact the substance of my adventure.

Now, for my wish list: I hope that love comes to me—at the very least—in the amounts I give. (I wish I weren't so weak).

CHAPTER 32

February 1990

Professor Parisien, you don't say...

Thuburbo Majus

The textbooks finally showed up! They are shiny and new, with lots of drawings...but I am not celebrating this good fortune. I can't, because the textbooks are...weird. They remind me, mostly due to the artwork, of comic books, dark comic books. The limited budget allowed for the choice of one color in addition to black. Red was chosen. Every image in the book, including the cover, is some jarring shade of gray and blood-red. It's unpleasant. However, it's the only resource I have and I am required to use it.

By contrast, the scenes and scenarios throughout the text (offered for the purpose of (re)introducing parts of speech) are boring, and the characters within them can't decide if they are English or Tunisian. They go from "tea" to "*mechoui*" (barbeque), from the "grocer" to the "*souq*," from the "loo" to well, you get the picture. A real identity crisis. My colleagues here in the department, a married couple from London whom I call Mr. and Mrs. Happy (being totally facetious here, as they are two of the most cheerless people I know), had a heavy hand in the book's creation. Because this was a home-made effort, mum's the word when it comes to criticism.

Scene: My classroom earlier this evening. In attendance, thirty-two false-start first-year students, ages eighteen to forty-five, scattered amid the theater-style seating. I am at my usual perch, sitting on the desk at the front of the room. It is a huge, old-school oak desk. It could have come from any elementary school in America. Other than those features, the room is utterly forgettable. There is nothing on the walls except for the whiteboard at the front and a speaker stuck up in the corner. The room is only mine for a few hours a day, so I haven't endeavored to uplift these surroundings. The classroom is drab, drab, drab.

Me: "Open your books and turn to page 19, please."

Students shuffle until everyone ends up on page 19. There is a crude drawing of a middle-aged couple, sporting Arab features, standing in a well-appointed, European-style kitchen. Their caricatures are not at all flattering.

Me: "This is a conversation between two people. Can I have two volunteers read it, please?"

In a flash, Abdelrazzeik and Souqeina, my class clowns in a class of clowns, are out of their seats and shimmying down the aisle over bodies. No one else stands a chance. Abelrazzeik plunks down on my desk; Souqeina takes up a position front and center. This enthusiasm is not for the love of English, mind you. These are my entertainers; I got their number.

Me: "Abdelrazzeik, you can be Salim; Souqeina, you are Lotfa. Go ahead."

Abdelrazzeik, as Salim: "I am hungry. Is it time for tea?"

Abdelrazzeik as Abdelrazzeik: "I don't understand. I don't eat tea."

Me: "In England, tea is a time to eat, like lunch or dinner. Continue please…"

Souqeina, as Lotfa: "Yes, I am hungry, too. Let's prepare bangers and mash."

Abdelrazzeik as Abdelrazzeik: "*Mademoiselle, shnuwwa* bangers and mash?"

Me: "Use English, please."

Abdelrazzeik as Abdelrazzeik: "Sorry, Miss. What is bangers and mash?"

Me: "I have no idea." (I should have asked the Mr. and Mrs. in the staff-room before class). Abdelrazzeik as Abdelrazzeik: "Do you eat bangers and mash in America?"

Souqeina as Souqeina: "Couscous is better."

Me: "I think you might be right."

Various students: "Couscous is *bnina* (delicious)."

"It is our national food."

"Have you had couscous, Miss?"

"You should come to my house. My mother can make couscous for you."

Me: "Can we continue? Abdelrazzeik?"

Abdelrazzeik as Salim: "I will help you cook. I can peel the…. the…the botatoes?"

Souqeina as Souqeina: "You? Cook? *Yikthb*. (He lies.)"

Various students: "*Yikthb*, ahhhh ha ha ha ha."

"You can cook, Abdelrazzeik?"

"*Mademoiselle*, can you cook?"

Abdelrazzeik as Abdelrazzeik: "*Shnua* 'botatoes?' (What are potatoes?)"

Me: "English please. Puh-puh-puh-po-tay-toz." (There is no "P" in Arabic.) "Potatoes are vegetables that grow in the ground, root vegetables. You make fries from them."

Abdelrazzeik as Abdelrazzeik: Shaking his head, still uncertain. "Fries? *Shnuwwa* Botatoes?" he asks the class.

No one seems to know.

Me: "*Ba-ta-ta.*" (Arabic for potato. I held out as long as I could. Complete immersion in my class? No way.)

Classroom: "Ahhhhh, *batata.*"

Abdelrazzeik as Abdelrazzeik: "*Shnuwwa* bangers and mash?"

Me: "Okay, instead of bangers, let's just say couscous, since you brought it up. Bangers is now couscous. Salim and Lotfa are going to make puh-puh-puh-potatoes and couscous. Carry on."

Abdelrazzeik as Abdelrazzeik: "We will also have *fil fil* (peppers) and *l ham* (meat) and *hummus* (chickpeas) with our *kus kus:i* (couscous)."

Classroom: "And, *sfinna:rya* (carrots). And *bsal* (onions)."

Me: "English, please. Lotfa is going to read. Lotfa, read please."

Souqeina as Lotfa: "Oh no. I forgot to market today. What shall we do?"

Lotfa as Lotfa: "*Shnuwwa* market?"

Me: "In English, please."

Lotfa as Lotfa: "What is market?"

Me: "Market in this case means to shop for food."

Abdelrazzeik as Abdelrazzeik: "Ahhh *mushkla kbir* (big problem). *"Mfammsh* puh-puh-puh-po-tate-toes." (There are no potatoes.) "I think no one will eat today."

End Scene

I cannot blame the disintegration of the lesson on the weird
book. In the hands of someone else it could quite possibly be the
holy grail of English instruction—for this setting, though, I doubt
it. At minimum, I hoped it would support me. With or without it,
truth is I have too many days like this: confused, certain of where
we need to go, but with no clue as to how to get us there. In my
classroom, the route to learning is indirect. We travel it together.
The students haven't tired of having me as their teacher. I get smiles
aplenty. I get feisty eagerness not entirely attributable to a passion
for learning English, but a desire to be here nonetheless. I sense
they are relishing the uniqueness of our arrangement as much as I
am. Our lives intersect for a time because we have much to learn
from one another.

CHAPTER 33

YSWF & Catholic—in an Arab world

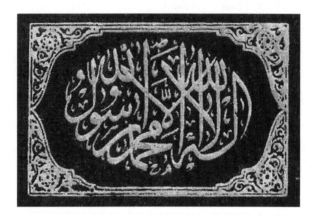

The medina gives up a secret: it is tucked away, a twenty-minute walk from 173 Rue de la Kasbah. The narrow cobblestone streets snake under archways, through echo chambers, in and out of sun and shadow, delivering me to wrought iron gates that wrap around a quaint lush and shady garden. Encompassed within is a church that could exist anywhere, but it is here, an anomaly with brightly colored stained glass windows and white spire reaching up to the light. I immediately attach to it as a place I inherently know. I have stumbled upon a safe harbor, one that offers a singular service in English and whose gates are always locked, except for two hours on Sunday morning. Attendance at the Anglican service is sparse. It lacks the pageantry and ritual that, given the context in which I find myself, would be comforting.

I spent my youth wrapped tightly in religious tradition, in the comfort of passive ritual, falling into harmony with a group in prayer.

After two decades of Sunday masses under my belt, I can effortlessly pour forth without hesitation or thought every required word and action of the mass, so deeply am I programmed. I completed every sacrament, attended every service, having long awaited the presence of God, felt or accepted. Faith, I was schooled, is believing even in the absence of direct evidence. Human that I am, I will always desire a more tangible connection to the divine.

That I have initiated a quest to find a church is worthy of note. In my childhood, I resented compulsory attendance at Catholic mass each and every weekend (previously stated) and with it, compulsory attendance at catechism. I despised the infringement on my liberty. I was quick to judge aspects of Catholicism I found abhorrent, things such the use of fear to enforce faithfulness, blatant and rigid gender inequality, sermons, monotony. I had no choice but to sit there, in that highly varnished pew, for—one—full—hour every weekend of my life. So, I cherry-picked. I distracted myself with things more entertaining: other parishioners, noting who sang and who didn't, clothing, hairstyles, boys, the smell and billowing of incense, the rituals, the glittery accoutrements and once in a great while, an occasion to accept communion from Father Tom.

Priests are supposed to be God's representatives on Earth. To me they were simply men in robes, except for Father Tom, who was so good at his job that he seemed to channel Jesus. When he said, "This is the body of Christ" and placed communion on my tongue, I swear it was Jesus looking out from those luminous green eyes. I was completely helpless, laid open, humbled and loved. I'd return to my seat in a daze of reassurance and resurrection; singular moments of authentic union, when however briefly, I was coupled with the divine. Sounds hokey, but these 'communions' were inexplicably, undeniably real to me. Amid a lifetime otherwise preoccupied, there have been precious few occasions of pure knowing. I am at one moment conscious in spirit and the next completely oblivious to it. This is the wishy-washy faith from whence I come. So, it's interesting that I now find myself on the search for a church, a sanctuary…a life raft.

Just beyond the entrance to the medina, at the top of Avenue Habib Bourguiba is an enormous neo-Romanesque Cathedral, built in 1882 and named for St. Vincent de Paul, who was once captured at sea by African pirates and carried as a slave to Tunis. Normally, the cathedral's huge iron gates are locked barring entrance to everyone. On rare occasions the gates open. But, passage is restricted by an elderly caretaker who requires money for cursory tours of the environs. It bothers me greatly that Tunis' two churches are largely inaccessible to me. Today one of the gates is wide open and there is no sign of the old guy. I quickly dash inside, expecting him to intercept me at any moment. It is very dark, enormous and cold. My footsteps echo as I make my way forward to a crucifix near the front alter. I kneel down in the shadows on the floor. I look up into the face of Jesus and instantly I am overcome with emotion. In the dim, on the cool marble floor, I cry uncontrollably for the first time since I left home. In a country where God is supposedly everywhere, he's been for me absent…until now.

The question of faith is a big one for many of the volunteers. Some have abandoned theirs altogether, others flounder in the absence of community. We are all challenged daily, bombarded by everyone in our path whose duty it is to educate us, save us from ourselves. It is a struggle maintaining this personal distance, protecting our doctrine, while attempting to integrate and engage with our hosts. These are serious personal affronts to each of us. In all of my conversations with other volunteers, I have yet to find one person who is navigating well in this particular arena. I had today one perfect moment of communion, one sweet moment of surrender. I cannot walk in the shoes of Islam, this I know, but, the old ones have never fit so well either.

• • •

I have solved the question of Nourdeen's intentions. He is a true believer with a singular goal. He wants to convert me and every last one of my infidel friends. He has glommed onto Daniel. Daniel, my guardian angel, generously saved me from bearing the burden of Nourdeen's speeches alone. It started some weeks ago, when Nourdeen was visiting me at the medina house. He and I were drinking English tea and eating fresh bread slathered with homemade butter. I was getting pummeled about the concept of the holy trinity and the crucifixion of Christ—just another casual visit from Nourdeen. The idea that God is anything other than purely monotheistic is blasphemous in Islam. "If Jesus was clearly a man, than how can he be God? God is infinite. Man is finite." Once again, I was on the hot-seat, until Daniel stepped into the conversation, pulled Nourdeen's strings at just the right moment, taking the pressure off me. This only fueled the man's passion: "a-ha, I can save two lost souls at once!"

Daniel is so good. People genuinely interest him. To him, every interaction is an opportunity to learn something. I can practically see his wheels turning when he engages. He makes the other person matter. There is no end to his patience, his willingness to entertain Nourdeen's relentless efforts. Now when Nourdeen visits, I can sit back and drink my tea, Earl Grey loaded with milk and sugar and watch the two of them go at it: Daniel, the master puppeteer versus Nourdeen the very willing pawn. Or vice versa.

CHAPTER 34

English, English everywhere

Hedi, the fixture outside my door

Today I formally requested a site change, to be allowed to move from the capitol to the city of Beja, two hours west. My primary motivation is the fact that in Tunis, I am regularly in the company of other Americans. Not that I haven't fully enjoyed the medina house's social atmosphere, the camaraderie has been incredible and I love my new friends. But, if I remain here, I will be deprived of the authentic, fully immersed Peace Corps experience that I really want. For weeks I have been considering the pros and cons of moving. Beja offers solitude, open air, access to nature, less bodies, less hassle, greater teaching freedom (if that's possible) and expanded opportunities to speak Arabic and plunge into the culture. However, it will be less convenient, lonely, not as comfy vis-à-vis living quarters, significantly less cosmopolitan and socially restricted. Plus, I will miss Besma. Additionally, there is the process of adapting to a new location, figuring out all over again where everything is, how everything is accomplished.

My formal site change request—a well-rehearsed sales pitch—to my Peace Corps boss included presentation of my "hotel registry." I have maintained a list of all of the visitors who have stayed in the medina house since the night of our swearing-in. The office doesn't always find it necessary to house volunteers in hotels when they require them to be in Tunis for various reasons. They have instead come to rely on the hospitality of the medina house. So, when I presented my record of 154 hotel nights as evidence of the overwhelming presence of Americans in my Peace Corps experience, little could be argued. In fact, in the past four weeks, we have gone only one evening without guests.

As it happens, one of the other factors that prompts my pitch is timing. One of the two positions at the Bourguiba School in Beja will be vacated by Molly, who is due to complete her service soon. I don't know much about Beja, or the school, other than Molly has been really happy there—motivation enough for me. There are four more months left in this, my first year of teaching. I wait additionally for approval from the administrators at the IBLV-Tunis who will ultimately determine whether I will remain here or venture further afield.

In the meanwhile, not content with being idle and ineffective in their respective sites, five first-year volunteers are requesting to be moved into the English teaching program rather than remain in their original assignments doing nothing. Keith is one such volunteer. He has approached me about helping him establish an English program in Aïn Draham, in the beautiful northwest near his site of Beni M'tir.

As a teacher I am required to occupy myself during the coming summer months with a Secondary Project of my own creation, one that requires, of course, the blessing of Peace Corps Tunis. Keith's brainchild found me making a second pitch to my APCD in as many weeks. I was given approval from the director of the Bourguiba Institute to begin work on what may become an Institute satellite school in Aïn Draham. All that is really needed are teachers, students and a classroom. Those five languishing volunteers previously mentioned? They will be my teachers…did I just say that? *My* teachers? Dare I presume I can teach what I barely know myself? I have enlisted help from Lisa, a member of the China Five group (recall they're the real teachers among us posers). She has happily agreed to join the adventure. Who could say no to summer in the temperate, cork forested, idyllic Aïn Draham? It's a win-win scenario: bored volunteers gain skills that allow them to fulfill their mission; students get free access to English lessons; and we all have a great summer!

· · ·

I shouldn't admit this. It is a guaranteed ticket home, dishonorable discharge worthy…I am moonlighting. For just a few hours a week, I tutor the executives at Tunisia's tallest modern hotel, the Hotel Africa. We meet in a professional conference room, all the top brass and me. They arrive with notebooks and focused attention—

shockingly different from the social club that is my classroom. We sail through the lessons with nary a disruption and afterward take our discussions anywhere we please, except of course in the direction of politics. The participants are keen on improving their interactions with the English-speaking business community. In particular, they seek to understand the "American businessman" who they see as impersonal and always pressed for time. Part of my program requires them to provide (in English) updates on current events in and around Tunis, as they or members of their staff might for a guest of the hotel. They get to practice and I get clued in to cultural events about town, like concerts by the Tunis Symphony Orchestra in the magnificent Municipal Theater, or the upcoming Carthage Film Festival, which this year will feature work by a Tunisian filmmaker.

Breaking Peace Corps' explicit rules about earning extra dinars is, I'll admit, foolish. Foolish because it weighs on my conscience, foolish because of the serious consequences I face should I be discovered, foolish because the English-speaking community is miniscule which raises the real possibility that I *could* be discovered. Foolish! Getting home for my brother's wedding has me crazy motivated, enough to assume the risk. Getting home on my meagerly stipend—without supplementation—is implausible. Once my ticket is purchased, I will cease my illegal activities forthwith. In the meantime, I lay low, skulk my way to the hotel and make more money in two hours than most professionals here make in a week, dirty rat that I am.

CHAPTER 35

March 1990

Ramadan

Spices at Central Market in Tunis

Part preparation, part warning, we've been issued a memo from our Peace Corps Director informing us that we are in our last lunar month before the start of the much anticipated, highly celebrated, holy month of Ramadan. We don't get much in the way of communication from our director; this must be important. "Dear Volunteers:...It's probably a good idea to get the word out, especially to first–year people...Be on your guard during what can be a difficult time for everyone...as the month goes on, peoples' fuses get shorter and shorter and sometimes, fights break out in public places...People who have been very kind to you all year will suddenly turn sullen and xenophobic." What kind of holiday *is* this?

In the classroom, anticipation is palpable as my socially-restricted students are suddenly downright chatty, almost animated, out of which comes: "Mademoiselle, are you going to fast?" In my classroom, conversations abruptly cease. All eyes turn on me. Here's what I know at this point. Ramadan seems an awful lot like Lent, with significantly more deprivation thrown into the mix. From sunup to sundown, able-bodied Muslims (the exempt include the elderly, travelers, small children and women in a certain condition) abstain from food, from drink, from tobacco, and from sexual relations, for an entire month. An entire month. For my students fasting (recall that it is one of the Five Pillars of Islam) is mandatory. Am I going to fast? I have a choice—they do not. I respond with my own question.

"Why do you do it (outside of the reality that it's required)?" Here's what they tell me. Fasting purifies the body and mind, allowing one to draw closer to God (a universally accepted reason). Fasting teaches self control. Fasting promotes kinship with other believers. By experiencing lack, as the poor do, fasting teaches empathy. Fasting is a good "regime." What? Fasting is good for the physique (Abdelrazzeik stands up and flexes his muscles in demonstration). Fasting is good for the health of the body—not synonymous with the previous answer. Will I fast? Perhaps.

Around 610 A.D., while wandering solo in the desert near Mecca, a caravan trader named Mohammed heard a voice from the heavens. It was the angel Gabriel, who informed him that he had been chosen to receive the word of God. During the month that followed, Mohammed received the verses that became the Qur'an. Ramadan celebrates this month through self-sacrifice and devotion to God. Fasting is a form of self-purification. Ramadan's intense spiritual power comes from marrying the fast to prayer. Mosques fill in the evenings, when a portion of the Qur'an is read one-thirtieth at a time, each night to month's end, until the entire holy book has been recited. Ramadan is also a time of charity and good deeds. With all this devotion and goodwill afoot, I am not sure where xenophobia and public fighting fits in. Only time will tell.

Along with the warnings contained in the director's letter were these words: "Some people say the only way to understand Ramadan is to do it yourself." I have claimed all along that I want to immerse in the culture. It's time to walk my talk: my "when in Rome" moment. My Carpe Diem. How hard can it be? A little self-control, a little purification, a little bit of struggle never hurt anyone. And, Lord knows I could use a spiritual tune-up.

At 4:00 a.m. on the first day the holy month, I hear the banging of pots and pans echoing through narrow the streets far below my open window. Accompanying the clashing is a booming Arabic voice calling all to wake and eat before sunrise. I am ready! I get up and eat enough pancakes to bloat me until nightfall. Everything has adjusted to accommodate the month of Ramadan. Food, coffee and smoking establishments, the core gathering places, are shut tight. Instead, the crowds pack into the Central Market, making it more frenzied than I have ever seen it; everyone in the throes of anticipation of the first evening's feast.

My teaching schedule has been altered for the holiday. I will teach only seven hours per week, instead of my normal twelve, in the afternoons instead of evenings. Seven hours per week! I might have to stay here forever. Of course, the Institute neglected to inform anyone of the schedule change and no one showed up for class today. I take it…in stride. The girl who once huffed and puffed all the way from staff room to coffee shop, now accepts certain things without question or fury.

• • •

Already I have cheated and it is just the first day. I had a glass of tea, behind closed doors, in the sanctity and privacy of my home. Oh, and a few licks from the spoon I used to mix coffee cake. I would never commit such an indiscretion in public. Nor will I mention the matter to anyone.

When the sun finally drops below the horizon and a length of black thread can no longer be distinguished from the white, deprivation is over. The day's fast comes to an abrupt joyful end. Feast and celebration ensue. Restaurants crank out food tirelessly until the initial wave of the starved masses, already seated at every table in every restaurant, has been fed. The cafes, closed during daylight, are finally open and are packed. The normally deserted late-night streets of the medina now see happy holiday goers, arm-in-arm, tummies fat & happy, filled with unique delicacies enjoyed only during Ramadan. Musicians entertain large crowds. Women are suddenly out in force, too. Not solo, mind you, but in cheerful packs. The lights are all on. Night becomes day. For an entire month.

A few days later... This Ramadan thing is proving rather challenging. I made the mistake of making peanut butter. Fresh peanut butter. The absolutely, most-incredible, best-I-have-ever-tasted kind of peanut butter. It just so happens, I have a little chocolate on hand. My willpower simply cannot bear these distractions in such close proximity. I cheat, just a teensy-weensy bit.

I don't think I am the only one doing things clandestinely. There are enormous black drapes covering the views into certain

establishments around town. I know there are people eating, drinking, smoking, doing all manner of the prohibited behind them. Today
I shall do better: today I fast in earnest. Interesting that Ramadan
coincides with Lent this year. Right now, as he does annually, Dad
is fasting, denying himself most everything, save bread and water,
for forty days and forty nights. He is a model of deprivation. I
wonder what he would think about my observance of Ramadan
(such as it is).

• • •

Tonight I break the fast with my neighbors. We share the stairwell and a small hallway that contains just our doors. There are five
in the family, including parents, two daughters, ages eighteen and
twenty-two, and a ten year-old boy, Ben Assan. The little one plays
soccer in the stairwell. I feel badly that this is his play area, that the
exuberance of the boy is being spent on a dark stairwell. Earlier
this week our front door was ajar and he wandered right into the
house, through the dining room and directly into my bedroom. He
didn't notice passing me as I sat at our table writing. He meandered
slowly, taking everything in, as if he was in a museum observing
great works of art. He was spectacularly innocent and open. I didn't
want to interrupt the moment, so I watched, saying nothing. His
eyes fell upon the tree painted on my wall. Sam's work is finally
completed. I have a glorious autumn tree in full color. From the
corner of the room, it climbs all the way up, curling long branches
around two walls. He let out a little gasp. His gaze descended to
the flowers I'd painted, growing out of the top of the chair rail tiles.
He traced his finger along the tops of them until he came to a ques-
tionable rendering of a violet. He halted, turned and walked back

across the hall, greeting me sweetly on the way out. I really like Ben Assan.

News of my fasting has spread and invitations to the evening meal are flooding in. To accept an invite to a Ramadan meal is to overdose on hospitality. I am *bintee*, my daughter, at once adopted into the family. I am waited on, hand and foot, reserved and served the best portions of the Ramadan feast. I cannot clear my plate; food replenishes as if by magic. Spicy macaroni, crisp salad, savory sauces, freshly squeezed orange juice, ubiquitous Coke, tea, sweets, piles upon piles of food. After denying myself every day until approximately 7 p.m., food takes on a whole new delight—every morsel is a celebration in my mouth. Different house, different night, same barrage of attention, every night for two weeks straight. My fasting for Ramadan has been an express flight deep into the culture.

· · ·

I am awakened for the second time in my life by an unmistakable "baaaa" echoing from somewhere very close by. I find it living in the stairwell, tethered to the handrail just outside my door. There is straw strewn all over the stairs and a little bucket with water. The neighbor's door opens. Ben Assan peeks out and smiles.

"We're having sheep for dinner. You can come." A few hours later, I watch the animal meet its end, right on the kitchen floor. My vegetarian inclinations are greatly tested here. The pressure to consume that which has been generously offered is potent. I haven't yet found an inoffensive way to decline the hunks of meat and gristle that show up on my plate.

· · ·

As the days wear on, I am beginning to understand what the director meant when he cautioned of the emergence of xenophobia and behavioral challenges. All day fasting followed by all night excess is taking its toll on the populace and my students, who complain that they simply cannot focus in class because of the fasting.

"Teacher." They say. "There is no ability of concentration. It is too difficult." I remind them that I am also fasting, but ready to work. The pep talk has little effect. They are unambiguously lethargic. They slump in their seats. Some even nap.

As for xenophobia, yesterday I was walking in the medina and a man walked right up to me and punched me in the sternum. I think he was aiming for the tiny crucifix I wear around my neck, which may have become exposed. I wasn't hurt so much as stunned. I also witnessed fully veiled women having a knock-down drag-out fight. They came to blows over a taxi, first shoving one another, escalating to spitting, climaxing in an all-out brawl. A police van filled with officers was parked just across the street. They observed with complete indifference; they didn't make a move to break up the altercation. They must be tiring of the frequent confrontations, flaring up out of nowhere. Finally, when one of the women was about to lose her shirt, two officers moseyed over and begrudgingly stepped in.

Ramadan feels less festive in these waning days; preservation instinct seems to be setting in. This is why our director felt it necessary to warn us. Like everyone else, I wait all day for evening's release. If I didn't have the support of many Tunisian friends, I'd given up long ago. They tell me how healthy I look, claim that my "regime" is doing me wonders. The phrase "live to eat" has taken on a whole new dimension. Some days are downright challenging. However, every moment of craving gets me closer to tapping into some of the mysteries and wonders of this culture.

CHAPTER 36

April 1990

Trampling the wildflower

Jasmine nosegay with rose

The hour is very late when I hear frenzied knocking at my door, too late for *louages* or buses to be arriving in Tunis rendering guests to the medina house; the pounding too frantic to be a visit of a casual nature. I open the door to see a women, wrapped head to toe in her *saf sari*, her wild eyes peering out. I don't immediately identify her until she asks me if Besma is in my house. No. I invite Besma's mother in. She has never been here before. I am surprised she even knows where I live. She is awfully agitated.

"Are you sure she is not here?"

"*W'Allah* (swear to god). No. What's wrong?"

"I need your help." She is desperate. "I don't know what to do." She explains that Besma and two girlfriends had gone out earlier tonight to partake of Ramadan's merriment. The streets were celebratory and bustling with activity (no doubt Besma wanted to be in the thick of it). Her brother, the ultra-religious believer, had spotted her flirting with strange men. I can picture her, laughing, playful, not sleazy. I can picture him, watching from the shadows, seething with judgment, plotting her punishment. Punish her he did. When she arrived home, he pummeled her to a pulp. There was nothing anyone in her family could or would do to intervene. The preservation of a woman's chastity is sacrosanct. This is non-negotiable. It was his duty to administer justice so that honor could be restored to the family.   Somehow, women are accountable for upholding the family's honor; the very sanctity of a family's name rises or falls with the choices made by the female members of the family. It isn't that Besma was grossly inappropriate. The "flirtation" occurred on a crowded Tunis street where generally some leeway is given. But, it just so happens, the most radical member of her staunchly conservative house witnessed the behavior and took her affront as a personal attack on his honor and the honor of his family. At the ready, he was more than eager to restore it. In the absence of compassion or ally at home, she ran away.

It would make sense that she would run to the sanctuary of the medina house, but she chose not to. She went underground.

"Please find her. Please." Her mother pleads with me.

The next morning, I head to the store where Besma works as a cashier. She hasn't shown up. I go to the homes of her friends, and friends of friends, until finally, I am led to the house of a stranger, who is helping to hide her. She is a mess, a terrified beaten child, hiding in a corner. She sits with her knees pulled into her chest, her head resting on her folded arms, as small and defeated as anyone can be. When she looks up at me, I start crying. Her eyes are nearly swollen shut and purple. She has deep cuts on her cheek bone and chin. He has beaten the beauty and joy right out of her, but her defiance is very much intact.

"I am not going back." She says. I'm not about to persuade her.

"I wouldn't either."

"I will leave."

"Leave?"

"To Paris. My mother will help me."

"How?" She explains that while her brother was pounding her, she had made the mistake of screaming her intention to run away to France. He stopped briefly. Then, he produced her passport, waved it in her face, set it aflame and set to beating her again. When the trouncing was over, she left, but not before locking eyes with her mother. She knew in that moment her mother would help her.

When I arrive to Besma's house with my news, her mother quickly ushers me into the family room. In hushed tones she tells me she had helped Besma obtain her passport in secret, but her son had discovered it. She knows that her daughter feels imprisoned living under the vigilant authoritarian eye of her son.

"My son is passionate...Besma must obey...or else." Or else, what? More beatings? Might he kill her one day? The subtext of her comments is too much to bear. Though she cannot comprehend her, Besma's mother loves her enough to help her escape. But even she is afraid of her son. She cannot not overtly help Besma. So, she moves in secret, without the knowledge of her husband or her children. She will save her wildflower daughter even if it means sending her, with nothing, alone, to a foreign country.

I never saw my sweet Besma again. She made her escape to Paris in secret. Over the years we have had sporadic phone conversations. She has a son. She is struggling. But, she lives without fear of reprisal. She lives on her own terms. Her jubilant voice is testament to a spirit in full force, one that has found a measure of the freedom she nearly died trying to claim.

CHAPTER 37

Khadijia

Khadijia was the daughter of the wealthy business merchant Khuwaylid and the first wife of the Prophet Mohammed, a most revered woman of Islam. For some reason, it is also a slang term catcalled to women of generous posteriors. I have a new roommate. Kristy abruptly moved out, but not before finding a replacement for Daniel and me. Patty hails from Oklahoma. She is a large animal husbandry volunteer who is working with area farmers and extension agents to develop successful farming practices with regard to their bovine. Patty's job has earned her the following term of endearment: Cow Patty.

She is the most unusual combination of things. She is smart as a whip, a computer geek, a farmer with an air of English aristocrat, hysterically funny and completely unpretentious. Patty moves through life as though hers is a sitcom. Generally, my funny bone is a bit dull. When jokes get told, I'm the stoic one. I wish it weren't so, but it is. Enter Patty, real, ridiculous and the first one to laugh out loud at her own absurdity. She is non-stop amusement, the source of deep belly laughter and to my great joy the newest resident of the medina house.

Patty is a full-size girl, very comfortable and perfect in her own skin. Yesterday on the walk home from the central market, a man sang out, "Ya Khadijia" in a rather suggestive tone after we had passed. We swung around to investigate and caught him leering at Patty, like she was a piece of steak (not altogether appropriate Ramadan etiquette).

"Khadijia? He wants you." I said. To which she replied, "I love this country!" I thought of Besma and her obsession with layering her wardrobe, claiming men do not fancy skinny women. She is….was…quite willing to suffocate herself in the middle of August to appear more ample. Most of her layers were acquired from my closet, as she would never be permitted to behave in such a manner at home. In any case, you lose no points for carrying a few extra pounds here—how very refreshing. Patty is free to be the goddess she is.

Patty also has wretched Arabic language skills, bless her heart, though she tries. In need of staples, we trek over to the Monoprix, the Tunisian version of a supermarket. One aspect of shopping that I love is the almost complete lack of packaging. This means many items, including all fruits, vegetables, meats, cheeses, nuts, spices, henna, incense, even butter, are displayed in bulk and can be evaluated, smelled, touched, even sampled. I can actually get close to my food without a veneer of Styrofoam and plastic obscuring its relative freshness. And, in a country that doesn't exactly have uniformity of garbage disposal, who needs more discards clogging the medina streets? Purchased in increments, the portioning, weighing and packaging of most food stuffs is done by the vendor. Everything is wrapped in paper or in pages from a magazine, rolled into cones or wedges or blocks. Shopping is collected in locally made baskets called *ghouffas*, the well-worn apparatus of daily living.

On this particular day in the Monoprix, the man behind the counter is serving a horde of Tunisian women. Being Ramadan, shopping remains the major undertaking of the day and all are engaged in the quest for tonight's ingredients. Accustomed now to the lack of queues, Patty and I cram ourselves into the mix. Ahead of us, there is a woman cloaked in her white saf sari, the edges clamped together in her mouth. When she places her order, it is through clenched teeth and layers of material:

"*Ki:lu zbda*" (one kilo of butter). The deli-guy quickly produces a colossal block of butter from which he will cut the customer's portion. Upon seeing this magnificent slab, the hugest hunk of butter you ever did see, Patty exclaims—at the top of her lungs: "*Shu:f, zib kbir!*" Every single head spins at once in Patty's direction. I am gone. Coward that I am, I leave her to face them alone. What Patty meant to say was, "Wow, check out the huge block of butter." What she in fact said was "Look at the huge penis." True story.

Safely on the street, Patty has no idea of the particulars, only that it is evident she's muddled something up. Patty is a smorgasbord of bloopers, like telling the restaurant host—in the sweetest lilting Arabic you can imagine—that her meal tasted like shit, when she believed herself to be paying a high compliment. What is eternally endearing, beyond her gaffes, is her ability to be the first to laugh at them, that is, if she is clued in.

· · ·

Patty and I are in Mornag, a village on Tunis's outskirts. We have plans to visit a volunteer friend here, but our rendezvous is falling apart, not unusual. Why I relied on Patty to direct us to Lisa's house, I can't recall. Patty has forgotten exactly where it is, but not before leading us astray. She is the Pied Piper and I, as well as every small male in the village, have fallen in line behind her. A parade wandering aimlessly to nowhere—what a spectacle.

"Oh dear." She says in her typical manner of singsong pronouncement. "Looks like we've gone and gotten ourselves lost. What a conundrum." Even when she is determined, she's never inclined to take anything too seriously, even now as we wander in the dark in a strange town. A little boy approaches us, furiously peddling his bike, clearly on a mission. I recognize him from the bus station. He was there when we arrived, zooming around, doing tricks, kicking up dust clouds like my brothers used to do on their BMX bikes.

"My mother said to come to my house." Call it a false sense of security, call it complete trust in the moment, call it foolish or desperate or starvation (I am still fasting) we eagerly accept his invitation without hesitation. Like two lost little lambs, we let him lead us right to his house.

We interrupt the Ramadan meal in progress. There are a dozen adults seated on the floor around a low table, feasting. Within seconds, the table is cleared for us and huge bowls of steaming *shorba* (spicy vermicelli soup), *tajine* (a quiche-y dish), lamb *coucha* (young lamb shoulder rubbed with paprika, cayenne, thyme and rosemary, then slow-cooked in an earthenware pot), warm bread, Coke (always), oranges, cheese and buttermilk are placed before us. Happy Ramadan! We sit to eat. Then…they tell us they are Libyan.

America and Libya have not been friends for some time. In 1979 the United States put Libya on the State Sponsors of Terrorism list and later severed ties with the country. In 1986, President Reagan lobbed a few bombs at Libya. On December 21, 1988, 259 people from twenty-one countries were killed when two Libyans blew up Pan Am flight 103 over Lockerbie, Scotland. Eleven more on the ground died when a piece of the plane fell on them. There was a Peace Corps volunteer on that flight, Steven Butler, a Peace Corps Tunisia volunteer, who had just completed his service and was going home. He is mourned here by the volunteers and staff he left behind. Many things in my programming have told me to be wary, including, more recently, explicit instructions to all volunteers to stay away from Tunisia's border with Libya—we are not to cross it under any circumstance.

Patty and I have been ensnared. We are vastly out-numbered, surrounded…and welcomed without hesitation to the table. This family doesn't look at all like terrorists. There isn't an inkling of angst, suspect or judgment. They are splendidly at ease, even with the addition of two complete strangers who they've plucked off the street. I wonder, would my parents invite total strangers, wait, Libyan strangers, to Christmas dinner? Would they fawn all over them, inundating them with food, sweets, deference? Sad to say, I think not.

Somewhere, I read this less than optimistic opinion: "If you join Peace Corps, don't plan on changing the world, just yourself." I am changing. I will act differently because of tonight. Because of things like generosity, an inherent Arab trait, and yes, charity. My experience is not unique. Without exception, we are being welcomed at the table. I don't for a minute believe that I cannot measurably impact the world. Truth and experience is transformational. Change is already showing up.

. . .

All is well with me. If I heard it once, I heard it a zillion times: Peace Corps is a wavelike experience. If that's true, I am cresting the wave, riding it out to the very last. Impermanent states find a compatible host in me. I am twenty-four, free from the clutches of kith and kin, living in altogether foreign terrain, all five senses fully engaged. I am nowhere near needing equanimity in my moment-to-moment existence. I am too busy amassing memories that will resonate for a lifetime and riding this wave wherever it takes me.

CHAPTER 38

Please don't ruin the ruins

Tom, Sam and Daniel atop the Arch of Septimius Severus

At long last, the end of Ramadan approaches and with it, a three-day bonanza of a celebration, Eid Kbir. Last night, Daniel and I ventured out into the hullaballoo underway right outside our door. We joined a throng of bodies moving slowly, heading deeper into the medina. Progress was slow. I was shuffling, inching from cobblestone to cobblestone. It seemed the whole of the medina had emptied and confined itself to this narrow corridor. We inched our way toward an intersection. Then, our mass converged with an oncoming one, coming to a halt in the center. People pressed forward from all directions, forcing one into one another. I became wedged into the heap and couldn't move. Bodies compressing, people pushing in a futile effort to move forward. More and more occupying less and less space. I could sense panic rising, not just mine, but from everyone helplessly jammed into the bulk. I counted at least nine different bodies pressing into me until I felt my feet leave the ground. I lifted my face in an effort to get fresh air. Then, a hand grabbed my tush. I spun my head around, prepared to cast my stink eye on the offender. Really? You want to play grab ass now? Now? The hand quickly withdrew. After a moment, it returned—squeeze. Again, I failed to identify him. The third time I felt it I was ready. I seized it in my grip. Fueled by rage, I thrust it upward twisting as hard as I possibly could, ready and able and quite willing to break it. This action brought me into direct contact with the distorted face of a man clearly in pain—my molester.

"I am going to break your fucking hand," I screamed. Just then, Daniel grabbed me and forcibly yanked me into the open doorway of a vendor's stall, to safety. We held out until the mess cleared and I recovered from my fury. Unbeknownst to us, while we were being squashed in Tunis, fourteen hundred Muslims making their holy pilgrimage in Mecca were smothered and trampled to death in a crowded passageway. Saudi King Fahd claimed the tragedy was "God's will, which is above everything. It was fate."

No misfortune can happen on earth or in your souls
but is recorded in a decree before We [Allah].
That is truly easy for Allah.
In order that you may neither despair over matters that pass you by
nor exult over favors bestowed upon you.
Surat Al-Hadid 57:22-23
(the 57th Surah of the Qur'an)

• • •

After last night's incident, any reasonable person would avoid going anywhere during these, the heaviest travel days of the year. Reason is something I don't do well. Besides, I've been itching to go visit Sam in his new site, Bir Chaabin. Plus, I will have company on the journey and we have a plan. About Sam's site change, I admire that he engineered the move; he is not the type to accept the futility of a poor placement or suffer stagnation. Sayonara Mateur—there's no love lost there, believe me. Though it means he will be far less accessible given the remoteness of Bir Chaabin, I applaud Sam's gumption.

I wake before sunrise so that I can beat the crowds to the bus station and secure four tickets south. Did I mention I hate the bus? Unfortunately, it is the only option that will render us deep into the country, through the Tell, the rolling high plains, into to the Dorsale, Tunisia's main mountain range. The Dorsale is a continuation of the Atlas Mountains which rise most spectacularly in Morocco. They cross Algeria and extend diagonally through Tunisia abruptly dropping into the Mediterranean at Tunisia's Cap Bon.

Getting the tickets for the bus is the easy part. When it rolls in thirty minutes behind schedule, the waiting crowd storms it. Travel here has taught us to be necessarily aggressive; be bold or get left behind. All four of us make it onto the bus, as do some eighty others, crammed in well past capacity. My traveling companions are Daniel, Tom (who, as it turns out, parted ways with Kristy just about the time she moved out of the medina house) and Leslie (a volunteer friend). For the second time in twelve hours, I am wedged between too many bodies, bodies already far too pungent for the earliness of the hour. The bus isn't going anywhere until a few dozen people volunteer to disembark. When it's clear no one is going to give in, we decide to take our chances on a second bus, rather than spend the next five and a-half-hours in a teeming armpit.

The next bus pushes out of the station within the hour and we are on it! At the very first stop, a multitude of people rush in bringing to overflowing the capacity of the second bus. Holiday-goers are not easily negotiated with, so the driver, after repeated petitions, refuses to depart until the climbers-on exit, which eventually they do. When we finally start to pull out of the station, someone manages to pry open the rear doors and a dozen people storm back onto the bus. The driver slams on the brakes and howls at the interlopers, which does nothing to dislodge them. So he throws the bus into gear and makes hastily for the police station, which solves absolutely nothing. Unwilling to concede, he drives to a National Guard post, then to a second, and a third. Finally, he returns us to the bus station and furiously demands that every passenger produce a ticket. Those who cannot are summarily thrown off the bus—literally tossed.

The journey to Thala is both long and unbelievably frustrating. We arrive too late to make it the rest of the way to Sam's site. We find the one and only hotel in the vicinity, an austere block of rooms, and close the book on this day.

We are blasted out of our sleep by cannon, by not one, but two deafening reports, heralding the end of Ramadan. Despite my minor indiscretions at the very beginning, I have completed the Ramadan fast. What, I wonder, has my commitment wrought? Am I purified? Have I learned self-control? Am I healthier? Most importantly, am I closer to God? I've had these many days to consider the process and to make comparisons (to Lent), or observations.

Here's my take-away on my Ramadan experience. A true Muslim does not let a single thing pass through her lips during daylight.

I did not deny myself water. So for that reason, I cannot say my sacrifice was pure. Regarding food however, with the exception of the first two days, I abstained during daylight hours. I had my moments, wrestling the hungries, fighting the inclination to (ch)eat when the presence of fresh bread in the house or *ghyrb* cookies (cookies made from chick peas, my favorite) threatened my resolve. Then, I'd hear Dad's voice in my head reminding me that I was in control: "mind over matter." His mantra worked fine, so long as I confined myself to my headspace…not something I am good at. But, do anything long enough, and with consistency, the acquired routine becomes a lifestyle. So for me, the self-control aspect was revealing, though time-limited.

All denial came to a screeching halt when the sun went down. Gorging on Ramadan specialties like *zlabia* and *mkarek* night after night can hardly be considered sacrifice (or health promoting). I have undergone no dramatic physical changes, to be sure, not even miniscule ones. So much for the benefits of "regime." Dad, however, has shed twenty-five pounds during his Lenten observance. Talk about denial.

I absolutely agree that fasting promotes kinship; compelling motivation. It diminished for a time the cultural barrier between me and my students. My fasting as a non-Muslim was supported and embraced without exception by my Muslim friends. It gave me entrée to homes and families, one after the other. This was reason enough to fast. The big question then remains, am I closer to God?

The small population of Thala, now fully awake (cannon fire will do that) emerges into the daylight, ready to partake in view of all a cup of coffee, a cigarette, each person bringing to an end the period of his own forfeiture or depravation, submission or journey to Allah. We purchase a few staples from a *hannute* while Tom secures us a ride in a *nakarifi*, eighteen kilometers in the direction of Sam's site. The roads are rutted from heavy rains, muddy and impassible. We travel only as far as the driver is willing. We slog the rest of the way.

The region where Sam lives is remote, extremely isolated and to my delight, the polar opposite of Mateur. We set out for Sam's feeling like pioneers crossing into new territory, trekking heavy laden with backpacks, sleeping rolls and water-filled containers. From the distance, eyes watch our arrival as we make our way along a two-track path, past the community well; Sam doesn't have running water. We follow the singular power line overhead until it and the track take a sharp turn away from the direction of Sam's house; Sam doesn't have electricity, either. Apart from perhaps fifteen houses sprinkled over the verdant landscape, there is nothing here. The meadows are blanketed with fiery poppies, wild daisies, buttercups and long grasses. Encircling the entire area are low lying mountains of the beckoning kind. We follow the track to its end, then aim for the solitary house painted stark white with yellow shutters and a yellow door, Sam's.

I want to stay and spend a few days in Sam's new world. But we don't because we have a plan. Well, Tom has a plan. Though before we leave, we make for one of those beckoning mountains swathed in long grasses and climb to the top, because it is right there, begging for it. This one is sheared level, like nature's table, providing a view to the south, the direction we will travel. From our vantage point, Sam's house is but a bright dot on an infinite harlequin plain. Lucky Sam.

We strike out on a three-day trek into Tunisia's hinterlands with Tom and his compass as our guide. The plan, which is entirely of his making, is to hike to the ancient site of Ammaedara, through the heart of the Dorsale, the range that marks climactic boundary between the lush north and the dry south. Of course, I have no real idea where we are going. Even if I did, I haven't informed anyone—outside of my companions—of my whereabouts. I'd put money down that my companions haven't either. Fear has no home in us; Tunisia is our playground.

We cross farmland and brush, rocky expanses that climb, roll and render us into dryer and dryer undergrowth. Along the route, we stop to speak with the few locals we meet. Each one zealously counsels us not to camp out of doors under the moon—very dangerous. "A ba ba ba ba ba ba..." they say, shaking their heads, gesturing emphatically. We are warned. We are told we are crazy: crazy to be traveling by foot, crazy to hoof such heavy cargo, but most sincerely...crazy to sleep outside. We don't heed them. Somewhere in North Africa, we sleep under a spectacular crescent moon that dangles above us in the black night. We relish the cool breeze brushing over our exposed cheeks, the comforting scent and crackling of campfire. We steep in the absolute intoxication of freedom.

For two days and eight blisters, we amble through countryside, becoming increasingly drier, rockier and monochromatic. When we arrive at our destination, the town of Haidra, we are immediately intercepted by a man who identifies himself as *The Director*, a man whose job it is to steer us to the youth hostel. The Director insists that camping is forbidden. He escorts Sam and Tom to the police station so that our renegade faction can be "registered," leaving Daniel, Leslie and I to scout for a camping spot well out of sight. We've come too far, lugged too much gear, consumed too many shitty cheese triangles to succumb to the comforts of a hostel. Sam and Tom ditch the Director and eventually find us. We set up camp about five kilometers out of town under a thick cover of evergreens. We sleep on the piney floor beneath a perfectly clear sky, outlaws that we are.

In the morning, we make our way to Ammaedara, one of the oldest Roman towns in Africa. History records that the Berbers were the first to reside here, until the Romans arrived and conquered them. The monolithic structures the Romans erected were part of a military camp established for the protection of the African frontier, under the jurisdiction of Augustus's famous Third Legion. Stories live in the remnants that lie here, partially buried. This ancient camp is ours for the taking, for the exploring, ours entirely. Towering over the site is the well-preserved Arch of Septimius Severus, a most imposing monument. It was built in AD195 to span the well traveled Roman road to Carthage. Not content to simply marvel at it, the boys scale their way to the very top, while I find a less regal perch from which to watch them. I have no desire to break my neck today thank you, or to climb the mausoleum or crumbling capitols either. I wonder about all the people who have passed through the arch in its seventeen centuries holding ground here. Soldiers, traders, travelers. I wonder how many of them ever dared to climb it.

We play in Ammaedara all day until we are apprehended by the police on our way out of town. We are detained and questioned. Our identification is confiscated and photocopied. Are we being arrested for climbing all over the ancient monuments? For wreaking havoc on the priceless cultural heritage? Nope. The only issue of great concern to the authorities: "You didn't sleep outside last night, did you?"

CHAPTER 39

May 1990

Shkshookah

Tom, Sam, Daniel & me

It has come to my attention that several volunteers are being closely surveilled by the secret police. A Tunisian friend, to remain unnamed, has a brother who works for the Tunisian equivalent of the CIA. The brother showed him an array, pictures of suspected spies and asked him if he recognized anyone. Several volunteers are among those being followed and photographed without their knowledge. Of particular interest is my friend Tom. According to my source, Tom's home in the town of Ras Jabel has been secretly entered six times and is currently being electronically monitored.

Why is Tom of such great interest? He is a beekeeper here... mostly. Despite his devotion to local apiculture, his first love is journalism. He's a major contributor to our Peace Corps newsletter, *La Cour*. In fact, we've worked together more than once compiling, editing and producing issues. He is at heart a serious journalist though, one whose compulsion cannot be met by the production of a monthly newsletter with so narrow an audience and subject matter.

Tom is the real deal, the intrepid muckraker—man of inquiry, man of pluck. No doubt conducting interviews with fundamentalist leaders and filing stories for U.S. publications from Tunis invites more attention than, let's say, living out in the middle of scrub brush somewhere in the deep south like several of our volunteers are doing at this moment and spending the days measuring bovine with a tool that has been affectionately named the "Peace Cord." Kicking the beehive (can't help myself) has got the bees buzzing, garnering Tom more notice than is perhaps prudent.

Tom's curiosity is what incited our visit to the PLO cultural offices. I wonder whether that little escapade helped boost suspicion of him and by association, me. As it turns out, we were well received in those offices by propagandists or freedom fighters (your pick) universally flabbergasted that any American might be interested in the Palestinian conflict. What is it about the combination of youth and travel that prompts the foolhardy to take a taxi straight to the PLO offices?

In any case, the secret police think Tom is a spy. Funny, I get asked all the time, point blank: "Are you a spy?" The American who abandons a life of privilege for one decidedly not is met with skepticism. The person who would leave family to live elsewhere alone is suspect. Our motivations are not very convincing, our explanations atypical. There exists nowhere in Tunisia's political or municipal landscape an equivalent of the Peace Corps volunteer, no such model or concept. Thus, our presence here is…curious.

Though I have no direct proof, I imagine that over its history Peace Corps has been infiltrated, by let's say, one or two patriots employed by the Central Intelligence Agency. The volunteer *is* perfect cover, with unique access to countries, cultures and communities around the globe. The very nature of many of the developing countries where Peace Corps does it work, is restless and unpredictable. Against this backdrop is the Peace Corps volunteer, exposed, pursuing a promise of altruism.

The reality is, there will always be monitoring from within and without. For obvious reasons, the Peace Corps goes to great lengths to segregate itself from other branches of government (to the extent that *that* is possible). Our safety depends on it. Recently a volunteer in the Philippines was kidnapped for political reasons. The Peace Corps pulled out of that country and suspended the program forthwith. As for Tom, he has to know that his activities are raising suspicion. Next time I see him, I am going to have to ask. By his own will, he is stepping into the fray for his passion. I admire that. As for the rest of my monitored brethren, they pursue, without intrigue, their noble endeavors.

• • •

The number of volunteers planning to attend my summer English teaching training has grown from five to twelve, which means I have a secondary project in earnest. Located in the Atlas Mountains fifteen miles from Algeria's border, Aïn Draham is insulated from the oppressive heat that sacks the rest of the country, making it the perfect place to while away a summer. The Ministry of Education has blessed the project by giving us a permission to use the school there. The responsibility for securing housing for our group has fallen to Keith, the local volunteer, the number one hoop jumper, the mastermind of this whole affair. In addition to finding two villas to rent, he is drumming up interest among potential students. In keeping with the way officialdom is executed here, the housing contracts have been traveling non-stop, hither and yon, from Tunis, to Aïn Draham, to Tunis, then to the American Embassy in France (who knows why) and back to Tunis, in a constant state of flux. I am crafting the curriculum and finagling supplies. I welcome the intense pace, even the copious bureaucracy. I am flush with productivity, which doesn't necessarily correlate to effectiveness, but always there is potential.

My transfer to Beja has been approved! *Il hamdullah*—thank God. The more the universe opens, the deeper I delve. The prospect of living alone in Beja has me giddy. But, before I get too carried away, there is first the matter of finding somewhere to live. I've made several hasty trips to Beja to follow up leads. My local experts are Jack and Molly. As I mentioned previously, they are getting ready to complete their service but are electing to stay in Tunisia under their own umbrella rather than return home. Talk about gumption.

Some months ago, on a particularly cold, gray and moody day, I was cocooned in my sleeping bag, drinking bowls of hot tea and attempting to exorcise the chill that had invaded my bones when someone rapped on my door. It was Molly. She was alone and not expected. She and Jack had just returned from their vacation in Morocco. Without exiting my sleeping bag, I waddled, she followed, into the kitchen where I put on another pot of tea. That was when I took notice of her feet. Her toes were unnaturally purple as they peered out from flimsy blue flip flops. I was enveloped head to toe in down, with just a blow hole for sipping tea and communicating. She had naked feet and near frost bite.

"Why are you wearing those?"

"I traded my Reeboks…and most of the stuff I had on me at the time, for a rug in Marrakesh! One more treasure for our genie room!" About the genie room, it is a magic space in Jack and Molly's traditional *dar arby*, a room that features eyes from Turkey, cloth from Iran, tapestries from the desert, archeological trinkets and now a rug from Morocco. "Purple toes are definitely worth it," she said.

From my perspective, I will call Jack and Molly successful volunteers: integrated, thriving, resourceful and very active. In an environment where complaint among volunteers is omnipresent, they pedal a brand of enthusiasm that is altogether catchy. They love this country, so much so they will stay here independent of Peace Corps. It is in fact their departure from Beja which paves the way for my move there.

We aren't just swapping cities (they plan to move to Tunis), I will assume Molly's post at the Bouguiba School. Come August, I will be the only American in residence in Beja—I am very okay with that. I am not okay with having thirty less dinars in my pocket each month as my monthly stipend will be adjusted for life outside the expensive capital. A paycut. As if the last week of the month isn't already an exercise in deficiency. Given this grim financial reality, I have narrowed my search to two houses. Do I choose spaciousness and semi-squalor for 70 TDs? Or, confinement and amenities for 100 TDs? Negotiations with the landlord Karima are underway for the latter.

• • •

What a fiasco it has been trying to purchase my roundtrip ticket home. The wiry little Yugoslavian man at the shabby Jat Airlines office keeps changing the price. Here I am, in his dinky little office for the sixth time, trying to secure my ticket. I got my wad of ill-gotten dinars in-hand and he requests 114 more. He gets up from behind his desk, shuts the door and launches—again—into the same conversation we have been having for weeks, the one where he ups the price.

"Ah ya." He says through his mangy moustache. "Dis is vat it cost now....you need to find a soloootion to da problem." This feels like a shakedown. But worse, there is a real possibility that no soloootion may be found and I will not be getting on a plane, unless I dig up more dinars—which has no chance of happening. My resources are depleted. And when or if I do step on that plane, it will be with zero dollars in my pocket, risky. Risky too might be the decision to fly on Jat. Yugoslavia's economy is in freefall and Jat is Yugoslavia's national airline. I had never even heard of Jat until I went looking for a cheap way home.

My own economic downturn, though serious, nevertheless finds me in possession of two very large hookah pipes and a small collection of all things Tunisian, gifts for family—but still no ticket. I've been living on the cheap and working underground. On his end, my eldest sibling, Mark—the only one in the know—is helping to orchestrate my arrival in secret. The only thing that stands between me, my pipes and America is that wiry little man and a three-stop swing through Yugoslavia.

• • •

I gave notice at the Hotel Africa. My moonlighting days are over.

• • •

The teaching year is plummeting to its furious end. It hasn't been easy cramming ten weeks of lessons into three weeks. Over the next few days, my duties will have me administering and correcting finals, oral and written, then passing or failing sixty students. I take no comfort meting out these verdicts given the debacle that was my first year of teaching.

My bags are packed. As soon as I can, I plan to slip out the back door and make my get-away. Who else but the guilty craft escape plans? I don't need someone to tell me I failed. Instead of a seasoned teacher, those in my charge got a student, a novice, even worse, a foreigner. I spent the whole year trying to embrace the rote teaching method and found it too small a box to endure. So, I deviated from the standard, made it up as I went along. To complicate matters, because I did not become the bitch the director encouraged me to be, I never did get control of the classroom.

That I did not measure up is decidedly not a win. That I am glad as hell *I* will not get a report card is most certainly a win. As for oversight, as long as my body showed up to the classroom, all was well. This is the vacuum in which I have operated for the past ten months, treading the waters of cluelessness and self-recrimination with nary an authority to witness. I made an honest go of it. But yes, I stumbled routinely. After Tunis there is Beja: new geography, new place, new students, a do-over, if you will.

• • •

Because my director at the Bourguiba School asked me to, I arrive to work early on the final day to complete paperwork. When

I enter the conference room, the entire staff, including the Secretary General, greets me with a going away party, complete with cards, gifts and fancy things to eat. It is a sweet send-off, though I am hardly worthy of it, embarrassing really.

• • •

At the close of the school year, I make a quick trip to Sam's site, Bir Chaabin. To be clear, there's nothing expedient about two louage rides, two bus rides, and a six-kilometer hike. At Beb Suika, the southern bus station, well over a hundred people storm the bus. Caught up in the tempest, I am groped; someone gets a handful of my chest.

"*Hram!*" I scream at my attacker (*hram* means "forbidden by Allah"). Surprisingly, I am offered a profuse apology, during which time a second assault, this time on my butt cheek, commences. Only eighty passengers are permitted to board—eighty! I spend several hours leaning against the driver with my feet straddling the gear shift and hands on the ceiling to steady myself against the lurching of the bus. Finally a driver demonstrates empathy—he opens the front and rear doors to allow air to circulate through the unbearably foul confines. He closes them each time we pass a police check point. I hate hate hate travelling by bus.

Bir Chaabin must be the quietest place in this whole country and the most isolated. I find myself walking the long track to Sam's house. People emerge from their houses to say "hello" or to stare. This is Sam's new fishbowl and he is doing swimmingly, living the model Peace Corps existence. I remember during training he struggled, perhaps more than most, with the language. The process was difficult. Yet, out here in it, he is probably more fluent than most,

right down to the mannerisms, the colloquial humor, the nuances—
the stuff hardest to get. Good for you, Sam.

We visit the village hot spot, the water source, where each day
Sam must trek and drop his bucket down into one of two very deep
wells. It is the social hub, where women gather to visit while beating
soaked wool with large clubs. The women stop toiling to come over
and speak with me. The prematurely weathered faces wear years of
strain and labor—they belie the youthful eyes that look out from
them. Rotting and missing teeth garble warm greetings.

"*A:sh bish tamlu bil su:f?*" What will you do with the wool? I ask.

"*Nomil burnus rajli: wa wildi:. Yixdmu; fi bara, fi rif, fi barid.*"
Says one of the eldest in the group. She is making *burnouses*,
full length heavy topcoats, for her husband and for her son who
work in the fields where it can get very cold. In fact they all are,
as the *burnous* is the predominant outerwear of the men of the
south.

"*Tnajim warini?*" I ask them to show me. The eldest walks me
over to a pile of wool that is being prepared for the upright single-
heddle loom, technology used since antiquity. I divide my attention
between the process and the oversized gold-hooped earrings weighing heavily on her aged drooping ear lobes. Each time she moves,
they swing back and forth slapping her neck. Her hair is flaming
red from repeated applications of henna, the province of women of
advancing years. It is hideous and unnatural. Who am I to judge?
I am hardly the picture of high fashion. My clothes are faded and
misshapen from repeated hand washings. My mom would call this
look "hobo." We, the female volunteers, have all succumbed to a
mode of dress that erases any hint of style. Garments that should
never show up on anybody—things like super-sized harem pants or
smock dresses—we wear with all regularity. One thing's for sure:

except for the clothing on my back, my wardrobe will not be returning to the U.S. with me.

At the well, those less social gawk at me and say nothing. After nearly a year here, I still have not adjusted to the fishbowl. It is not comfortable feeling one gets from being conspicuously inspected at close range. In this remote village, where few outsiders roam, I am a novelty. A man arrives and pours a half bottle of bleach into each well. In the distance, a young girl with black braided hair and red dress sailing in the late afternoon breeze tends to a flock of sheep. Mules tied to a broken line of spigots await heavy cargo. More red haired women supervise one another in the construction of a loom. Small children follow me wherever I go. I am thankful to have a friend here, through whom my access to this faraway peaceful village is granted.

Sam and I have no agenda for this visit. For me, it is enough to be in his company, enjoying simple things. We read, write letters home, listen to the BBC and prepare food together in the quiet of his country abode. We've been in-country for a year now..."together" for a year. He tortures me with his inconsistency. When there is no one else around, in the space and protection of privacy, he is an unabashed lover. Outside of this context, he is indifferent, cold even. Yet, I cannot break free from him because despite my private pain, I am in love. Living here has forced me into the present, has taught me that in any given moment, the moment is all I really have. So, this "thing" with Sam, I—either in the blip of bliss or the bloat of longing—take it as it is, and him as he is.

CHAPTER 40

June 1990

Aïn Draham

Teachers and students in Aïn Draham

Tunis is in the rear view and already I am feeling nostalgic. I will miss Daniel, my inquisitive and protective friend. Miss seeing his cheery pie-in-the-sky face. Miss our late night ritual of writing and listening to music and munching on mandarins or pomegranates. He is on his way back to Minneapolis, finished with his studies here. And my blessed comic relief Patty, who one night joined us at the table to write her first letter home in months and months and then let it nearly catch on fire because she left it too close to the candle. She abandoned her letter because there was a perfect crescent moon hanging over Tunis and call to prayer was beginning to ring out in the medina. We leapt from our seats ran quickly up the rickety steps to the terrace, like many nights. The chorus of voices over the old city is a concert not to be missed, though how could we possibly, with seats smack dab in the thick of it. Voices ring out like a round, one after the other, "Allah hu akbar..." God is great, a calling undeniable, even to us: the three keepers, for a time, of the medina house. During our many months in Tunis, these wonderful companions have helped me experience more of this country than I possibly could have alone. I will miss them dearly.

The medina house. Ten months never saw one lonely moment in that house, so filled with comings and goings. More hostel than home, mother ship, safe house, flop house. Open twenty-four hours a day, seven days a week. And just outside my door, life teeming as it has for a thousand years. Brothers Habib and Farid, the owners of the *hannute* below us, the one we flooded, are always open for business (even in times of disaster) serving up fiery hot local flavor fast and on the cheap. For years they have watched the processions of Americans through those double brown doors, polite to me always, but purposely distant. Aziz, the snaggle-toothed cigarette vendor, and others like him have been here perpetually. For a brief moment I shared in the life that flows through these streets; it will live in me forever.

Before I left the capital, someone thieved 220 dinars from my secret hiding spot in my room. I had just cashed my living allowance check for the coming month. The check is supposed to cover rent to my new landlord and allow me to LIVE. My living stipend, my food allowance, mysteriously lifted by someone I know. This should bother me, especially given my struggles with budgeting, but it doesn't. I don't know why, but I am not angry about it and certainly don't wish to expend energy pursuing suspects. I plead my case to Peace Corps and was allotted 50 percent of my pay, enough to get by. Thus, I move on to Aïn Draham a little light in the pocket, while all of my worldly goods moved without me to Beja.

After my dubious teaching performance this past year, it is nothing short of a coup that I should be spearheading a five-week secondary project to train teachers. There is a great deal of interest and support in Aïn Draham for our English school. When I arrived in a louage with Lisa, my partner in this enterprise, we were within minutes escorted by a local to *our* villa. News of our presence has spread quickly.

Twelve trainees are participating in the training. Here's another one I've heard countless times, "Peace Corps is the longest vacation you'll ever endure." I don't think that's the case for those in my charge. They are not about to endure anything. They're fed up and moving on. Fed up with "assignments" that did not materialize or weren't remotely productive. Case in point, one of our attendees has been "working" in a women's center. Outside of making and selling pottery, there isn't enthusiasm for much else. For education, however, there is always interest. Teaching may not replace her primary role at the center, but it does give her a vehicle to stay and enhances her capacity to positively impact those in her village. Each one of the attendees is determined to make something of their two years. Is not our "can do" spirit what typifies Americans?

I love our ensemble. Immediately compatible, energized and motivated. I've let go of the notion that I am not qualified to lead the training because the aspirations of my fellow volunteers fuel my own and have me believing I have something to offer. I believe this will be good for all.

The initial two weeks are focused on introducing the Tunisian standard of rote learning—the model, the standard, the very system

I abandoned in favor of fly-by-my-seat tactics. It is how Tunisia delivers education and therefore must be explained. As a teacher within that system, the Audio-Lingual Method triggers in me sheer boredom: who wants to parrot information, all day, every day? I cannot see how repetition furthers understanding. To me, memorizing and repetition is about compartmentalizing, which is synonymous with pigeonholing. Forget about creativity, or critical thinking, or just plain thinking. Hence, this is the pool into which we have jumped and success here will come to those who tread water best.

Over 150 students signed on to participate in our program and more show up every day! Beyond the challenge of accommodating them, we have a range of proficiencies—from absolute beginners to advanced speakers—to manage. We have not turned anyone away; we just expand as we go. As I watch from the back of the classroom, I find myself longing to be up there teaching, a realization which shocks me. Though it is my role to critique my peers, I am really just one of the many faces before them, soaking it in. They are teaching me. The unabridged passion of everyone connected to this program is proving to be the highlight of my tenure here.

Outside of the classroom, our group of teachers is congealing splendidly. One of our bonding experiences included a henna fest. One-half kilo of henna found its way onto hands, feet and the hair of two of our male attendees. We moved all of the mattresses into one room and slept side-by-side immobile with plastic bags over hands and feet. A night of endless chatter was fine entertainment for all, an opportunity to learn about the divergent experiences of my friends. It's being rumored one has gone off and married a Tunisian man in secret. Another volunteer refused to go into Tunis for his required immunization, so the Peace Corps nurse showed up at his door with it. Apparently, she was shocked by his living conditions.

Seems he takes his vow of asceticism a little too seriously. In his house she found little more than a mattress, a cook top and a few cooking utensils.

Over the weekend, our henna-ed entourage leaves the comfort of cooler breezes in Aïn Draham to head for the beaches in Tabarka. We lay claim to a perfect deserted stretch of beach far east of Les Aguilles, the Needles, sixty-foot pinnacles of jagged rock that dominate the landscape near the popular beach. A perennial on-shore breeze soothes the intense heat and dries for a time my sweat. No sooner do we settle in and begin to disrobe down to our bathing suits when we are joined by a slew of male gawkers who take up positions a few feet from us. Unlike the German tourists who are quite cozy sunbathing half-nekkid on any of the shores in this country, we have gone in the opposite direction. It is no longer enough to be culturally sensitive; we strive to be culturally appropriate. In my case, I arrived with a deeply rooted and overblown grasp of modesty, which has after living here for a year, intensified exponentially. In my mind, lying around in a bathing suit is akin to posing for Playboy—sure to get attention…which is why we picked an uninhabited area. The staring is so intense, to escape them we seek refuge in the sea, go into the salty depths up to our necks.

They follow us in. I call them "disco boys," young men of a certain age, jobless, directionless, forever on the prowl, they brazenly append themselves to us in the hopes we'll bite. They are everywhere in Tunisia, loitering, ogling, unabashed, the products of high unemployment and of course, Islam, with its severe restrictions on socializing. Sometimes I throw out a few choice phrases in Arabic, like my favorite, *shbi:k* (what's your problem) or, when my powers of discretion fail me and I am more desperate, *Allah bish ysharrig ain:k* (God's going to rip out your eyes). To which I get a range of reactions, mostly surprise and oftentimes laughter. That a foreigner would know and use their own language against them is something most unexpected. Magically, a few well-chosen morsels will terminate most intrusions. As a rule, I ignore the behavior, conceding its omnipresence in my life for the interim.

• • •

Just when we think we've found nirvana in our heavenly outpost, one-by-one we succumb to the ravages of some kind of parasite. Poor Lisa has been sacked by giardia, a severe infection of the gut being blamed on the water in Tabarka. One of the more unpleasant aspects of her condition is the prevalence of intense sulfur burps which send us running. She is forever apologizing, dear girl, as we leave her alone to dwell in her cloud. There we were in Tabarka, happily splashing away in the surf when out of nowhere a man ran up to us and motioned us out of the water, screaming that it was contaminated. Little did we know, when we ignored him, that the microscopic protozoan would wreak such havoc on us. I wonder if the disco boys who chased us there are also up shit's creek.

• • •

If you're an agricultural volunteer, you have the luxury of being issued a motorized bike to assist you in reaching the distant farmers you aid. If you are teacher, you don't get wheels. Given the condition of the mobylettes, there isn't very much to envy, as they have a tendency to break down a whole lot. They whirr obnoxiously. And, Peace Corps requires its operators to wear an enormous bright yellow helmet. But those things aside, mobylettes can be good fun...

when they are operational. So Tom and I (Tom is here for the summer), fully recovered from our maladies, commandeer Keith's "hog" and take off into the hills. Tom has become my friend in adventure, always revealing to me things I might not have the courage to find on my own. I've come to trust him and his plans. Today we journey due west until we reach the heavily patrolled Algerian border; we turn south and ride into the boonies. We buzz through the cool cork forested mountains under an evergreen canopy, through clouds of loam and laurel. We pass sporadic towns, wind in our faces, deliriously free, even at times, laughing out loud. We land in Hamman Bourguiba, a village known for its hot springs and other equally sizzling offerings, like hot Coke, which we eagerly guzzle out of battle-worn 9-oz bottles. On our return, we make it only two kilometers when our ride peters out: one dead spark plug, plus one flat tire. We hitch a ride in the back of a government truck and are deposited within one kilometer of a National Guard post because, as our driver informs us, he cannot legally transport civilians. A second truck ferries us all the way back to Aïn Draham, lifeless moped and all. The demise of our transport notwithstanding, to venture with abandon—come what may—while possibly reckless, is completely intoxicating. If it takes beating the life out of a dying mobylette to get my "drink" on, I am happy to oblige.

• • •

Our classes are overloaded with students. More come every day. In keeping with our policy, we are quite happy to squeeze them into our expanding schedule. Our teachers have gone from teaching with their partners for ninety minutes, to teaching solo for three hours per day. I am supposed to be providing critical feedback. Instead, I am taking notes, digging the way our teachers work the rooms and stealing their ideas! Tom has his students writing poetry. Keith has his performing skits. Lyn is lyrical and lovely to watch. Robb is a master of American resourcefulness, making props from stuff lying around the villa. JoAnn, one of our elder volunteers exalts her *azu:za*—old woman status; she has no discipline issues in her classroom. Each of them has easily stepped into the role of teacher; and their students overwhelmingly welcome them. I know it is too early to call, but this is a huge win for all of us.

• • •

After five weeks in the idyllic Aïn Draham, it is time to say goodbye to a town that embraced us. Almost two hundred people attend our final day of classes, after which we celebrate by hosting a *hafla*, a party. There is traditional music performed on darboukas, *mizwits* and *ouds*, dancing and even a game of "Simon Says" for the whole assembly. Lisa and I present our teachers with apples carved from olive wood. They demonstrated tremendous spirit and commitment in making the program a success, en route to meeting a fraction of our mandate here.

CHAPTER 41

August 1990

Home Sweet Home: Michigan

Dan & Melissa

The groom has adamantly rejected the idea of having a bachelor hoo-ha, specifically, the notion of parading a scantily clad woman before him in a rite of passage many before him have embraced. I am hiding outside, while my family assembles with Dan, front and center. Their chatter turns to expectant giggles as the Arabic music I've supplied to the elder brother fills the air: my cue. Wrapped head to toe in a bright purple sari, I negotiate the steps and enter the front door. The heavy silver bands about my ankles and wrists clink together, bringing focus to my henna-ed feet and hands. Through the sari, I see Dan displeased, his arms folded defiantly across his chest. Just beyond him is the bride-to-be, clearly amused. I quickly scan the room—the whole family has come. Dad has the video camera fixed on me. My legs defy my intent, which is to be sexy, alluring and convincing. Instead, I move awkwardly toward Dan, gyrating around, shaky lumbering, not looking the picture of professional. I stand before him, move in close until my veil grazes the skin on his cheeks. Hips swaying, arms swirling, smile hiding. Through the veil I watch Dan cast steely disapproving looks to my brother, Mark. Mark—the one who set him up. I cannot prolong the moment—I am too eager. As gingerly as I can, I unwrap the first layer of sari, encircle it about Dan's head, concealing us both to the room. I peel the layers until we are nose to nose.

"Oh my God!" he cries. He throws his arms around me. "Is that Lora?" Mom asks incredulously. Dad drops the camera. Ann starts howling. I am quickly engulfed in a massive family hug. The shock value alone makes all the haggling with the wiry Yugoslavian worth it. I am back in Michigan…for a visit. Oh, and I never paid the little Yugoslavian the extra money for the airline ticket, not because I was hardheaded on the matter, but because I never had it to spend. Turns out, it *was* a shakedown.

I am out of sorts, out of place in America, land of my birth and home of my rearing. I take exception to things which were once the stuff of everyday living. I am overwhelmed with the trappings of American life, things that are suddenly indulgent, even obnoxious. Case in point, huge cars, too shiny and new. Or lampshades which seem ridiculous and foo foo. A trip to the grocery store almost sends me off the deep end; the sheer variety of goods overwhelms me. I reach catatonia in the cereal aisle; one row entirely comprised of boxes upon boxes of morning morsels in every conceivable confection, shape, color. Even my sense of propriety deceives me. Ann expends great energy trying to get me to remove a layer or two of clothing, convincing me that bearing my knees is acceptable and necessary. It is August.

"Aren't you frying in all those clothes? Don't you have anything with less...material? You're making *me* hot—you need to change." I try shorts; I feel naked. I am out of sorts.

Dan and Melissa's wedding is beautiful, but I spend most of it on the fringes feeling estranged. My conversations are brief, are of little interest to those who exist in this reality.

"Say something in Tunisian," they ask me. "What's the weirdest food you've eaten so far?" "Is Akim, Mohammed, etc. giving you a hard time over there?" "Now you know, America is the best!" I get filled in on what has or has not transpired since my departure. Everyone's still working at this or that or the other thing. Going through the motions. Why do all the people in my life suddenly seem so inert? So boring? Why am I hypersensitive to the stagnancy and the dullness of living in America? Beyond my reassurances that the henna on my hands is not infectious, there is little to be said. I cannot entertain the lackluster, the uninspiring. Nothing has changed, except for me. I am no longer at home at home. I am antsy. Uncomfortable. I want to go home...to Tunisia.

Tunisia? Home? When had this transformation taken place? Not very long ago it was aversion I felt each and every time I stepped out my door to face streets populated with tormenters. They're still there in good number, as grating as ever, but they no longer get the better of me. The flirtations, while exceedingly annoying and overconfident, are completely harmless attempts to get my attention. A Western woman does not convey the protections that Islam provides—she is fair game. It is pointless to take anything personally. In fact, I am significantly safer walking the streets of Tunis than those of Detroit. My struggle, the stuff of fierce internal combat, took place in my head, as the throes of culture shock (now long subsided) had me convinced Arabs were either unknowable or not worth knowing, or both. Plus, there were a number of aspects to the culture that repelled me. Then I began to notice that one by one, they no longer did, or didn't nearly as much. Like the moment I realized that Arabic music, at first jarring and cacophonous, was harmonious and lyrical. Or Arabic, initially super-syllabic, hyper-conjugated and unattainable, was in fact starting to dominate my dreams and fall easily from my tongue. With regard to Islam, a force that at times is uncomfortably intrusive and meddling, I've found deference and consideration. Islam is still intrusive and meddling, but it is also balanced a great deal by grace and peace.

Awareness is something I've had to learn to cultivate. It gives me a perspective from which to view Tunisians as they are, not as I am, to view Islam as it is, not as my "faith" is, etc. etc. I don't know when it happened, but at one point I stopped swimming against the tide. My feet are up and pointing down river. I am sailing through the rapids with a huge smile on my face. I cannot wait to get back to it, to them. But while I am here, I will savor my family, the smell of freshly-cut grass, the rumble of muscle cars going past the house, the plush carpet on Mom's living room floor and blessed anonymity.

• • •

"So how are you doing over there, really?" Dad asks one morning over toasted tomato sandwiches.

"It's a rollercoaster ride, Dad. You either love it or hate it." I tell him.

"So, which is it?" he asks, stirring his chocolate milk with a very long-handled spoon.

"Well, I'm in love right now."

"What's the hardest part?"

"I don't know, probably the psychological stuff, not my living conditions, or even my job, which Lord knows has been tough enough."

"Like what, exactly?" He asks.

"Islam. It's like a lead blanket, a little suffocating."

"Hmmmm. Quite the metaphor."

"You mean simile. I am an English professor, don't cha know."

"Mai oui bien sur, Madamoiselle professeur! (But yes of course, Miss professor).

"Here's a metaphor: I've spent the first year in the defensive zone. But, now I believe I am finally moving into the neutral zone."

"Said like a true hockey player," he chuckles. "The neutral zone is just fine. Remember what happened when you were at college?" He says with a wink. He is referring to the semester I got myself wrapped up with a group of Pentecostals. I got a little too curious, and instead of studying, I went to healings and witnessed prophesies and started digging into the book of Revelation with apocalypse "experts." This is what happens when a Catholic girl gets let loose. She either stays straight or takes a walk on the dark side. Thank God for Dad. He gave me a much-needed course correction. He didn't rush up to school to rescue me—though it killed him not to. Instead, he wrote me a letter, a twenty-one pager. I still remember a few of the lines: "You will never completely understand love and there is no one who can explain it to you. You will never completely understand hate and there is no one who can explain it to you. Religion is so much in the same category. Is there anyone qualified to tell you how God wishes to be loved?" So healing, those words, and so true even now.

• • •

At home, the maelstrom I left has quieted some. Mom and Dad are still working things out and doing a good job of concealing their stress. With the wedding and my return home, all attention appears to be focused on these happier events, and not on the fact that Dad has refused still to give up entirely his other woman. Mom seems to have regained her strength. Anger is a powerful motivator. It has a way of building resolve and fueling intention. One way or the other, she will survive this. Dad, sweet, overly emotional, damaged—even more than Mom—may not.

• • •

August 2, 1990, Iraq invades Kuwait. It takes Saddam Hussein's 100,000 soldiers and 700 tanks one day to overpower the emirate. He promises to turn Kuwait into a graveyard if anyone challenges his takeover. The U.S., the first to take up the challenge, demands an immediate and unconditional withdrawal. Six days later, the U.S. launches Operation Desert Shield. Baghdad responds by announcing that Kuwait is now part of Iraq and closes its borders the very next day. The Arab League tentatively commits Egyptian, Syrian and Moroccan troops to join the Western troops. I am stateside in my parent's living room watching it unfold on TV, watching the black hole of conflict suck everything into it. On August 25, the UN Security Council authorizes the use of force.

I call Peace Corps Washington concerned that Tunisia could get swept into the fray. I am told that I should not return.

"Tunisia is on high alert," the desk officer tells me. "All of our programs in Muslim countries may be suspended at any moment. You should wait it out in Michigan." Not a chance. I go back anyway.

CHAPTER 42

Cast off

I don't know how long I've stayed in this hotel room in Tunis, dying from my broken heart, days I think. I can't free my face from the pillow, can't raise my eyes to the day, can't face the truth that has finally caught up with me, bludgeoning me once and for all. Sam was here in Tunis waiting at the airport when I got off the plane. Too late to catch a louage to Beja, he accompanied me to the hotel. I threw open my suitcase, eager to hand over the gifts I'd collected for him at home. Something in his reluctance to accept them caused me to inquire. The fickle heart wants what it wants and this one wants another. He did not abandon me immediately. Instead, he attended to me over the long night while I died inside. Died so hard, I imploded before him. Before he left, I gave him the journal I had been keeping for the past year, the dumping ground for my unrequited emotions. It was my garbage disposal, into which pieces of me that could not be used or ingested got churned instead. I've been laying here since he left. I am destroyed, defeated, utterly incapable of movement. The great Sufi master Hafiz said "Don't surrender your loneliness so quickly. Let it cut more deep. Let it ferment and season you as few human, or even divine ingredients, can." This is exactly what I am doing. I am marinating in my grief, bathing fully in it, until I can bury Sam's imprint in so deep a place as to never expose it again.

Dear God, Allah, Universe, ad infinitum: heal me. Remind me that all is perfect, even when it wounds, even when I am complicit in wielding the knife against myself. Grow hope in place of loss, effort out of incapacity and momentum, so that I can move forward out of smallness. Remind me that I can be fearless, boundless. Lead me not... into anger, but deliver me toward love.

This is not the homecoming I envisioned.

The heart is right to cry

Even when the smallest drop of light,
Of love,
Is taken away.

Perhaps you may kick, moan, scream
In a dignified silence,

But you are so right
To do so in any fashion

Until God returns
To you.

--Hafiz--

CHAPTER 43

September 1990

Welcome in Beja

Beja

After seventy-two hours of festering in Tunis, I manage to get my sorry self to my new site. Fifteen minutes outside of Beja, the road climbs to a soft peak revealing a first glimpse of the clustered metropolis sprawled across its verdant landscape. It takes fifteen more minutes to ride the dip into the valley to reach civilization. Something about the very final stretch of road lifts me for a moment from my funk. So welcoming with its column of stately trees opening to receive all travelers who pass through them—the final gateway into Beja. I am home. I take a long and luxurious breath in and follow it with a deeper exhale. The scene is splendidly pastoral. This could be Tuscany or Provence. Well, except for the huge sign that reads: *Marhababik fi Beja*; *Bienvenue á Beja*; Welcome *in* Beja (confirmation that a bit more English instruction is warranted).

Beja was once the heart of the Roman bread basket. The fertile lands of the Medjerda valley in the foothills of Djebel Acheul provided much of the grain that fed an empire. Everywhere there are vistas of rich green and in the spring fields blaze with vibrant poppies. Peace reigns supreme here, though this has not always been the case. Over history, Beja has been assaulted and brutally destroyed by the armies of Carthage, Numidia, Rome and by Vandals. It even saw fierce combat during World War II when Germany demanded surrender and the locals refused. Within twenty-four hours, a British battalion parachuted into the valley to defend Beja. The Germans responded by bombing Beja to smithereens. There were massive casualties, both civilian and military, but in the end the Allies were victorious and Beja healed once again from its wounds. I think in this place I too will rise from the ashes.

While the growing of grain is still a major enterprise here, it has given way to the production of sugar cane. The large sugar refinery in town spews a sour smell incongruent with its core product. There is also a blue jean factory which churns out both a Tunisian brand of denim and lesser known products for the high-end Dolce & Gabbana brand.

My new digs are located in the quiet neighborhood of Jebel Axdhir, which means "green mountain." I am living behind my landlord's house in a cozy studio apartment that shares a breezeway with his family. The very private family compound lies within a locked gate that is "guarded" by Wahid, a little man in dark blue peasant dress. There are beautiful gardens, a blooming jasmine tree and a Bougainvillea bush just outside my window. Khalil, the head of the household, is falling all over himself to accommodate me, exclaiming profusely at any opportunity how happy he is that I am here. "You will be my daughter," he says during repeated visits to make certain I have everything I could possibly desire. Already he has supplied me with a gas bottle so that I can cook and has offered to replace it when it becomes depleted—great news given that gas bottles are extremely cumbersome and the journey from Jebel Axdhir into town is a steep trek down and a staggeringly wretched climb back up. He has also provided gas for my heater, which transforms my little dwelling into a cozy warm space, though it smells like a garage when it's lit.

Khalil's wife Karima is lovely and very respectful of what is now my space, which I appreciate given my penchant for over-emotion these days. There are three teenage sons, Mohammed, Iyed, and Nasir, all rather studious and polite. They too keep a fair distance. Dinner hour however, is the exception. We gather at a long table in the courtyard under the dark night sky, feasting and sipping absinthe or whiskey. Mostly it is Khalil who partakes of cocktails; he seems eager to demonstrate his European sensibilities to me, at least behind the high wall of his compound.

"*Ishrub, Noora.*" He wants me to drink. He pours absinthe into a delicate glass, stands up and delivers it to me at the opposite end of the table. "*Ishrub.*" The taste of pure black licorice coats my tongue. I inhale the vapors and want to cough. "This is the finest," he explains. "It comes from Belgium." I'd hate to sample the crappy absinthe.

"She doesn't like it." Karima is laughing. "Look at her face."

"Doesn't Islam forbid alcohol?" I ask.

"But you are not a Muslim?" Khalil responds. Now, everyone is laughing. "What is *hram*," (forbidden) he explains, "is losing control of your mental faculties. That never happens to me."

It is comforting to be a part of this close-knit group. It is also reassuring to observe that Islam has just as many gray areas as any other doctrine. Or rather, that people are people: we will interpret for ourselves those things which suit us and redefine or reject those things which do not.

I am safe. More importantly, I am climbing hand-over-fist out of my misery. On the rollercoaster ride that has been this past year, I alternate between clutching and throwing my hands in the air, navigating each dip of despair or elation as it comes. Truth be told, I am profoundly grateful for each moment of either, because in the bearing of them I know I am fully alive. It isn't a very equanimous state of being, somersaulting through life this way, but, it is the only way I know how to be, fully engaged and flying madly forward.

CHAPTER 44

Exploring the Roman bread basket

The souk in Beja

With several weeks left before the new school year commences, I have plenty of time to explore Beja. One of the first items on my agenda is to locate an appropriate place to run. I find the sports stadium, a walled-in soccer field encircled by track.

It is vacant in the cool hours of the early morning. I start running there.

After only one week, Khalil asks me to stop. Apparently, news of my activity has spread and, unbeknownst to me, I've become a spectacle. Males are gathering beyond the walls to watch me. Khalil heard about it when he was in town and rushed home to put an end to the scandalous display. The incident in Aïn Draham taught me nothing. For several nights, I had taken to running within the walls of the soccer field there, until the evening I noticed a man sitting on the wall pleasuring himself, eyes locked on me. Up to now, I hadn't wanted to consider that my plodding about might in fact have some measure of erotic distraction for desperate young socially restricted men.

At Khalil's behest, I've given up running in Beja's stadium and started running at the girl's school. But then, one of the physical education teachers sees me and requires her students to run with me. My hour-long runs do not make me popular with these girls. My activities there end abruptly as well. However, one girl emerges and offers to run with me on the outskirts of town, so long as I teach her English along the way. I will never take my freedom to run in the U.S., whenever and wherever, wearing shorts, spandex, or whatever, for granted again.

• • •

Just a short distance from my house is a cemetery. It cascades down the hill in uneven rows of raised gravesites. Islam requires that a Muslim be buried immediately after death. The body is wrapped in cloth and buried on its left side facing the direction of Mecca. To date, wherever I have traveled in this country, I have found cemeteries to be remarkably idyllic and sacred, especially those containing the graves of WWII casualties. The cemeteries of fallen soldiers are immaculately maintained imparting stately honor to those who found their final rest so far away from home. The notable exception, however, are the Jewish cemeteries, which are shockingly desecrated and ignored. There is one here in Beja. It is hidden behind very high walls. Even the walls that hide it are in tumbling disrepair.

The cemetery atop Jbel Axdhir is the perfect spot for contemplation or just taking in the view. From here I can see the whole of the valley, its green fields rolling all the way to the horizon. It is peaceful most days, with the exception of Monday when small groups of women, or those mourning solo, come just after daybreak to wail at the sites of their departed loved ones in a haunting ritual that was at first disturbing. The women spend hours graveside, sprinkling the tiled graves with water, having lunch there, attending to the site and then, finally leaving offerings to the soul of the deceased. Walking down through the cemetery is the quickest way to get to the town below. On Mondays I am sure to keep my pace measured and mindful.

• • •

Across from one of Beja's larger cafés sits a man who daily occupies a little table covered in flower buds, sticks and string. As I am walking past his table today, he invites me to join him. He crafts jasmine bouquets, or *machmoum*. I watch as he meticulously winds red thread around individual jasmine buds and affixes each bud to short lengths of straw, eleven buds per stick. Next, he ties four finished stems together and voila: a mini jasmine nosegay. He sells them for five hundred millimes, about fifty cents each. Painstaking work for something that will last just one day. But jasmine, with its intense perfume, is a culturally iconic cherished flower.

Pronounced "yaz meen" (its translation means "gift from God"), jasmine's cultivation is so ancient that its country of origin is unknown. It's prominence in ancient Tunisian love stories propels it to this day as a symbol of romance. It is a bloom worn and savored. It is not unusual to see men with jasmine festively tucked behind the left ear, denoting availability. So informs my friend, the jasmine expert, Amir. But, it can also be worn simply to express joy.

Speaking of joy, it is common to see men walking arm-in-arm or hand-in-hand, behavior confined to few places in the U.S., as the connotation in my culture is clear. Not so in Tunisia, where the practice of linking of arms is routine and absent of romantic relationship. Friendship can be expressed without fear of judgment, reprisal or insinuation. Why is this so? Because homosexuality in Islamic culture is considered deviant and therefore strongly discouraged. Nevertheless, it does exist here, well under the radar.

I am all for displays of friendship in any context, including mine with Amir. I take liberties and risks given that I am a single woman openly meeting this man in public. A proper Tunisian woman would never be so…sleazy. Outside of that which is sanctioned by marriage or chaperoned by family, even the simplest of interactions are stringently restricted. Honor must be safeguarded. As I have already seen, families will go to extremes to do so. I take these liberties because I can; I sully only myself with my blatant fraternizing.

Besides, Amir is paternal; I cannot help but to gravitate to his protective and kind influence. I like his ability to be fully present in our conversation, without for a second sacrificing the speed of his hands as he ties blooms, one to the other, to the other. I like the way he hails the barista from well across the street and demands that he bring me a cold Fanta. I like how he plays the gatekeeper, fending off with a stare the disco boys that wander into our space.

"I will make it my mission to marry you off to a Tunisian man so that you can stay here forever," he says. I don't mention the futility of this, given that I have already declined the most attractive offer I am going to get. I change the subject to the only other topic that garners his attention, Beja's soccer team.

• • •

Like Tunis, Beja has an ancient medina that is the center of commerce and life here. It is also where I do the bulk of my near-daily shopping and exploring. Because there are essentially no tourists in Beja, I enjoy the freedom of milling about without having shopkeepers attempting to lure me into their shops. There aren't *those* kind of shops here anyway. Beja is altogether more rugged and practical and gritty. Today the streets of Beja's medina are muddy and pocked with puddles from consecutive days of rain compelling each of us to carefully consider our footing. Some women lift their white *safsaris* high to the calf. But most don't bother; mud finds its way onto low-hanging fabric, onto *shleka*-clad feet, up to ankles. I buy bread, rice, tomatoes, carrots, peppers, onions and cheese from four different vendors, collect the items in my sturdy two-dinar market basket and decide I can keep shopping. I must manage my haul carefully, lest I get overloaded. Plus, the road conditions are dicey. At the end of every shopping excursion is the trudge up Jbel Axdhir, tallish and steep, and today sure to be slick. I follow the smell of popcorn until I find a man selling it packaged in paper cones.

"*Salaam wa leykum.* Can I buy a kilo of…(crap, what's the word for kernel?)" I finagle my request. "Not the cooked stuff, the before stuff…"

"Do you know how to cook popcorn?" He is astonished. "No one has ever asked to buy "raw" *qitanya!*" *Qitanya!* Some words shall forever remain in my lexicon. We speak awhile. I answer the standard questions about my origin. I have secured a supplier for *qitanya*…good thing 'cause my popcorn habit is well established. A kilo of kernals puts me at capacity, my shopping is done.

An old woman crouched on the sidewalk gestures me over to her. "*Ogud baha thaya fi GAAAAA.*" She pats the ground next to her. I sit down and consider how much the Beja accent trips me up. After a year of fine-tuning my ear, cultivating specific sounds and refining pronunciation, I am at a place of relative comfort with Arabic. That is, until I leave the capital. Accents vary from region to region. In Beja, crispness and refinement is replaced by crude heaviness, Arabic at its most guttural. I struggle to decipher words I already know. I sit with the old woman, Habiba is her name. Together we watch a pack of shoppers pick through mounds of fresh oranges, a sausage vendor force ground lamb through a metal funnel into casings, a group of young boys disappear into a *hannute*. I say my goodbye to Habiba. She confers blessings on me and then asks me for money. I give her a dinar. She blesses me all over again. Then she asks me for my clothes. I'm not quite ready to part with them.

• • •

Thinking my cheese can hold out a bit longer, I stop to visit with Amir at his jasmine table. We are joined by two others who begin busily constructing jasmine bouquets of their own.

"Is America going to go to war with Iraq?" One of them asks.

"*N'shallah*, no." I haven't heard very much regarding the Gulf crisis since my return. We spend a few moments speculating on events to the east of us before Amir shifts the conversation to matters of greater import to him, namely his quest to find me a husband.

After the slog up the hill, I deposit my shopping and go back out for one more item. Just around the corner from home is my closest shopping source, a cinderblock structure about the size of a walk-in closet with a corrugated steel door. Inside there are simple staples, non-perishables mostly, cans of tomato paste and *confiture*—jam (quince mostly), sugar, flour, olive oil, and my new favorite, raw milk. There are just a few items, but they are immaculately displayed, artfully lined on three shelves, the well-kept space of budding entrepreneur. The proprietor is Leila, a school girl, who claims to have a cow tethered behind the shed. Since I discovered the lusciousness of raw milk warmed slightly and sweetened with sugar, I've had to make daily visits for my fix. I still haven't located that bovine, though. Everyday it's the same thing: "How are you? How is your cow?" She laughs hysterically…every time…which makes me laugh…every time.

This is life, Beja-style, a slow, deliberate meander through the parcels and parts of a simple existence. I wondered, albeit briefly, if I would be lonely here following the whirlwind social life I enjoyed in Tunis. My newfound solitude is enhanced by a fellowship that does not rely on Americans. It is what I sought coming here. Welcome *in* Beja *indeed.*

CHAPTER 45

Amoebas and the true measure of friendship

I lost seven days of my life to a despicable amoeba that invaded my body and nearly killed me, or so I was convinced. Over the weekend, I headed into Tunis to participate in the thirtieth birthday fête for my dear friend and former roomie, Patty. From all corners of the country, volunteers converged, including several who somehow managed to pilot their rickety mobylettes over eleven hours from great distances. Now that we have been in-country for over a year, our assemblies have become family reunions, and rowdy ones at that.

The revelry included the standard foul-tasting booze, an eclectic collection of homemade this and acquired that for all night eating, midnight scooter rides into the blackness and a once in a lifetime happening of swimming very late night in a phosphorescent sea, an experience akin to floating in liquid pixie dust.

In the morning, I was not so well. I assumed it was due to my excessive intake of *boukka*. So naturally, there was not a great deal of sympathy to be had. Within hours however, I was acutely ill and my temperature shot north of 104 degrees. It is incredible what an ailing body can produce and mine was especially unwell, spewing things unnatural. Finally, the Peace Corps nurse was summoned to my aid. Though I was delirious when she arrived, I distinctly recollect being shot up with valium. There were two other injections, of what I do not know, but one of the three caused numbness from my shoulder to elbow.

Many days later, the feeling in my upper arm has yet to return. Patty reports that I was overly preoccupied with the notion that I had left my motor home unattended somewhere in a Tunis parking lot and was determined to return to it at once. I faintly recall being put into a bathtub filled with ice cubes. I clearly recall thinking I would die, that it would be a welcome release from the misery of my condition. I was attended in my deluded state by Patty and our friend Christian, who, in a demonstration of pure humanity volunteered to transport my bodily samples into Tunis for analysis. Tests confirmed a diagnosis: severe vegetative amoebic dysentery. Source: grapes. Apparently, soaking grapes in a mild bleach solution for half-an-hour is not enough protection against the microscopic bastards which inhabit them. This I did, after I purchased them in the souk two days ago. I thought I was covered.

Worse than the horror of melting from both ends is what I did in my malaise…something I deeply regret. Someone snapped a Polaroid picture of me, slumped against the wall, cheeks sunken in, dark circles under my eyes, looking fifteen pounds (to be exact) lighter. I sent it home to my parents captioned thusly: "having a great time, wish you were here." When good sense returned, I placed a call to assure them I am still alive and no longer resembling the wreckage in that photo. During training, we were told that letters to home, written under duress or in times of stress, should have an incubation period, should be delayed. By the time these letters reach the parents, the issues that prompted their writing are almost always long gone. Case in point: my amoebas. In the interim, parental concerns are inflamed and Washington gets calls from frantic parents like my Dad, who freaked out. The sending of that photo, as my brothers would term it, was a bonehead move…and I regret it.

CHAPTER 46

Love & Marriage

Raodtha & Chehir

The moment I return to Beja, Jack and Molly meet me with news. They are moving into the medina house, bringing to twelve the number of years Americans have occupied that property. I am thrilled that our home will stay in the family! Jack and Molly are in Beja to attend the wedding of one of the sisters from their adopted Tunisian family. They invite me to come along. I haven't been to a wedding yet, so I seize the opportunity. I wonder what it will "look" like. I wonder how one is "performed." Are there similarities to weddings at home? I somehow doubt there will be any smudging of cake or dreadful nonsense involving garters.

We attend only part of the six-day celebration. This portion takes place in the decommissioned church in the center of town. Inside, there is a large stage at the front of the gymnasium-sized room. In the center of the stage, there is an empty bench. Behind the bench, there is a temporary wall covered in faux flowers of all colors and encircled by gaudy flickering lights. To the right of the bench a small orchestra plays traditional *malouf* music. Below the stage are rows and rows of chairs occupied by women only. The women are decked out in all manner of finery ranging from flashy gold lamé and sequined affairs to old-school prom dresses—very frilly and fluffy. There is even one woman sporting a fox stole in high summer! Men congregate behind and alongside the rows, not as adorned as the women, but looking dapper enough. Molly and I take seats near the back and wait, while Jack takes his place with the men. We wait. And wait. And wait some more.

Finally, the bride appears. The dress. Wow! Every square millimeter is covered in silvery sequins—she is a spectacular glittering extravaganza. But the dress is not a dress at all. It is actually two sequined-laden pieces: a bustier and pants so wide-legged that they appear to be a full skirt. Is that a belly I spy? Yes, and cleavage, right out there. From my distant viewpoint, I can see the bride's heavily caked make-up: eyebrows drawn on, a flash of intense cobalt eye shadow, heavily lined eyes á la Cleopatra, rouge streaked across each cheek and lips so crimson and lustrous they look as if they might drip off, if not for the black liner clearly defining their borders. Her hair is a sculptured masterpiece, twisted and spun and coated with tiny flecks of silver and gold which twinkle at each movement of her head. An enormous swath of veiling poufs out from within her coif. As for her manner, she appears drugged, catatonic, joyless. Her spirited entourage, mostly family, bolsters her from all sides, half-carrying her along the center aisle toward the stage. It is clear she will not make it under her own power. She is an overly medicated, reluctant drag queen, being conveyed against her will to a future she can't help but concede. At least, that's what it looks like to me. She is escorted up the stairs to the stage and onto the waiting bench, at which time a dozen women seize upon her, fussing, arranging, smoothing, fluffing, primping; hands fly everywhere for ten full minutes! When they are finally satisfied with their masterpiece, they leave the stage. The bride is now propped up on satin pillows. Her veil is a halo, spread and pinned in a large semi-circle to the wall of flowers behind her, leaving her little wiggle room. In one hand, she swishes a feathered fan back and forth in front of her face; the other holds a jasmine nosegay. She is melting under the weight of her bridal costume and five pounds of makeup. What is this?

I find it a little strange, a little awkward that the bride is, well, miserable. I assume she is marrying against her will. Arranged marriages are very common in Tunisia, where the family of the groom plays a large role in determining who is best suited for their son; where the family of the bride secures important alliances in the community. Negotiations between families are commonplace, but rarely if ever do they involve the potential bride. In an increasingly modern Tunisia, women have a greater voice. In a culture where no man is an island, women are barely atolls. Women need family support from cradle to grave. That being said, few women make the choice to move against the wishes of family.

Here's something that helps to clear up some of the confusion of the evening. Molly tells me that even if a bride happily enters into a union, she cannot openly display her joy on her wedding day. She is required to appear solemn, to bury her smile, to not register in any manner whatsoever a smidgen of delight. She must instead communicate grief at the leaving of her family. She sits alone on her throne in all her finery, a sourpuss, while her audience sits and watches her.

Some time later, the groom makes his grand entrance. He, in stark contrast, is all smiles. Triumphant in his Western suit, he is escorted by a large group of men; one holds an arrangement of flowers over his head. They lead him to the stage to join his stoic bride. Someone hands him a jasmine bouquet. Situated together on their throne, they look out over their constituency, not speaking to or hardly acknowledging one another. Meanwhile, Molly and I sit and watch them. I admire the ease with which Molly and Jack melt into any situation, any environment. Nothing seems to trip them up, even the brutal honesty of a handful of well-meaning students who walk up to Molly, first to greet her warmly, then to let her know her new haircut is *xa:yba*—ugly! But Molly, fresh-faced and adorable in her pixie, laughs off the commentary.

"*Mush mushkla, bish yikbir.*" No problem, she tells them, it will grow back. The hacking off of her glorious locks confuses her students, as it is simply not something Tunisian women do, go from long locks (the norm here) to drastic. Not ever. "I love my new do!" she tells me. "It is going to stay short." And I love my sassy unflappable friend.

Eventually, small groups head to the stage to have their pictures taken with the happy couple. The bride is detached from the wall and stands with her groom, while ensemble after ensemble has their turn at the photoshoot. The couple doesn't move from their spot for over an hour. Baklava is served, as is Coke and Fanta, too. We are still sitting and watching...for hours. Then it ends. That's it. The uniting of two people in marriage; a strangely unenjoyable kind of celebration.

Molly and Jack stay with me overnight. We spend the evening talking in candlelight. Jack gives me an update on Charlie, our friend in Tunis. Charlie has been my guide through Bulla Regia, Carthage and Dougga. He has taken me past every column, every pedestal, every mosaic, discharging history and breathing life into the ruins. He is well-loved by those of us lucky enough to know him. He is also an example of how it is possible to live creatively and gracefully here, despite, I'll add, having very little money. He opens his heart and home to volunteers, often hosting large banquets, where every hand partakes of making the feast. He smokes too much and dines almost every night at the same crowded French restaurant, the Cosmos. Lucky Jack is going to help Charlie create his legacy, work by his side as he masterfully documents Tunisia's buried mosaics. Jack is the perfect companion for the task at hand, equally curious, bound by nothing.

We chat into the wee hours about Charlie, about travel, teaching, spirituality and astral projection. I've never heard of astral projection and have to have it explained to me by Jack, which prompts Molly to interrupt.

"Want to hear something funny?" She explains that a group of volunteers were playing Ouija board in Sousse (someone actually brought a Ouija board to Tunisia), when during the course of the game, the séance or summoning or whatever it's called, the board clearly spelled out: "G O I N G H O M E." The board was then asked "Who is going home?" It responded by spelling out Molly's name, first and last. "Isn't that hilarious?" She chuckles. "I am the last person planning to go home." Indeed, Jack and Molly are digging in. "The best thing about Peace Corps is that it teaches you how to live overseas," Molly tells me. She has no desire to leave.

• • •

Molly and Jack's offers of comfort and gluttony are enough to lure me to an upscale Tunis neighborhood the following week. They've been asked to house-sit for a U.S. embassy employee whose business takes her out of the country for a spell. Even though my visit to Michigan raised the red flags of excess, something about the pursuit of luxury in Tunis is profoundly different. The decision to join my friends in the lovely villa, one equipped with CNN, movies, air conditioning, all manner of amenities and stocked with a variety of edibles is an easy one to make. What better way to utilize my waning days of vacation than spending time with two of my favorite people, eating what I please, catching up on events in the Gulf and living in the lap of luxury, Tunis-style?

We go to The Bardo where Jack disappears among the mosaics leaving me to catch Molly up on the Sam situation.

"So how are you doing with all that?" she asks me.

"I already met the new gal. Guess what? I like her." I tell her. It's true. I met her at the Peace Corps office in Tunis, walked right up to her an introduced myself. Spent a few minutes asking her about her experience of Tunisia, and then looked up to see Sam standing in the doorway observing us, mouth agape.

"Really? Huh. I didn't see that coming." She is surprised.

"Neither did I. But Allah works in mysterious ways."

"That's for darn sure," she says. "Well, good for you."

"Good for everyone."

We go to Alif, Tunis' best book store and comb through gorgeous photo books and exquisite Arabic language books. I buy a children's version of a book that introduces Arabic script.

"Are you going to send that to your nephew?" Molly asks.

"Oh no, this one's for me. I am still working on the script. I keep slanting my letters in the wrong direction. I need more practice," I admit.

"I'm thinking of studying French," Molly muses.

"Now there's a benefit to living in Tunis. You will have ample opportunity to practice here. I know of the perfect teacher, too: Hichem. He's still here studying law."

We spend two days hitting our favorite Tunis haunts and three nights enjoying a standard of living out of reach for most residents of this country, enjoying it gratis—all thanks to a woman I have never met. It's another of those "I am so grateful to be here" kind of weekends.

CHAPTER 47

"The spirit returns to the God who gave it"

Molly

It was during the aforementioned hedonistic weekend that we made plans to meet two weeks hence at Cap Serrat on the north coast for a few days of camping. But Jack and Molly fail to show. I am disappointed, but reset expectations. For this is the way of things in a country whose ubiquitous expression, *n'shallah*, clearly delineates a lack of control. After three nights without an appearance, I secure a seat in a louage and return to Beja. I spend those hours trying to remain Zen while the holy driver blows Qur'anic music through tiny radio speakers. I will never appreciate quantity of sound over quality of sound. It is only when we enter the tree-lined boulevard leading into Beja that I find a measure of silence that sustains me as I walk from the louage station.

Beja is lovely; I am at home here. I take in the familiar: cafes of men spilling into the boulevard, the clusters of uniformed school girls en route, *saf sari-ed* women conducting their daily shopping, a donkey conveying hummus to market. I approach the long hill to Jbel Axdhir and follow the path that leads past and through cemeteries, one in disrepair, the other a living memorial. I love the diversity of architecture that greets me at the top, including the wedding cake French architecture and ancient Moorish mosques I see with my bird's-eye view, to the blend of traditional and modern homes before me. The presence of one home in particular, where no one appears to live, always gets my attention. I stop at the gate, as I often do, and peer in through its spaces and wax romantically about it. For some reason, I want to live here. Despite its shabby condition and obviously abandoned state, I am fond of the atypical red tiled roof, pitched and poking through clusters of green, the wraparound scalloped portico. I am drawn in by its seclusion, by the dense grove of overgrown olive trees that encircle it, by the very high walls that contain it.

My neighborhood, in fact, is a series of walls, but magnificent ones at that, walls smothered in cascading bougainvillea, completely blanketed in brilliant fuchsia and coral. Life on this hill is quiet and predictable. So, when I turn the last corner I halt at the sight of something very anomalous, a large black American car, idle in front of Khalil's house. Peculiar. Tunisia is the land of beat up Peugeots and diesel Mercedes. American vehicles are the sole province of the American Embassy. They're not in the habit of frequenting this neighborhood...or this region, for that matter. Before I can put my key into the locked gate, Khalil opens his front door.

"Someone is here to see you. Come in." He ushers me inside his house. I recognize John, our volunteer coordinator. Robin Soprati, embassy official (and owner of the lovely villa I'd recently enjoyed so much) introduces herself. Well, that clears up the question of who owns the monstrosity parked outside. I am suddenly aware of the eerie quiet in the room and the stiffness of those in it. At this point, I'm quite sure I leave my body, because everything following becomes murky. They motion for me to sit down.

"Molly was in an accident. She died." No prefacing remarks, nothing to soften the blow, just out with it. I hear the words, but they don't register.

"What?" No. No... But the anguish on Robin's face is irrefutable. Then John explains what happened. It had been dark and rainy in Tunis that day. At the kasbah entrance to the medina, so close to the medina house, a spot where hundreds of times I've caught taxis and watched buses sweep in to load and unload passengers, in that very familiar place, Molly stepped into the path of an on-coming bus full of tourists. She tried to jump out of the way but fell back and hit her head on the curb.

"Jack?" He must be crazy with grief, in shock. He and Molly are a package, hard to conceive of one without considering the other. They'd been living in the medina house just one week when Molly went missing. She left that morning to go to the Ministry of Education to sign her new teaching contract. She never made it. At home, Jack waited for her. As the hours passed into the evening, wonder gave way to fear and he could wait no longer. He went to the police, but got very little assistance. By late nightfall, he was frantic. So, he went to the Peace Corps nurse for help. Together they went from hospital to hospital until they finally found Molly in a public ward. She was naked from the waist up, covered by a sheet from the waist down. She was peaceful, without a scratch on her. She was in a coma. After two days in that Tunis hospital, they moved her to the military base in Frankfurt, Germany, where she died.

This moment of absolute reality ruptures my heart. Jack, Molly's family, everyone who has ever known her will feel this deep in the gut, this raw anguish. For Molly was luminous and most beloved. My head pounds. I cannot speak. Hurt invades my chest. The body succumbs entirely to grief. This cannot be happening.

This was why they never showed up in Cap Serrat. I didn't give it a second thought at the time. There are always arbitrary disruptions here that prevent even the best-laid plans from being carried out, random things, transportation snafus, intestinal matters, obligations that materialize out of nowhere or better invitations even. It's part and parcel of living here, expecting the unexpected and sometimes gracefully, sometimes with effort, going with the flow, moving on. But this, this is inconceivable. When they didn't materialize at our rendezvous point, not for one second did I consider tragedy. Days ago, we were poking fun at Raquel Welch's sexercise video at Robyn's villa. In between convulsions of laughter, Molly pantomimed her breathy provocative instruction, the sultry leg lifts and suggestive stretches. Molly was very much alive; in pure physical form. Her laughter is still in my head, as is her face, as is every moment of friendship I have been privileged to share. She is not absent of me. That I will never set eyes on her again is unthinkable.

John hands me a note from Jack:

Dear Lora,

What can I say? I wish I could've had you here with me. I'm sorry I didn't call but things were very hectic. I did think of you often though and knew how upset you'd be. I want you to know

Molly considers you her best friend here and all prayers will be heard by her and by the Lord.

I am sorry to be the bearer of news such as this, but I wanted to leave you my words as I was definitely thinking of you.

Please visit the Jabbzura family and let them know I will be writing. Thanks.

Love, Peace and Happiness.

Be in touch

Please pray.

Love Jack

Visiting Molly and Jack's adopted family in Beja is the first thing I do. Telling them the news is impossible. I hadn't even known the Arabic word for "die" until now. I am back at Robin's at her request, for the interim. I am vaguely aware of the ride to Tunis in that big black car. I never expected to return to Robyn's villa. She gives me a box of Kleenex, a pack of cigarettes and her phone so that I can call anyone I need to. Everything has come to a screeching halt. I have no sense of time or place, only that this couch is yielding to my weight, softly curling itself about me. I am bound in sorrow. I will stay right here, burning through smokes and tissues, as loss too profound to name begins to take up residence in my heart.

I return to the medina house for the last time, to pack up all of Jack and Molly's belongings and ship them back to Ohio. It sucks. Molly left all her remnants of daily living with expectations of return. These manifestations of her existence echo proof of life. I trespass into territory much too personal, her make-up, her jewelry and her clothes. Each object takes on an aspect of sacred. Touching them borders on desecration. But, she is gone and they are now artifacts. Jack's journal lay open on the table; his last words are desperate and frantic.

Another violation of holy space! I close the journal, wrap it carefully. On the receiving end of this shipment will be my friend mourning the loss of his perfect match. How does one navigate through this?

I take the medina house rent payment to my former landlord and explain that his new tenants are gone. I don't want to give him Jack's money. I will not elaborate on the details associated with the logistics of Molly's passing, on the exorbitant cost of getting her back to her family. Suffice it to say, because she was no longer a Peace Corps Volunteer, she was without a blanket of protection when the accident occurred. Given these realities, I feel more inclined to return the money to Jack than pad the old Haj's pockets.

"I am the last person planning to go home," she'd said about the Ouiji board nonsense. Indeed, this was never part of her plan. As I write this, her body is already back in Ohio. But her spirit is everywhere. How does the saying go, 'The spirit returns to the God that gave it?' To celebrate her and to say goodbye, we gather at St. John's Church in Tunis for an eclectic memorial service that Molly would have loved. We play her favorite music, including this from World Party, a song she played incessantly:

"...See the world in just one grain of sand,
Better take a closer look, don't let it slip right through your hand.
Won't you please hear the call.
Put the message in the box,
Put the box into the car,
Drive the car around the world,
Until you get heard.
The world says,
give a little bit, give a little bit, of your love to me,
'cause I'm waiting right here with my open arms.
She says,

give a little bit, give a little bit of your soul to me,
cause I'm waiting to behold your many charms."

One of Molly's friends, a young Tunisian woman, performs a dance. Her movement mesmerizes us, an expression of grief and celebration communicated through flowing arms and swaying hips. I give Molly's eulogy. She was exquisite. She lived her passion. She was fearless. She was my friend.

Qoo len you see ban ail le ma koo tee ba Allah oo lena:
You have to know what happens to you is God's will;
only what is written by God for us…"

CHAPTER 48

October 1990

In the first week of October, 1990, Germany unites: Deutschland is whole again.

On the seventh day, my friend slips away.

By mid-October, Western troops in the Gulf number 226,000.

On the 15th, Mikhail Gorbachev wins the Nobel Peace Prize for his role in bringing an end to the Cold War and helping to open Eastern Europe. We can sure use some peacemakers in the Middle East.

By the final week in the month, this:

UNCLASSIFIED STATE DEPARTMENT COMMUNIQUE OCTOBER 1990:

RESIDENTS AND TRAVELLERS TO THE MIDDLE EAST, NORTH AFRICA AND SOUTH ASIA BE ADVISED THAT INCREASED TENSIONS DUE TO THE IRAQI MILITARY INVASION OF KUWAIT MAY LEAD TO DEMONSTRATIONS OR OTHER ACTIONS THAT MAY BE DIRECTED AGAINST THE U.S. AMERICANS ARE URGED TO KEEP IN MIND THE POSSIBILITY OF SUDDEN CHANGES IN THE SECURITY SITUATION WHEN MAKING TRAVEL PLANS TO THESE AREAS...

Iraq's invasion of Kuwait leads most newscasts. It is interesting to be in a position to monitor so many divergent viewpoints. In Iraq, the word is America will not dare attack. The "gentle and compassionate" Saddam Hussein can do no wrong. The United Nations embargo against Iraq broadens to restrict air movements. It's very serious. Iraq refuses to withdraw from Kuwait. The United States leads the pack, backed by the U.N. War is a threat. Saddam, the secular, grows ever defiant and calls for a holy war against America and her allies. Caricatures of Saddam in Arabic newspapers show him as Rambo, heavily muscled, often brandishing a machine gun, courageously, singlehandedly facing down his Goliaths: America and Israel.

• • •

I am on a bus bound for Jendouba, a city west of Beja, the city where Hichem's family lives. The man sitting to my right catches me trying to read his newspaper. Indeed, I *am* well into his space, leaning in to get a closer look at a large picture of President Bush addressing American troops in Saudi Arabia. He rashly turns the page, clearly offended by my intrusion. I squeeze to the furthest reaches of my seat, quite content to bear the whole of the ride in silence, when into *my* space appears the paper. He points to a second photo, this one showing Americans gathered in protest of the United States' involvement in the Gulf crisis.

"Of all the people...I get stuck next to an American..." and something else involving God that I can't quite make out. Though his voice is raspy and his words jumble when he spews them, it is clear he has pegged me as an American (which never happens... usually people believe me to be Lebanese). He isn't too pleased to make my acquaintance.

"*Shnuwwa tiktib?*" He asks for an interpretation of the photos, particularly what is written on the protesters' placards. "*Get the HELL out of there!*" "*All for our precious Big Oil!*" I translate, though I leave out the part about hell.

"Ha!" he says. "Americans want war. You are driven by your own economic interests. This is proof!" He begins to seethe. He is angry. What a sticky wicket this is. Stuck on a bus with a guy who hates Americans. This could get ugly. I try to clarify, to explain what the people in the photos are trying to communicate. He doesn't buy it. For him it is simple: people + placards = support for the president (government, policy, etc.), not opposition.

In Tunisia, the only voices that had better show up in the streets are those of the president's admirers. Period. I haven't lived most of my life under the stern rule of a dictator. I don't know what it's like growing up in a police state. When Ben Ali seized power, he stole it from his mentor. All my seatmate knows is what he has experienced and seen. From his viewpoint, maybe there *is* only one interpretation.

My interpretation? I am relieved at first. Here is a regional Arabic newspaper that has the gumption to print an American protest photo. Arabs (at least a few) will see that American support for a war is not universal. The relief is short-lived.

My seatmate starts polling the people around us. By the way, Tunisians are quite free to debate matters that are not local, especially regarding those that involve entities ostensibly ganging up on Islam. Before too long, everyone from the mid to the rear of the bus is engaged in the debate over the pictures, which inevitably leads to discussion over the role of the United States in a probable war, which ultimately leads them to the lone American on the bus.

Screw this apolitical stuff. I have an opinion. It lives in my gut, that inexplicable place deep inside that informs my truth. It is a powerful voice. But for all its power, it cannot shed light on things like United Nations resolutions that go unheeded and what is to be done about it. My gut tells me unequivocally that war is not a choice.

For the better part of an hour we deliberate, one random American and many random Arabs, about events which affect us all. No one is hot-headed. Even my seat mate ultimately concedes that it is entirely possible that not all Americans support the conflict. Everyone is thoughtful and engaged. Far from being zealots to some Pan-Arab contest, I find Tunisians to be calm, almost neutral and open to having the conversation. A fraction of peace is peace nonetheless.

CHAPTER 49

Do over

The beginning of the school year in Beja has gone almost pre-
dictably. I arrive at my new school on the appointed day ready
to meet my one and only colleague, the sole person with whom I will
have professional interaction—the *other half* of Bourguiba School-
Institut des Langues Vivantes, Beja. He is a no-show. There are
however, some of Molly's students waiting for me. In speaking with
them, it is clear her creativity and openness left an indelible mark on
them. She was their Mrs. Watson. You know, the favorite teacher,
the one you never forget, the first teacher to really see you. Mrs.
Watson was my fourth grade teacher, the first to inspire me to learn,
to reach, to be the best me I could be. Molly's students know what
they lost. These are difficult shoes to fill.

Back at home, I sit in flickering candlelight thinking about things beyond my control, like Molly, like another false-start school year and my monthly allowance late for the fourth month in a row, my missing Pap test that ended up in Zimbabwe, Mom and Dad's sad life in Detroit—perfect subject matter to accompany the terrific storm that has settled over Jbel Axdhir. The sound is huge; thunder rattles my house and my nerves. Lightning illuminates the night for stretches of time, creating enormous shadows on the wall that flash in ways menacing. Cold gusts whip past my open windows. This is a full orchestra, booming, resonating, filling every space.

It takes returning to the school every day for two weeks to finally meet Sofien, the other teacher. Our introduction is unceremonious and brief and decidedly not a coffee hour, get-to-know-the-staff ice breaker. There is no small talk whatsoever and Sofien stays just long enough to give me my assignment: three classes, two first year and one second year, a total of 120 students. Then he exits.

In the first week (actually the third week), no one shows up for classes. The new teaching year has begun: weeeeeeeee're off and running. Because one year of living in this country has softened me to the degree required by this culture, I am hardly fazed by these events. My impatience, along with the burning need-to-be-productive has mellowed dramatically. I am liberated.

It has been five weeks since I have received even one letter from the United States. Apparently, I am not the only one. All the volunteers are experiencing a stoppage. Cannot help but wonder if it has anything to do with the Iraq situation. Maybe not. It's not unusual to see letters that have originated in the U.S. arrive with postmarks from South Africa or Tanzania or other random locations on the vast continent. What does raise my antenna is the news that I have been followed on several occasions, so says Khalil. He has asked me to curtail all nighttime travel, outside of my return from evening classes. I am aware of one known pursuit, when a man in a BMW trailed me from the louage station. I noticed immediately and took steps to outmaneuver him. Everything I know about Beja I learned on foot. I had no trouble zigzagging through streets and passages where he could not follow, up through the cemetery. When I reached my neighborhood his car rounded the corner. I slipped into a narrow path and snuck home through the back. As I closed my door, I heard his car pass. A game of cat and mouse. I don't know whether to attach more meaning to it or not.

• • •

I am awake very early on a crisp Beja morning. I have pomegranate seeds with sweet milk for breakfast, tie my sleeping bag to my backpack and leave my house. I make my way down through the cemetery. It must be family day today, for everywhere there are men, women and children gathered around the gravesites, mourning and washing the tiled graves with water. I pass horses hitched to wagons and carts, their snouts buried deep in feed bags. I'd hate to be in that set up and sneeze. At the louage station, there are over twenty people waiting for a ride to Tunis. I snag a seat in the very first louage—I am shamelessly aggressive. The driver is erratic, passing on the shoulder, forcing others off the road. It is too early to have my body pitched so violently. Too early for Qur'anic recitations crackling through the radio speakers. Too early to stomach smoke from too many cigarettes, wafting right up my nose. And definitely too early to repel the "I know you can't resist me" look on the face of the guy sitting next to me. I turn my attention to the green landscape flying by. Just outside of Beja at the edges of farmer's fields, there are

Bedouins camping in thatched dwellings covered with large sheets of plastic. They are endlessly fascinating to me. I would like to find a way to get a closer look.

. . .

I am lying under a full moon in Islam's fourth holiest city. Behind Mecca, Medina and Jerusalem, there is Kairouan. Ancient and holy, it is said that ten visits to Kairouan is equal in religious merit to one trip to Mecca. I wasn't an immediate fan of Kairouan. It's just a little too staid for me, a little too sober, maybe even grim. But my friend is here and she says "it grows on you." If not for Lisa, I would have missed Kairouan altogether. One visit would not have been nearly enough, for it required a bit of digging in before I found my measure of reverence. I've come by my devotion the long way, through skepticism and exposure, unlike the faithful pilgrims drawn here through the ages. If I were keeping count, and if rumors are to be believed, I am well on my way to securing "Haja" status, for I have returned willingly to Kariouan for the sixth time.

For over thirteen hundred years, Kairouan has been an Islamic settlement, sustaining the oldest mosque in North Africa and the world's oldest minaret. For all of its ancient history, it has been a sedate and serious place. Consecutive visits do little to change my impression of Kairouan's distinctive sober personality; Islam is serious business and never am I more aware of its stronghold than when I walk these streets. Kairouan is in the middle of nowhere, a vast desolate plain. The army who traversed it back in 670 had no intention of putting down roots here. It was to be a temporary military camp, that is until Uqba ibn Nafi, general of the Islamic conquest of North Africa, made an extraordinary discovery. While walking the barren plain, he happened upon a golden goblet and recognized it as one he had lost in the holy fountain of Zem-Zem in Mecca. When he dug it out, a spring of water gushed from the dry earth. A miracle. The water is believed to be connected to the same source as Zem-Zem. "Kairouan" means "caravanserai," a resting place for camel trains. This forsaken tract of land, distant from any shore or trading route, this consecrated ground, was enshrined to be for all ages a destination for the faithful.

In this city of legendary mosques dwells one that is home to all Tunisians, The Great Mosque. It is a fortress to God. An architectural achievement. A monument of pure devotion. On visiting Kairouan one hundred years earlier, the great French novelist, Guy de Maupassant said:

A race of fanatics, nomads scarcely able to build walls, coming to a land covered with ruins left by their predecessors, picked up here and there whatever seemed most beautiful to them, and, in their own turn, with these debris all of one style and order, raised, under the guidance of heaven, a dwelling for their God, made of pieces torn from crumbling towns, but as perfect as the purest conceptions of the greatest workers in stone.

Over the centuries the Great Mosque has grown to monolithic proportions, its caretakers expanding, enhancing and even recycling materials to nurture this spectacular shrine. Its sheer size, the strength that it conveys, the perception that it has been here forever and will be here forever more makes me feel small and insignificant. This is the only mosque that I know of that permits non-Muslim visitors. Even then, wanderings are limited to the periphery. More than house of worship, this holy ground seems anointed by God.

I was groomed to believe that God dwelled in churches and that the Roman Catholic Church is *the* sanctuary, *the* asylum inviolable. When I was very young I thought God lived in the ornate golden box that sits atop the alter, front and center. Because I was a mere mortal, I never was never permitted to see inside the box, though I always tried to steal peeks when the priest pulled back the small curtain to retrieve or return the golden chalice housed inside. I knew churches to be sacred and with them each and every relic, symbol and candle. But it was the box, the Tabernacle on the alter under the enormous crucifix where I believed the pure essence of God lived— that is what my faith told me.

For Uqba ibn Nafi and countless pilgrims, it isn't a question of faith, but one of reason and intellect. The presence of water where none should be is reason enough to stay. Though communication with God doesn't require a stately building, believers erected one of the most enduring here. Just because this is not my house doesn't mean I cannot feel at home here. It is pure reverence that washes over me now, where I am a stranger, but no longer an infidel. For "infidel" has an interpretation that goes beyond non-believer. The label also includes those who lack thankfulness or gratitude to God for the gift of life—I dwell in gratitude. I walk in meditation, weaving in and out of the columns that wrap around the prayer room; there are four hundred of them. From a distance, the layout is all perfectly symmetrical. The columns are uniform in size, but as I touch one, I notice a diversity of marble, then capitals and friezes from Roman, Phoenician and Arabic collections. Everywhere there is exquisite stonework and archways that play with sun and shadow.

I move quietly in this holy place; there is a clear line between discovery and intrusion. Some believe my presence as a non-Muslim defiles this hallowed site. For me, it's an honor to share the sacred space. God no more lives in a box than he is the sole property of a people, wherever he dwells.

• • •

It is an expensive journey from Beja to Kairouan, given that 20TD is all that remains of this month's living wage. Plus, my November check is going to be late because Washington cannot seem to agree on a budget. I wonder if those fat cats in D.C. know that their inability to come to consensus reduces to zip the already meager living wage of Peace Corps Volunteers around the globe, to say nothing of all those military families with loved ones who have been dispatched eastward. By now, I am adept at surviving on scraps, as my budgeting skills have not improved, but my hobo skills sure have. I am flush with two cans of beans, some milk, a half kilo of tomatoes and half an onion that I brought with me. Together with Lisa's rice, peppers and cheese, we have all we need for a Mexican fiesta. This is mastering living on the cheap.

Along with getting my "holy" on, I come to Kairouan for camaraderie and connection. When we're not exploring or perusing Kairouan's extensive selection of carpets, we idle away on Lisa's terrace, watching the street life below, children rolling bicycle tire rims, a steady stream of shoppers at the produce stand across the street, or men loitering around the same *tabac* where we buy our long skinny brown cigarettes. Neither of us has an established smoking habit. In fact, the only time we smoke at all is when we are together, on Lisa's terrace, in private. Our big secret. Yes, and that one time after Molly…I was a chimney then.

It is always good to hook up with Lisa. She is a lovely mixture of intelligence, composure, and confidence. Her position as a university teacher affords her a front-row seat to some of the most dramatic student demonstrations in the country and unfettered access to the sometimes rebellious, often challenging voices that give rise to them. In Beja, the only time passions flare is when my students feel they are due an additional day of vacation. So they organize a "strike" and skip school for one day. Nothing is ever said about it. It is but a ripple in the pond. Meanwhile, in another part of the country, Kairouan's students erupt.

Political and social tension creates a flashpoint; the students are ripe, energized, involved and willing. As mentioned previously, things like freedom of expression and association, criticism of government and radical dissent are severely restricted. In September, a student was shot by police during a demonstration. He died. The incident triggered even more demonstrations and authorities responded by arresting scores of Islamists, which sparked even more protests. In the end, hundreds were arrested. Dozens were held without access to family or legal assistance. Many were tortured and some died while being held in detention. To campaign in Kairouan, whether instigator or curious looker-on, is to hazard harsh and arbitrary repercussions, imprisonment, harassment and intimidation or worse at the hands of a swift moving government. It is interesting that at the last moment Lisa was pulled from the China group because of civil unrest that garnered the world's attention. Though it is not being played out on the world stage, the drama here is no less intense.

Speaking of eruptions, I wonder if George Bush will keep his cool, or if he truly believes that the U.S. should come to the aid of a monarchy. As far as my hosts are concerned, America looks singularly focused on her inalienable right to cheap oil. King Hussein of Morocco has called for an emergency Arab summit. Iraq sent an envoy under the conditions that it will have a place on the agenda and the Palestinian question will be discussed. The U.N. Secretary says he is losing room to maneuver for a peace process because Iraq is still "stiff." There are no English newspapers in Beja, so I have resorted to scanning Arabic language newspapers which are consistently dominated by depictions of Saddam as a beefy superhero. He is widely regarded as a champion, both for standing up for the rights of Iraqis and for shining the world spotlight on the Palestinian situation. As for preoccupation with the unfolding events in the Middle East, where two or more volunteers are gathered, conversation inevitably turns to speculation of the U.S.'s involvement in the crisis. Should the option of war be exercised, we can't help but wonder how the inevitable ripple will affect us.

CHAPTER 50

Life in Beja

In my kitchen in Beja

Dogs of all tones bark endlessly as night falls, disturbing my
peace. In the daylight hours, cats rule Jbel Axdhir, roaming
freely in search of scraps. Today two wandered in through my open
door. I closed it behind them. It is time, I concluded, to befriend
my feline neighbors as they are always lurking about in great number
and appear starved for attention. They hissed violently at me, mak-

ing it clear that affection is not on the menu. They rely on humans to provide their food, yet they are utterly distrustful. I liberated them. They are not pets.

• • •

Teaching is new and exciting. I enjoy far more autonomy here (if that's possible), crafting my curriculum without having the need to teach to "the" book. One of my three classes is comprised completely of male students, average age: fifteen. Why Sofien thought it reasonable to assign this particular class to me has more I suspect to do with his personal entertainment. The students are a rambunctious lot and discipline is proving to be my most significant challenge (again—still). More effort is expended wresting control than imparting lessons. "Be a bitch." Words of advice ricochet in my head. And though I don't dare turn my back on the ocean that is my classroom, I am simply not ready to go *there* yet. I'd like to inspire engagement without resorting to threats and wielding meanness to achieve it. So despite the fact that this particular class is more happy hour than academic undertaking, and I am more jester than educator, I show up, every time.

• • •

I join a student on a visit to his grandparent's house in the "*rif*," the country. They live outside the town of Bou Salem, to the north. We travel in the back of a *nakarifi* to a random location and are left there. I follow Walid on a path that leads from the main road, past fields of pomegranate trees, over a trickling stream, through a lemon orchard and beyond.

Situated behind an enormous thicket of prickly pears is Walid's grandparent's farm house. It has all the signs of a home in serious decline. Vegetation is overtaking the rear of the structure. There are huge swaths of mortar slapped onto areas where the block construction is crumbling. Scraps of corrugated metal are tacked roughshod onto the roof in three places. Instead of a door, there is a *hammam* (bath) towel. Walid's grandparents are both stooped with age, weather-beaten, and wearing clothes drab from too many seasons of wear, filthy from too many days of wear. This is a very poor family. His grandfather takes my elbow and ushers me to a tree, then holds up his wrinkled hand to "say" wait here. He spreads out several coarsely woven wool blankets under the tree and motions me to sit. Walid brings out a tray. On it is warm *tabbouna*, hunks of fatty meat in a chipped bowl, thick potato fries in old newspaper, sections of oranges and the sweet dessert, *bsisa*, also in a chipped bowl. He sets the tray down. His grandmother hands him a ceramic pitcher—the handle is missing. He walks away to fill it, not toward the house, but back in the direction that had brought us. Walid grew up here but moved into Beja last year to be closer to school. There are a couple of chickens about and a horse with serious swayback and protruding ribcage tethered to a random post, a pathetic sight. I look to the food and know I am being given the very best this household has to offer, including the time and attention of my hosts. It is one of the more humbling moments I've had.

"Are you married to a Tunisian?" Walid's grandmother inquires. And so it goes. "To an American then? Are you a Muslim?" The standard menu of burning of questions about my marital status and religion leaves them with this: unmarried, non-Muslim woman, far away from family. Always the puzzle. I weather the inquiries well enough—I am used to them, can have this conversation in my sleep. "We are happy you are teaching Walid English." She changes the subject. "He doesn't want to be a farmer, like his father, like his grandfather. He has ideas of his own." Walid returns with the pitcher. He has walked to the community spigot, somewhere in the vicinity of the lemon orchard.

"Walid will go to university." Grandfather speaks for the first time.

"*N'shallah.*" We say in unison.

Education is *the way*. The best way someone as impoverished as Walid can change his circumstance. Indeed, I think he will. He is motivated. I've been tutoring him before class several days a week. I put the offer out to all my students. Walid is the only one who shows up consistently.

"Teacher," says Walid (a much better fit than professor, but still not as comfy as my name). "Yesterday in class, when you talked about…" He stops mid-sentence, quickly drops his left ear to his shoulder and brings it back upright at the exact moment that I do. We start laughing and we can't stop.

"*Shnuwwa? Shnuwwa hetha?*" (What? What is it?) His grandmother puzzles. From the beginning, Walid has insisted that all conversations we have take place in English. His English is excellent, except that he shares a common Tunisian stumbling block, the habit of adding an extra syllable to certain past tense words, for example "talk-ED" or "walk-Ed." It's so rampant among my students, I've had to come up with tactics to eradicate it. In my classroom, whenever someone brings "Ed" into the conversation, I twitch, bobble my head as a way of giving them a chance to self-correct. It's caught on. Savvy students bobble right along with me. I'm fairly confident twitching has no place in the Audio-Lingual Method, but it seems to be helping.

Walid's grandmother insists on sending me off with two loaves of *tabbouna*, wrapped lovingly in a cloth. To not have accepted her gift—Lord knows, they need this food more than I do—would have been an insult. Believe me, I tried. So, I take the loaves. I feel like a buffoon.

• • •

With great emptiness, I find myself contemplating Molly when I pass the street where she used to live and when I teach in her classroom. That I won't see her again breaks my heart anew whenever her memory is conjured. Haunting me is the pervasive notion that each time I leave my house there is the possibility that I won't return to it; that someone will find it as I left it and have to sift through the remnants I have left behind. Before I close my door, I turn and scan the room for my imprint as if to say "goodbye." Molly, leaving the way she did, when she did, reminded me how impermanent I am; confirming for me that the dream of my life is ever-fleeting.

• • •

I find myself once again wading through the deep waters of Tunisian bureaucracy, as it is time to renew my Carte de Sejour. Khalil escorts me to the Belladia, several municipal offices and the police station to submit our housing contract, signed months ago. At the police station, Khalil is particularly anxious. His hands tremble when we are made to handwrite two separate copies of the contract in addition to the original. The police take me to a private room and question me for over an hour, quickly honing in on Khalil's cautious and evasive demeanor. Of greater interest is my frequent comings and goings over the past five months, which they clearly seem to be tracking with great accuracy. Sometime during my detainment, Khalil leaves. In the post office, my next stop, he suddenly appears.

"What did you tell them?" He is restless, uneasy. "They're going to interview you again." He says nervously. He doesn't elaborate. He leaves it to me to learn that my arrival in September (the month I became a Beja resident in earnest) coincided with the arrest of eight spies. That I am a person of interest is of no particular interest to me, such is the fog of naïveté in which I dwell.

• • •

Providence has sent me a kitten. I discovered him upon investigation of a peculiar noise coming from underneath my bed. He is tiny, severely malnourished and nearly fur-less, save thinning patches of black here and there. It was his screech I heard; he cannot meow, not even a teensy bit. The pathetic little creature must know my penchant for black felines. He's affectionate and attached. He likes to curl up on my shoulder when I read in the shade of the courtyard or when I move about the house. I introduce him to Karima, a bona fide cat person. She is always leaving scraps of food outside for the wild ones, which is why we have a preponderance of them roaming around the garden. I explain how Moses (I named him for my childhood cat) appeared mysteriously in my house, how he adopted me. She is a little taken aback:

"You named your cat after the prophet?"

• • •

I've received a letter from Nejla, one of the students from the program in Aïn Draham. It read:

Hello. How are you? I hope that you are fine. I am happy to write you this letter and to know your news. I had think to write you before now, but the number of tests were important and I think that with a number like this none can find a moment to write a letter.

Lora I hope that you haven't forget the marvelous days in Aïn Draham in the last summer. For me I will never forget this weeks, they were very nice and you were friendly and kindly.

If I will go to America one day, it's not because I like this country, but because you live there and I like to know more about your real life. If you want, write me something about life in America because what I have seen in T.V. was horrible and marvelous at the same time.

Write me soon.

Miss Nejla

CHAPTER 51

Smadhi

Former President Habib Bourguiba
pinning the Order of Republic medal on Mehrez Smadhi

In Sanskrit, Smadhi means "beyond waking, dreaming and deep sleep, a conscious experience of union." In Beja, Smadhi is the name of my newly-adopted family. At the close of my very first night of teaching in Beja, a student approaches me and introduces herself as Bchira, which means "good news." She tells me point blank that she doesn't have any friends her age, nor any that are her intellectual equal. Her admission is so honest, so undaunted, I am happy to oblige her invitation to dinner at her house—on the spot. We make the long walk in the dark to the Smadhi's modest home near the kasbah, the imposing Roman fortress that sits atop a hill opposite Jbel Axdhir. Across the street from her family's home, sheep graze in a rocky field that ascends to a dense assortment of sumac shrubs. Kitty corner is the local office of the RCD, the Constitutional Democratic Rally, (formerly known as the Socialist Destourian Party), the ruling party. Inside the gated wall of the Smadhi home, we are greeted by Omee, mother to a crowded household of women. Her head is bound in a red scarf and tied into a bow below her chin. She wears an ornately ornamented green velour robe, her housecoat. She takes my face into her hands, looks right into my eyes and lovingly kisses me four times on the corners of my mouth, as though I am a long lost daughter. Then she quickly disappears into the kitchen at the back of the house.

I meet Bchira's four sisters, who range in age from twenty-six to twelve. My immediate impression tells me that Bchira is the serious one. Right now education is her focus. She is going to be a nurse. Her older sister, Raodtha, is boisterous and plump, fun-loving and loud. Sonia is aggressive and sociable. And Intessar and Rejeh are innocent, curious and delightful. There is also Grandma, bent and wheezing, with flaming orange "henna-ed" hair. She keeps a can of Tunisian snuff in her hand and dips, frequently. I'm told there is a brother who lives in Italy. The patriarch arrives, Mehrez. Known as "Bubba," or father, he sports a brown woolen fez, a well-endowed pot belly and a very large gold tooth, front and center.

"*Marhaba! Marhaba! Marhaba!*" Again and again he welcomes me warmly. He leads me into the family room and guides me to sit on the floor near a low table. Omee enters the room carrying a heaping bowl of couscous, for just me. The entire family takes up positions around me. After countless meals in the homes of strangers, I still find eating with an audience to be awkward. I convince Bchira to share some of the feast. In between bites, I answer questions. Bubba tells stories. The conversation goes well into the evening, so late in fact, I am asked to stay.

I've been adopted. Because they cannot fathom why I, as a single female, would leave my family to travel around the world to live alone, they have taken it upon themselves to ensure that I endure as few solitary hours as possible. I am "*mskina*," a pitiable and misfortunate girl too far away from family, in an unthinkable state of being—one they cannot allow. I dine with them, spend nights with them and generally take my place in their very active household. Except, they won't let me do anything to help. They wait on me, endlessly. While I sit with Grandma, wrapped in a blanket, they bring me slippers, tea, my dictionary. They clean around me. I feel foolish. Then came the afternoon I decided to join them.

"Sit! Sit! Sit!" They insisted.

"I've watched you enough; I think I know how it's done." Now I am tossed a broom or a wash cloth without a second thought. And the fine-tuned machine that is this household of women cleans every room in the house with speed and muscle. On the terrace someone beats the carpets, while in each room, buckets of water are thrown on the floor and every square inch is mopped and squeegeed. This is what happens every morning, this concerted effort with all hands—and now mine, too—on deck.

As soon as the house is immaculate, the work of mealtime prep begins. We spend a lot of time chopping and dicing and chattering in the kitchen. The atmosphere fills with overlapping voices in multiple conversations. The smell of sautéing garlic, onions and tomatoes in pungent olive oil saturates the air. So many delicious dishes begin with the same simple ingredients. Naima takes no shortcuts with her food. Few Tunisians do. Convenience foods are non-existent. So, grains are wrought by hand, steamed and carefully massaged with flavors and adorned with fresh vegetables purchased each day in Beja's open air market. I stand at Naima's side as she demonstrates her recipes from memory. She is so habitual, so deliberate in her actions, I have to guesstimate her measurements, as I transcribe her process for making authentic dishes like couscous and *salata* (salad) into my journal. My one and only attempt to share American cuisine, in this case carrot cake, was met with great skepticism.

"You put carrots in a cake?" They were aghast. I ended up taking the cake home with me because they couldn't bear all my effort going to waste on them. I know it was because carrots do not belong in cake.

We also spend good chunks of time on the floor crowded around the low table, sharing meals from one large bowl, drinking cool water from one pitcher—"*Arby*" style—and talking, well, mostly Bubba talking, late into the evenings. Mealtimes are chaotic, and lively. This is cherished time.

I love Bubba, as the paternal figure, as the defender of his women, as the driver of our family conversations, especially political ones. He is open and exceedingly non-confrontational and very good at keeping everyone engaged in debate. He surprises me. He is my reminder that I assume too much of some people and too little of others. It would be easy to gloss over a man like this, assume his life is as simple as anyone's could be, without a great story, without tragedy or triumph. I did. I meet him as a loving father, devoted to his family and now, even to me. His simple life is good enough. His clothes are simple. In fact, most days, he wears the same thing, his faded blue uniform and brown fez. His home is strikingly simple, unadorned, adequate. His day is going to and coming from his job as a supervisor of the *barrage*, a massive dam that holds and controls the flow of freshwater to the whole of the north and eastward toward Tunis. Work and family. Simple Life.

But nothing about a former freedom fighter is simple, especially one that has been scarred by conflict. Military service shapes and hones a man. But war sears the memory center, rendering everlasting hurt and wounds felt forever. Like my father, Bubba goes cloudy at the remembering of war, eager to tell the overarching story, but with stops and starts and omissions. And just like Bubba, Dad lives the picture of boring, so it's easy to assume he is a simple guy, too. Once upon a time though, my dad was a drill instructor teaching hand-to-hand combat to hundreds of recruits heading to Vietnam. Through some tragic error of judgment, the vast majority of the recruits got sent directly to the front lines after leaving Dad's training. Hundreds perished. Deep pain, the never-ever-go-away-variety inhabits Dad, bubbling up when conversation veers there. I see it also in Bubba. Their sorrow affirms how I feel about conflict. No good can come of it.

Bubba has a photo. In it Tunisia's first president, Habib Bourguiba, is pinning the Order of Republic medal on Bubba, decorating him for his part in helping wrest control of the homeland from France in the early 1950s. He showed me his stunning bronze ornament, with a five-pointed star highlighted with green and red enamel, finely engraved with silver lances encircling a coat of arms, with a ship, the scales of justice and a lion, topped by a crescent moon and star. *Republic of Tunisia* is embossed in Arabic. It dangles from a green and red striped ribbon. Side note: it is curious that the decoration—celebrating Tunisia's independence from France—was fabricated by the house of Arthus-Bertrand, medal makers to the world since 1803, located in Paris.

In 1960, Bubba served in the Congo as part of a United Nations peacekeeping operation whose primary function was to ensure the speedy withdrawal of the Belgian military from the newly independent Republic of the Congo. For his participation, he was conferred a medal that bears the logo of the United Nations on its face. On the obverse, it simply reads "In the Service of Peace."

Bubba's exploits come as a surprise, given his lovable demeanor and easy way. He does not fit the picture of a military man as I know it. He is not at all authoritarian or regimented or orderly. Quite the opposite. He is soft, in every way. One thing's for sure, though he is the undisputed head of a household teeming with females, he is too yielding, too responsive to be its supreme ruler. That role falls to Naima. Bubba is surprisingly relaxed, progressive almost about his girls. That he supports Bchira's professional education is significant. That he says his girls will have a say in who they marry is a liberating avowal. Marriages are negotiated between families. Long before the marriage contract is signed, good mates are heavily prospected and vetted on both sides of the equation, and too many times the bride is not consulted. Bubba will not negotiate away a one of them.

He calls me daughter, tells me "as much my daughter as my other five, and as such I will share all that I have equally with you." Instinctively, I think of Dad. He would never compromise his fidelity to his family, especially never to an outsider. Never so callously dilute the holy relationship of father-daughter for someone not of his blood. I know it sounds dramatic, but so's my dad. I look to the sister's faces, Raodtha, Sonia, Bchira, Intessar and Rejeh, looking for hurt or dissent. There is only unanimous agreement.

Omee is the Arabic for word for "my mother." Naima, Omee, is mother to me in the way she pulls me into her fold protectively without hesitation. Looks to my needs before her own. Locks eyes with me in a way that confirms connection. Lays hands on me each day in prayer pleading to Allah on my behalf for protection, which makes sense, given that she is this house's spiritual head. She is a devout Muslim, who quietly makes her way to prayer, never missing when summoned. Sometimes, she invites me to sit near her while she prays. I love these moments, communing with her and God/Allah, just us three. She rolls out her prayer carpet in the salon, to face the east, which, in this case is the TV. She has washed her face, her mouth and nostrils, her arms, hands and feet. She is purified. Her hair is covered. Her eyes are closed. She raises her palms to heaven and begins to whisper her prayer. She kneels, places her forehead to the floor and rises, returns her forehead to the floor and rises to standing. This pattern of prayer looks to me like an offering of an open heart followed by a show of submission. It goes on for several minutes. If Islam has a tranquil voice, than Omee, is it, gently weaving the protective web of faith around her family and me at all times. Islam sustains her, and is the very lifeblood of the family she sustains. In a world gone crazy, where the only Muslim voices that get airtime are the nut-jobs, the overwhelming majority of them pray thusly, in whispers, move thusly, in humility, act thusly, with grace.

Omee is also this house's supreme ruler in other areas of import. The whole of the household budget lives in a tiny change purse she keeps tucked in her bra. From it, she dispenses the monies needed to fund food, education and the stuff of day-to-day living. Nothing is purchased without Omee's explicit approval. I have even seen her dig for dinars for Bubba. If something is needed for the household, one must first hold court with Omee, possibly bring witnesses, even American witnesses. How I factor into the purchase of new pair of *shlekas* (fancy flip flops) or fancy cakes for a gathering, I shall never know. In the end, Omee must approve all acquisitions which are shared equally among all the members of the household. In the face of overwhelming female energy, Omee quietly leads, setting an example for five daughters who will one day have to do the same for their own.

Family is the collective hug of belonging. I have a family. I bask in the embrace.

CHAPTER 52

November 1990

That which you resist, persists

Omee

The ladies have henna-ed my hands and feet numerous times, and even though it is too cold for anyone to see my feet, they insist. They invite me to the *hammam*, the public bathhouse, for the ultimate in bonding rituals—one I have managed to avoid until now. To be honest, I am not keen on sharing a practice which is best performed solo, behind closed doors. The Smadhis have a bathtub, but it is not plumbed for water. It is never used. As far as I can tell, there are no plans to remedy the situation, either. So, once a week, the girls pack a suitcase and go to the *hammam* for ritual bathing and socializing.

As soon as I enter the *hammam*, a blast of steam strikes me in the face and sucks all the air out of my lungs. The rank stench of skin, damp and fetid, curls into my nose. Humidity settles on my face collecting in beads on my forehead. I am instantly clammy and claustrophobic. How can a bathhouse make me feel so…unclean? The first room, the changing area, is very large with a raised platform around the perimeter and mattresses lay end to end. In this room, we strip down to our undies and empty the contents of our fully-packed suitcases.

With our buckets, plus a variety of soaps, loofahs and potions, we step onto the tile floor. It is heavy with slime-coat. Thank goodness for *shlekas*! The sauna room is a crowded echo chamber, packed with rambunctious children and women engaged in lively conversation. We spend twenty minutes steaming in our soggy underwear until Omee deems us sufficiently moistened and leads the charge to move on.

We proceed to an area where we collect scorching water in our buckets and head to the washing room. Never have I been in the company of so many naked uninhibited women. There are perhaps one hundred, all in the various states of cleansing. They stare at me. Suddenly, I am self-conscious of my albino skin. I stare back at the incredible array of shapes and sizes on display, doing all manner of what should be accomplished in private. I am, I admit, rather out of my element here. One of my students recognizes me and greets me with four kisses. It's hard not to feel self-conscious about a public kiss with a woman, when between us we're not wearing enough material to make a hanky.

But then, this isn't really considered public space, not really. This is the feminine space. Women of the Middle East have a long history of collective living, wherein much of what makes us women is shared, experienced in and supported by the community of women. This is very natural for them; not so much for me. I envy the woman who can find comfort in this space—which is to say every woman here, except me. It is curious to me that Tunisians seem to have no notion of privacy. For the state of being alone is never preferable to being in the company of another, especially if that company is a family member. Communion is preferable to isolation. This collective mentality, coupled with the natural separation of the genders under Islam, results in a society of women that is strongly—and intimately—connected.

It is about this time when I begin to lose total control over my bathing. Every few minutes, my student brings me a bucket of fresh water. Omee supervises while I wash and condition my hair. She makes me repeat the process three more times. I watch women using coarse loofahs to scrub each other's bodies raw. They lie on tiled platforms while mother, daughter or friend scrubs aggressively from nape of neck to feet, working up large balls of skin. The bodies are doused with a bucket of water and the process gets repeated, again and again, until no more skin can be exfoliated. Wads of skin join nests of hair on the floor traveling along in a stream. Disgusting.

"Your turn!" orders Omee, as she dons a loofah mitt and positions me against the wall. She scours every nook and cranny of my flesh until balls of soft tissue form. "Tsk, tsk," she mutters, as if I am uniquely unclean. The pressure of her hands is so robust, I have to work to brace myself against the wall. My skin begins to sting. She instructs me with all the compassion of a drill sergeant: "Do this! Do that!" Suddenly, I am four years old, incapable of independent action. After she removes my epidermis, she has me wash my hair... again. We spend two-and-a-half hours bathing! Despite some of the more repellent aspects of the *hammam*, I feel more pure than I thought possible and certainly cleaner than I have ever been, ever.

CHAPTER 53

A decisive step

The cemetery in Beja

The Prophet Mohammed said,
"After my disappearance there will be no greater sources
of chaos and disorder for my nation than women."
Abu Abdallah Muhammad Ibn Ismail al Ismail al-Bukhari.

Karima, my landlady, stares down at the red checkered table cloth on the little table in her kitchen. I slowly sip the thickly sweet Arabic tea from the shot glass, occasionally fishing out a pine nut floating on top. Not once does she bring hers to her lips. Instead she enfolds her hands around the glass until the glass cannot not be seen at all.

302 THE MEASURE OF A DREAM | Begin

"I have so many problems…" Here it comes, the explanation behind the rigid posture, behind the rather uncharacteristic pensive behavior of the last thirty minutes. I've heard the frequent heated confrontations from across the breezeway. Arguments erupt out of nowhere, jarring me from my sleep, my thoughts, my peace. The cheap disco boom box I bought in Tunis does a poor job of running interference; our proximity is too close and their outbursts too piercing. The eavesdropping can't be helped. Anger is a universal language that doesn't necessitate translation. I don't need anyone to confirm for me that there is serious trouble in this house. When Karima and I see each other after one of the explosions, we behave as though all is right in the world. I am amazed at the grace with which she carries her conflict—she is forever smiling and buoyant, without a hint of what lies beneath.

Today she is confessing...to me. And it goes like this: Karima's marriage was arranged by her parents; the contracts were signed when she was just fourteen years old. She had barely completed school before being taken as a bride. It was a terrifying time for her. She begged her parents to change their minds. Her tears were rebuffed. Her father shunned her. The groom? He was some twenty years her senior. The bride lacked experience, emotional maturity, higher learning, but she knew enough to know these things she lacked would hurt her. She was forced into the marriage.

It has been twenty-eight years of sorrow, each one piling up on the other, each one further fueling resentment over the usurping of her dreams. When she gives voice to her aspirations to be more than a housewife and mother, her husband quickly reminds her of her responsibilities. For her role as a submissive—as cook, as maid, as hidden wife and mother is well-established. She pleads for change. She campaigns for employment or any opportunity that would allow her to function in an intellectual capacity, anything that could help compensate for the hollowness she feels. He is unrelenting in his refusal. He staunchly resists any deviation from the status quo. These things which "are" shall not be changed. Period.

She rarely leaves the spatial boundary of the family compound. She is not permitted to drive despite being in the highly atypical position of owning not just one, but two vehicles. Her duties have changed little over the decades, breeding mind-numbing monotony. She has had to internalize her dreams of liberation, living every day in service to her family, while waiting for her children to mature. Waiting for a freedom that may never be granted.

Islamic culture does not sympathize with her. "The meaning of marriage is the husband's supremacy...Marriage is a religious act... which gives the man leading power over the woman for the benefit of humanity" (Sheikh Ibn Murad). Thus, her duties as a wife, as a mother of three are clear. She must remain and accept her confinement. She must not complain. Her family is indifferent to her cries. Hush daughter. Hush wife. Hush mother.

I see now that she is a woman who carries both fire and sorrow at all times, though she is expert at concealing it. In the early hours of the morning, she tells me, she writes her story. These are the only private secure hours she has. These are also the hours during which she plans her departure without aid of anyone, because it is wrong to abandon one's family.

She asks me to help her find a job and an apartment in Tunis.

Every Monday she strings the wash on the line. Lunch is served every afternoon promptly at 1:00. The house and garden are immaculate. This semblance of order masks the confusion that has infected their household, and now mine.

This is the second time I have found myself pulled into a situation that has overwhelmed me. What is it about my presence that incites freedom-craving Tunisian woman to self-determine in ways atypical of this culture? In me they find camaraderie around a shared value. The dynamics of a culture balancing on the tightrope between tradition and modernism leave many struggling to maintain footing. Some simply cannot.

Besma wanted only a taste of the freedom I've known easily all my life. Her veiled sisters misunderstood her. Her parents tolerated her. Her brother beat her. She had no one until I came along. I was the drug that hooked but could not sate her. We became so entwined that accountability for the choices she made seemed to belong to me as well. Now I have been swept up into the storms that are raging through this household. It hasn't been any overt word or deed of mine that has caused this instability. It existed before me. I am the lightning bolt, the disruption in the Force. I am the Western influence that protectors of tradition throughout the Middle East fear and avoid. My presence snags the cultural fabric toward a ruinous outcome. Besma escaped. Karima plots.

By the time I return from class tonight, she'll be gone. Bailing after twenty-eight years of marriage, like my parents. How strange it will be once silence reigns, no arguments, no shaking of the rugs, sweeping of the terrace, rattling of pots and pans, watering of plants…the sounds of freedom will ring glorious.

• • •

It's very quiet around here. Karima is gone. I didn't have to live here very long to recognize how deafening this silence is. Khalil comes to my door, taps lightly.

"Do you know?" I nod, yes. "Did she tell you?" I nod again. "She has everything, clothes, trips to Sousse, her home and children. She's sick in the head. Her mind is deteriorating." Hmmmm. If freewill looks like illness, then indeed she is most afflicted. "If anyone comes here, please tell them you don't know where she is," he asks. "I don't know where she is." He shakes his head and shuffles away.

"Change is shaking the foundations of the Muslim World. Change is multidimensional and hard to control, especially for those who deny it. Whether accepted or rejected, change gnaws continuously at the intricate mechanisms of social life, and the more it is thwarted, the deeper and more surprising are its implications."

-- Fatima Merniss, *Beyond the Veil*

With timing not to be believed, the phone rings. It is Mom. Dad's moved out.

Wedded Wasteland

The destruction of our unit
is his to account for.
Anger festers and lingers…
All the days to follow shall never be enough to heal the breach.
She made a black circle her closing date…
in time it came to pass.
"My warranty has expired," she said,
As though one not in a precarious place.

His mind sprays
Too long compartmentalized.
In the end,
The weight of his untelling
Lost him more than he could ever redeem

Wicked, this storm
The tragic hero has squandered his gifts;
Years of effort laid open
To the wind,
ripping and tossing everyone in proximity
To the far corners
"She'd rather be a widow," he says
As one in a most precarious place.

CHAPTER 54

Asylums & Sanctuaries

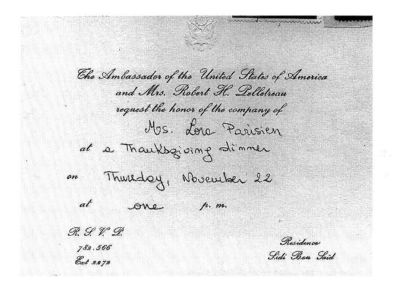

The Ambassador of the United States of America
and Mrs. Robert H. Pelletreau
request the honor of the company of

Mrs. Lora Parisien

at a Thanksgiving dinner

on Thursday, November 22

at one p. m.

R. S. V. P.
782.566
Ext 2272

Residence
Sidi Bou Said

I've received an invitation to dine at the home of American Ambassador Pelletreau for Thanksgiving, an act of pure charity to be sure. The Ambassador lives high on a bluff overlooking the port with a view to Cap Bon in the hilly village of Sidi Bou Saïd. Lucky man.

Sidi Bou Saïd has always been a popular place. Its geography made it the entry point for invading Roman armies and colonists in 146 BC and a thousand years later, the ingress for Louis IV of France and his entire army. Today it is home to Tunisia's local and international elite and overrun with tourists. It isn't history or the bevy of "authentic" Tunisian trinket and artisan shops that draws them by the busloads to swarm the well-worn cobblestone streets. It is beauty of the most breathtaking variety that lures them, and me. And Thanksgiving dinner.

Sidi Bou Saïd is the perfect mixture of architecture and environment: seascape and sky, simple lines and delicate details. Like Hergla, it is awash in stark white, the perfect canvas for random splashes of a singular accent color mimicking the sea. Unlike Hergla, the residences are grand edifices, inspiring awe and yes, jealousy. Intricate iron scrollwork painted an eye-popping turquoise adorns windows. Windows also boast ornate flower boxes, painted the same. They overflow with plantings and fresh blooms. Grand Andalusian style keyhole doors, some turquoise, some bright yellow, mark entrances. Bougainvillea in fiery crimson cascades over walls.

Most popular is the Café de Nattes, the legendary Moorish coffee house with its red and green palette, rush mats and commanding views. It may well be dominion of men and tourists willing to climb the steep steps, but it was mine too, for a time. When I lived in Tunis, it was an easy retreat to zip here for a day to have my fill of views. Sidi Bou Saïd is, bar none, the most charming village in all of Tunisia. It is obvious why the wealthiest of the wealthy live here. When I am too old, too feeble, please set me to rest overlooking the Bay of Tunis in Sidi Bou. Though I am not really on track to purchase my retirement home here, now am I?

In the Ambassador's elegant residence, I am seated for the feast between Colonel Marc Powe, Defense Attaché to Tunisia, and a woman whose name I can't recall, a member of the U.S. Embassy's Political Council. The colonel indulges my probing questions about the predicament looming east of us and admits that Iraq's failure to respond to the diplomacy of the day is troublesome, even for us. Now I have even more fodder for my preoccupation. We spend an hour talking on the subject of whether we will we go to war with Iraq.

I have speculated myself into a tizzy. On the one hand, I am feeding on the news, consuming each and every nuance, gorging. On the other, once the radio is off, newspapers and *U.S. News and World Report* (subscription courtesy the U.S. government) are put away, I am rendered unconscious to the world outside my door. Day to day I am unaffected by disputes beyond these borders, preoccupied instead with the stuff that informs my life in this moment. The prospect of war doesn't have me conflicted: I am against it. My home nation is meddling in the Islamic world; no good can come of it. I straddle the world of my now, with a darker one that might be.

CHAPTER 55

December 1990

Something wicked this way comes

It is December and the United Nations passed a resolution author-izing the use of force against Iraq if they do not voluntarily pull out of Kuwait by January 15. Saddam Hussein has agreed to meet Bush for a high-level dialogue. While the U.S. demands an uncon-ditional withdrawal; Saddam raises Arab grievances, particularly the Palestinian issue. Here in Tunisia, the Palestinian problem is front and center and the number one concern for many—not Iraq, not Kuwait, not the U.S., but the plight of the Palestinians and their desperate need for a homeland. For the record, Tunisia opposes American support for Kuwait, regardless of the fact that the U.S. provides economic and military aid to Tunisia.

As a precaution, Peace Corps has provided the volunteers with an evacuation strategy should it become necessary. In that plan I have been designated as an Area Warden, which means I am responsible for the fourteen volunteers in my region, the closest volunteer being forty-five minutes away. There are three levels of alert. Level One, the Stand-fast Phase, is just that. We stay put at our sites, in our homes until further notice. In their words: "no movement authorized." Level Two, the Consolidation Phase, requires that volunteers congregate at a designated area. All of the volunteers in the northwest would converge here. I have been provided with a list of staples—though no funds with which to acquire them—that I am required to collect and have on-hand should visitors suddenly show up for an extended stay. Level Three, the Evacuation Phase, requires an immediate departure from our sites to Tunis. There isn't great detail beyond that. There is only inference and obsession.

Living under the threat of evacuation makes each day here especially precious. Not so for everyone. Today we lost another volunteer to early termination. This brings to twenty-three the number who have bailed, 50 percent of my group. Usually I hear about the departures after the fact. I rarely learn of the reasons volunteers give for leaving. I think of the trials I've had and know with certainty my friends are facing challenges, too. I cannot judge those who have made the choice to go.

• • •

It is very late when Dad calls. Our conversation is emotional and heart-ripping. Things do not go well between him and Mom.

Afterward, I lay in the dark with it, buffered only slightly by the great distance between us. Then, I hear a key turning in the lock on my door and footsteps approaching my bed. I spring up and recognize Khalil, my landlord, in the darkness.

"Who was that on the phone?" he asks. The line that serves my house originates in his. Because he doesn't understand a word of English, I have dismissed the obvious eavesdropping on the rare occasion I use the phone. "I heard you crying." Suddenly I am aware of his closing proximity and my very limited attire. "*Mski:na.*" He says. Pitiful. He puts his hand on my face. With his fingertips, he follows my jaw line down my neck to my chest where he lays his hand flat. Alarm. I step back, throw up my arms instinctively swiping his away from me, but his finger gets caught on the spaghetti strap of my camisole (the one fou fou item of clothing in the whole of my dumpy wardrobe) and it lifts practically off.

"*Imshi!*" GO! I command in a tone that surprises even me, authoritative and forceful, the likes of which I should have been using in my classroom all along. It gets his attention. I cannot believe what comes next. He looks like a wounded puppy, as if he has some real expectation that I would welcome his solicitation. He is clearly disappointed. He turns and leaves me. I don't know what to make of this violation. It splinters my sense of security and puts my future in this residence into question. Not that I expect Khalil to take a second swing at bat, but, his uninvited entry into my space makes an already awkward situation—the absence of Karima— especially problematic.

In the morning, I go to the Smadhis and tell them what transpired over night. They are furious. They won't let me return to my house and insist I move in forthwith. I do spend most of my free time in their company, sharing meals and household chores, watching bad Egyptian dramas on TV, marketing and squeezing my body in between two sisters on a shared mattress on the floor many nights. Going from the quietude of my dwelling into the frenzy that is this house will be an enormous adjustment. My home has served as a necessary refuge when I just can't bring myself to utter one more syllable of Arabic or gracefully deflect another bathroom intrusion as I hover over the seatless toilet (closed doors are meaningless) or entertain the presence of constant company.

As mentioned previously, the concept of privacy extends to the family unit, not to the individual within it. Homes are sanctuaries, fortressed to the outside world behind high-walled enclosures. Once inside all notions of retreat vanish. In fact, it is considered strange to isolate oneself from the family. I am rather attached to my alone time, especially in this environment. I have a place where I can retreat when I need the solitude to refuel. Plus, I can whistle to my heart's content there. Grandma Smadhi says whistling is *hram*, forbidden, because it invites the Devil. I never realized how often I actually whistle until Grandma Smadhi brought the dangerous habit to my attention. It looks as though the only choice before me may be to leave Jbel Axdhir, move next to the kasbah with the Smadhis. I have to accept that not all refuge is found in solitude.

• • •

It is Friday night and we are all gathered in main salle of the Smadhi home watching an Egyptian film with French subtitles. There is so much conversation going on around me, I can hardly concentrate on any one person. The TV adds to the incessant chatter. There is a terrific debate underway over whose turn it is to receive a new pair of shoes. The fervor with which each girl debates her position would lead one to believe there is something far greater at stake here than a pair of shoes. There is outburst and fury, tears and flailing. Everyone except Grandma weighs in. Tunisia's homes and streets are filled with the boon and boom of conversations like this, expelled at the top of lungs, delivered on the most passionate of breath. Tonight it's about shoes. Tomorrow the eruption will revolve around something else too trivial to merit dispute, let alone ruckus. These emotional displays exhaust me. Though I have to wonder: what has the silence in my family—a lifetime of silence—cost us?

Days pass and I am still here, reluctant to return to Jbel Axdhir ever since the intrusion. Omee makes coffee from powdered roast beans that have been boiled in a traditional Arabic pot. She fills my small cup. I wait for the dregs to settle to the bottom before I take my first sip, not too fond of sludge. She steps behind me as she does every day, places her hand on my head and says her prayer over me. Then, she looks into my eyes as if to say "okay, you're covered for a little while." Mattresses are already out in the early sun. Carpets are cast over the walls. Blankets are folded and stuffed into the armoire. Floors throughout are doused with water and squeegeed. In a house bustling with activity, only Grandma sits stationery, wrapped up in blankets until it is time for prayer. She rises slowly, sets out her prayer rug and takes her place on it. She is a very old eighty-three, so getting down on her knees is a painfully slow process. But she does it five times a day, alone. When she is finished, she returns to the couch, pulls out a dip, utters God's name every so often and shouts orders in between wheezes and moans. A wisp of orange hair peeks out from her crocheted scarf.

In the afternoon, Rejeh and I walk to my house to collect a few necessities. I am relieved to not find Khalil in residence. I quickly grab a few changes of clothes and open three cans of food for Moses, leaving them just outside my door. We depart stealthily without being seen, walking beside the tall walls, walls that secret the well-kept homes of the neighborhood and now, two less women. Today is perfect, cloudless, the sun high but not blistering, casting long shadows from the flourishing trees overhead. I have never minded the walk from my house to the Smadhis. It is like traversing a 'W' from its starting point in the quiet dusty roads of my hilltop neigh-borhood, down into the heart of Beja buzzing with life, up along zigzagging pathways, down through a rocky field strewn with trash and goats grazing on green thickets, then up past homes plucked into the hillside to the very last one, the Smadhi's.

A note about architecture and cultural values. Homes every-where are in a state of ongoing construction and the Smadhi's is no exception. A home develops along the specific trajectory of the family who dwells within it, with floors added as family members are added. When sons marry, their brides move into a space built for them. The clan expands; the dwelling expands to accommodate. Though, because the economics of expansion are so difficult to meet in any expedient way, it is done as it can be afforded, brick by brick, fixture by fixture. While Bechir, the one and only son, is in Italy, the Smadhis prepare a place for him and his future wife and their off-spring. Marry the man, marry the family. I shudder to imagine the families I might have been conjoined to. Because I was not raised here, this aspect of culture is troublesome for me. I cannot fathom moving in—permanently—with in-laws. The idea of separateness is too strongly entrenched, and with it, independence. These are the crux of my American identity: the right to liberty, autonomy and choice. I am an individual unit. Again, the contrast throughout the Arab world where the smallest measure of a person is her family, and every single act reflects upon the whole, is one I struggle to reconcile.

But, with the group comes interdependence and the banishing of loneliness, and the spreading of responsibility and security. It is the reason entities like retirement homes are non-existent and matriarchs like Grandma Smadhi live out their days among their progeny. It is the reason there is very little mine or yours, only ours. If not for this shared existence, this single American woman who clearly needs looking after would not have been so easily embraced.

Rejeh and I pass the *kusha*, one of the many bakeries that serve up piping hot loaves of bread—yours for a dime—from enormous ovens all hours of the day. We stop to gather our stockpile for the family dinner. Coming up the road, we pass an old man seated sidesaddle atop a donkey. He coaxes the beast, snorting under the burden of a portly driver and a wooden cart piled high with garlic bulbs. School girls in navy blue smocks walk in clumps. In the rocky hillside sheep seek green patches. A feisty conversation floats on the air, the hard consonants and exaggerated inflection of Arabic have become familiar. Beja thrives and I in it. It is big enough to reveal something new to me at each turn, yet quaintly manageable. Even though my living situation is in flux, my decision to move here was a solid one. I love Beja.

Bchira meets us at the door when we return. She asks me to join her in taking Rejeh to the doctor. Rejeh discovered a series of strange lumps on her body, one of which happens to be on her left breast, if a twelve-year-old has a breast. In his stark office, the doctor makes his examination and calmly announces:

"*Kibrid.*"

"*Kibrid?*" Even Bchira, a trained nurse, is a bit stunned by the diagnosis. Apparently, the arrival of bumps all over Rejeh's body, with a particular nod to the one little bud in a particular location, is a clear sign that Rejeh is on her way to womanhood. We leave his office and chuckle all the way back home. Once there, I direct everyone's attention to the table where I have filled a bowl with hot water. I produce four capsules.

"Medicine?" Omee inquires.

"Yes, for Rejeh, for her illness. Here Rejeh, drop them into the water." The whole family gathers in close around the bowl. Plop. Plop. Plop. Plop. The capsules dissolve. The tiny sponges compressed inside begin to morph into a lion, an elephant, a camel. We wait for the last one, which is taking a long time to expand, drawing out our anticipation.

"*Hallu:f* for Rejeh!" I announce. A pig. The room erupts in laughter. Pig, being of course, absolutely HRAM—forbidden by Islam. This is why I love this family. This reaction. And everyone thinks Muslims can't take a joke.

For an undisclosed number of days, I have sought refuge in this household, where there is rarely peace, where so many bodies share so little space. I miss the solitude of my abode, which feels evermore like a sanctuary given the frequent and disruptive family squalls; disputes that always have more drama than substance. Today there is a doozy underway. It has to do with an obligation to attend a gathering. Raodtha is demanding Bchira attend, though she is not feeling nearly well enough to go. The fight has escalated. The room has filled with fever pitch barking and I am trapped like a puppy in the corner, having to bear witness while the "alpha dogs" battle it out, once again. When suddenly they turn to me:

"*Nimshi:o?*" Are we going? And just like that, the clash is resolved. We are going to a reading of the Qur'an at an unknown time, in an unnamed location, with any number of people I have never met. The outcome is fine with me; it's the prelude that I find exasperating. I don't know what annoys me more, that I cannot understand the nuances of these disputes or that I cannot abide the frequency or force of them. In point of fact, I cannot remember the last time I had a spat...with anyone. I learned conflict avoidance from two masters: I am the product of parents who have never argued, who were the products of parents who never argued, ad infinitum, which means my predilection for pacifism, my aversion to conflict is generations in the making.

This house has its share of supercharged confrontations and fiery altercations—and they're all very dramatic. I have to constantly remind myself that raised voices, tears and fervor are the persuasive tools of argument; they demonstrate true passion. Emotion is honored not avoided. More and more, I am seeing that just because something appears chaotic or unreasonable or even irrational, it doesn't mean there isn't logic underlying. What does my discomfort or my flight response say about me? Judgment always seems to have a way of creeping in, coloring my view one way or the other. I keep trying to be mindful, to see things as they are, to remove the judgment. My hope is that I end up at a place that looks something like this: not good, not bad, just different. No matter what transpires in the day, all the drama is done by the time we meet at the table. All is healed before first bread is broken, before we feast from one bowl and drink from one pitcher. And that is the way of things here in this home.

CHAPTER 56

The bully in the sandbox

Sitting in my doorway, Beja

In the Gulf, 480,000 Allied troops wait.

Students in Beja began striking earlier this week because there are only eleven days in the coming holiday instead of the usual fourteen. They became violent, breaking windows and destroying school property. The National Guard was called in and the disturbance was quelled. I wish I could post a few Guardsmen in my classroom, armed, fatigue-wearing, lesson-enforcing sentries.

Without a doubt, as has been mentioned, my greatest weakness as a teacher is controlling my classroom. I have on more than one occasion walked out...on my classroom of boys. My two other modules are populated by industrious, agreeable students. Our time together is productive and valuable. In fact, I would even say I am satisfied with the work being accomplished therein. What a debacle is that classroom of boys, however. They are obnoxious and I am outnumbered. I should have stepped up and negotiated a better deal at the start. Instead, I let Sofien off-load this group of rascals into my custody without a single word in contest. Talk about a set-up for failure. I am not a big enough threat to force conformity, not a big enough "bitch" (still) to wrest control. Night after night, my classroom is two hours of mêlée, with me teaching to the air. Hello? Anyone? I can't figure out why they bother to show up at all. Not for the education. Not for English. Not for the girls—there aren't any. Must be the entertainment.

One thing's for sure, when it comes to these guys, I am quite depleted of patience and nearly bankrupt of investment. I have sought counsel from the best at my disposal—spent three long nights consulting, note-taking, ranting—with a master teacher from the China Five. I've become more practiced at creating effective lesson plans, just not adept at breaking through the brouhaha. There was one breach though. I have a cassette that I bought for one dinar from a Tunis street vendor. It features the sweet voice of Cat Stevens singing his hit *Father and Son*. He was born Steven Demetre Georgiou, but is better known to my students as Yusuf Islam, the successful musician who abandoned his career, auctioned his guitars for charity, converted to Islam and dedicated his life to causes in support of the Muslim community. For a few perfect moments, there was rapt attention and the sparking, ever so briefly, of unity and learning. If I had at my disposal an enormous library of music (preferably comprised entirely of pop stars who have converted to

Islam) I could deejay my way through the semester. I haven't been able to re-create that shining moment and in so doing have lost my students to the static.

Tonight is the beginning of the end, the culmination of failure—theirs and mine. It begins when one student, Chedly, to the delight of his audience, starts darting around the classroom, swapping seats whenever I turn to write on the board. With each swap, the roars of his contemporaries escalate. I ask him to stop. He doesn't. So I ask him to leave. He refuses. I walk over to his seat. He stands up. Again, I ask him to leave. He doesn't budge. Instead, he folds his arms across his chest, thrusts his hip out like a woman would do and gives me an "I dare you" look. More sassy than threatening. More punk than menace. His heavy black lashes rim provocative eyes; even the mole on the bridge of his nose is insolent. An experienced educator would know what to do in this moment, would have any number of tricks up her sleeve, would be unruffled, imposing, powerful even—would know what to do.

I opt to leave. I make a hasty beeline for the exit, cross the hall to where Sofien is contentedly conducting lessons for his compliant darlings. I rap on his door.

"I am ready to hand them over to you." I unload about Chedly, discharge four months of frustration in two minutes and paint him a target in the doing. "Can you do something?" Big mistake. Sofien storms into my classroom and ambushes Chedly. He yanks him like a rag doll from the desk and pummels his face with a closed fist, punctuating each blow with admonishments. Chedly crumbles under the assault while I stand frozen. Sofien then drags a whimpering, broken Chedly from the room.

I can't move. Not one inch. I can't speak. Not one syllable. I can't meet their gaze, not one eyeball, but I can feel every last one fixed on me. I skulk to my desk, too numbed by the violence to be outraged. Though I didn't administer the punishment, it is my fault. I set the perfect stage, let matters spiral to this predictable explosive end. I invited it. Then, I watched it without lifting a finger to stop it.

I gather my things and walk out without looking back. Shock. Weakness. Shame. Of the moments that articulate my life, this one will remain among the most raw and painful.

Needing a space of quiet to ruminate over the horrible scene in my classroom, I sneak back home for a few days. I will sit with it in the dark. I'm still stunned. Ashamed of my action; my inaction. I was complicit. Was I expecting Sofien to correct my mismanagement with a few magic words? I am pissed. I am obsessed with confronting Sofien—with calling him out on his despicable deed. Before I can face him however, I have to resolve my complicity. I don't know that I can. The self-righteous part of me has a speech, prepared and rehearsed, delivered with such authority as to command penitence. But the soul of me shrinks with culpability.

I pass a group of Chedly's classmates in town. They greet me as if it is any other day, without hint of malice or disappointment. My first thought is "thank God…thank God Chedly isn't with them." Then it hits me, why aren't they mad? Or sheepish? Or judgmental? Why aren't they anything other than absent memory of it? If there is something cultural going on here, I clearly misunderstand. The beating was brutal. Of all the scenarios I create in my head, the hardest to conjure is my apology to Chedly. I should have stopped it.

• • •

The avoiding of Khalil goes on, as I attach myself to the Smadhis and melt into their daily routine. This morning we make the winding journey down into the markets, Omee with all of us sisters in tow and me struggling to conceal the great effort it takes to walk in a pair of stupid shoes. Raodtha insisted I wear the much-coveted, fancy silver-sequined *shlekas*. As common property, these favorite sandals grace the feet of all the females in this house. By extension, what is theirs has become mine and vice versa. Several items of my clothing have been adopted by my sisters and are oftentimes worn for days on end, sometimes finding their way into the bottomless heap in the family's armoire. By decreeing me today's "chosen," Raodtha circumvented the inevitable scuffle over the stupid shoes. There's no negotiating with Raodtha, who by the way, is giddy-pleased that I am wearing them.

In the streets people amble in all directions simultaneously. Some carry *ghouffas*, hand-woven baskets overflowing with peppers, tomatoes, fennel, pumpkin or maybe a chicken with feet bound. Noisy mopeds zip about. We walk to the *freep*, which features its own brand of madness, like a mall on Black Friday with everyone on the prowl for bargains. The *freep* market serves up mounds and mounds of donated second-hand clothing on sale for pocket change. This is the mainstay of the communal wardrobe and of many a Peace Corps Volunteer. It is also a source of treasures and surprises. I once found a University of Michigan sweatshirt buried in a heap as big as a car. It cost me about a quarter.

We begin sifting, burrowing and over-ending the piles in search of something useful or unexpected. Bchira and I are on a mission to find a few skirts. She has a discriminating eye, checking stitching, examining lining. She knows what she wants. Meanwhile, I am digging away in my own pile when suddenly Khalil appears from behind a bundle.

"*Aaaa...wi:nik?*" Where have you been? In a millisecond, my entourage encloses me, presses me to the back, creating distance between him and me, thus absolving me of the responsibility for having to answer his inquiry. Omee, front and center, begs him off, pivots around on her heel and corrals us in the opposite direction. Through the long edge of her *saf sari* gathered between her clenched teeth, I hear "What is he thinking? I won't allow it! " Plus a few things lost in translation. Mama has spoken. Our freep-going comes to an abrupt end. Into the protection of my family, I take temporary refuge long enough to determine how and when I will orchestrate my exit from Khalil.

CHAPTER 57

In flux

Dougga

January 15 approaches. The world waits. Will there be war or peace in the Gulf? Today American troops are being inoculated against anthrax. President Bush insists it will not be another Vietnam. He believes he will gain the support of the American people for this unpopular war if the U.S.'s victory is decisive with few American casualties. I am outraged…at the prospect of war…at the overt waging of it…because I feel helpless.

• • •

The two-week teaching break coinciding with Christmas affords me the opportunity to steal away to Tunis; to Robin's for camaraderie and for the lavish dining, spoiling and debriefing that accompanies our visits. It is Robin who swept me to Tunis following Molly's death, providing me a place to mourn the very first friend I have ever lost. Out of that tragedy has come our friendship and days like this of flash and flurry, of off-loading our adventures of living in and among Tunisians and working for our respective offices of the federal government. Truth be told, I cannot help but be drawn by Robin's expert whipping-up of delectable gourmet offerings. You'd think I was a starving dog given the greedy manner and unabashed way I beg at my master's table. Indeed, Robin is someone to whom you give a wide berth. In her well-equipped kitchen, she is both virtuoso and witch inspiring masterpieces and crafting with fire and brimstone. She dices tomatoes and drains capers simultaneously, while she rages about the uglier aspects of her job. Call it culinary therapy: the frantic whisking, the well-directed but violent chops at the butcher block, beating the poor garlic to a pulp—I stay at a safe-distance letting the master "dish."

As a Foreign Service lifer, Robin has lived and worked abroad for decades in Burma, Italy, Kenya, Paris and now Tunis. I covet Robin's world: wanderlust as a way of life with the means to sustain it. Though I see it is solitary, acrimonious even. An absence of sustained belonging might cause one to grope a little further down the food chain for fulfillment. Enter me. Robin and I bonded over the loss of Molly, over two boxes of tissues and a few packs of smokes. She was a haven to me even before we met.

The smell of sautéing garlic and dissolving anchovies reaches my nose. As she vents, I can see that a great deal of passion is going into my food and perhaps a few too many red pepper flakes. Her unapologetic spewing and the appearance of tears belie the tough figure she otherwise cuts. No doubt...she has had to be hardy for a very long time. Don't we all need just one person who will compassionately absorb our occasional rants? Who won't try to fix a single thing? A loving witness? In this moment, I seem to be that person for Robin. I occupy my stool, lifting not one finger in the preparation of this feast, but sustaining its creator in any case. She is both easy and rash motion, tossing parsley and olives while fixating on a New York posting. She presumes that politics and nastiness will vanish with a change in venue. She plates the pasta, dresses it in fragrant Puttanesca and retires for now her fury.

• • •

I am having confession with a Benedictine monk. As far as sacraments go, this is about as informal as they come. There is no confessional room, no screen secreting our identities, no vestments or ceremony. There is a man in the guestroom. He wears blue jeans and a t-shirt...and he has a face I already know. The man is my Program and Training Officer's identical twin, visiting from his order in Europe. Can I unburden my soul to a guy who looks exactly like the guy who gives me Pop-Tarts? Tell my deepest darkest to a guy who looks exactly like one who happens to be my boss?

In the room, he turns away from me. He unwraps a burgundy cloth that contains the sacred scapula, kisses the scapula gingerly and then places it around his shoulders. When he faces me, he is a holy confident, more spirit than man, open to my soul's admissions.

"Forgive me Father, for I have sinned. My last confession was... two years ago? Three?" I let him have it, every misstep I can recall over a period of time that I can't recall. My sins.

"Dominus noster Jesus Christus te absolvat; et ego auctoritate ipsius te absolvo ab omni vinculo excommunicationis et interdicti in quantum possum et tu indiges. Deinde, ego te absolvo a peccatis tuis in nomine Patris, et Filii, + et Spiritus Sancti. Amen."

(May our Lord Jesus Christ absolve you; and by His authority I absolve you from every bond of excommunication and interdict, so far as my power allows and your needs require. [*making the Sign of the Cross:*]

Thereupon, I absolve you from your sins in the name of the Father, and of the Son, and of the Holy Ghost. Amen.)

Whether or not one can be truly absolved of sins by the confessing of them to someone of this world, someone acting *in persona Christi,* I don't know. In Islam, the repentant Muslim asks forgiveness directly from God—there is no middle man. Here I am again, at the intersection of faith, questioning whether it is better to go to the source or to his intercedent. My whole life I've been confessing to men behind screens. Today will be my last. This yoke of guilt is no longer my requirement to bear, nor shall it be anyone else's to absolve. Though, there is something truly powerful about face-to-face reconciliation, when the intercedent is truly benevolent and inspired as I believe mine is today. Absolution is absolutely divine, but it will, until furthermore, come from the divine.

On Christmas morning I attend service at Jean d'Arc, my first Catholic mass—in English—since my arrival. How easily I slide into the cadence and rhythm of the mass, with not a misplaced amen, signing of the cross or droning of prayer. Dare I say it is comforting? Somehow I end up at the lectern to deliver a reading for the sparse congregants—Miss Johnny-come-lately, the one who once co-conspired with her brother to skip church in lieu of burning off hangovers at McDonalds. This is what happens when one finds herself in a culture that daily calls into question her programming or the doctrine of her faith. My "faith" ebbs and flows. Ever am I either fleeing from or racing into the grasping arms of religion.

· · ·

We have taken over four floors of the Peace Corps office for a two-night slumber party. At least thirty volunteers have arrived from points all over the country. We pull foam mattresses from storage and sling them everywhere, along with our backpacks, deposited wherever. The eclectic mixture of holiday munchies reflects foods adapted, like a potato gratin and brownies baked in the shape of the Palestinian oven (if it's baked, it's round) and local favorites like *baklawa* and *makrudth*. Balancing out the sweet, there is a selection of fresh and grilled salads. One thing's for certain, this country is flush with good eats. I have always had access to good food, be it via the hospitality of my hosts who cannot sanction a single woman living or dining alone, or, through the blessing of economy. Healthy, fresh, local fare is available and affordable. In addition, government subsidies ensure that bread, the mainstay of every meal, is affordable.

Five years ago, the former President Habib Bourguiba made the mistake of raising the price of bread from 8¢ to 18¢. Riots erupted. Mobs rampaged through the capital. A state of emergency was declared and the army was swiftly dispatched to quell them. The President went on television to announce that he would immediately return price of bread to 8¢. And peace immediately returned to the land, but not before fifty people died in the Bread Riots.

The only thing more bountiful than our holiday buffet at this Christmas gathering is our chatter. Clusters of conversation pop up everywhere and go long into the night, as most of the volunteers are eager, after weeks of speaking Arabic only, to discharge in our native tongue. This is where we share our lore, our individual adventures, our colossal failures or cultural clashes. My favorite is when we share the myriad ways we embarrass ourselves here. Someone admits that her underwear, stretched from repeated hand-washings, dropped around her ankles in the middle of the *souk* one day. So that's the reason Peace Corps suggested we arrive in-country with extra elastic! Another volunteer drove her moped all the way through her town never realizing that the back of her skirt had somehow flown up and gotten tucked under her helmet. She was mortified to discover that she had flashed everyone on the street. When you consider that her bright yellow gargantuan helmet (standard issue and required) is already an attention magnet for the lone American in residence there, it is guaranteed they saw her coming...and going. Her story has become the stuff of legend.

At midnight, five of us steal up to the rooftop terrace to smoke a doobie. We can see the walls of the American Embassy from our vantage point. Directly across the street a minaret peeks up from a mosque. The conversation briefly explores the ramifications of getting busted with grass in Tunisia. Someone gives an account of a young U.S. citizen who came to Tunis by way of Amsterdam and was busted at the airport with his souvenirs. He was tossed into the jail in Jendouba, not exactly Midnight Express, but close. Lost to the world for a time without benefit of Arabic or a single contact; it was two years before anyone Stateside got word of where he was. He is still incarcerated. True story (confirmed later by Embassy folks in the know). We linger for a time on the terrace contemplating our defiance, triumphing in our rebellion, until we hear someone a-nosin' at the door and our sneaking around comes to an abrupt end. *Suma:r ellayali*, which means "night community," is the name we give this memory. I shall speak no more on this.

A rather orderly system allows the thirty gathered to share one phone line. Calls from family are received in turn; mine comes at 4 a.m. Christmas morning. I am dozing when someone leads me to the black receiver lying on the desk.

"*Joyeaux Noel*." My father's voice. I perk up instantly. At home, the phone is passed to everyone in my family, including our newest, still bald at one-and-a-half, Sean. Though I have found a home in Tunisia, if there is one day a year to be spent with my own tribe— even with all of its challenge and heartbreak—for me it is this day. We do not speak of the chaos at home. Nor does anyone mention the prospect of war in the Middle East, or any matters of great substance. It is enough to connect, for a moment in time, on the one day a year it would be unforgivable not to.

From Tunis, I leave with friends to the sparsely inhabited north and the secluded village of Raf Raf on the splendid Mediterranean coast. Bucolic. Absent of outsiders. We have the boon of experiencing a location that without entrée would have been inaccessible to us. Our resident host is Paul, a former rebellious volunteer who was "separated" from Peace Corps some years ago. Rather than allow his butt to be booted out of Tunisia, Paul severed his ties with the agency and stayed in-country. And, to the chagrin of those formerly in charge, proved himself to be a most capable and enterprising young man.

I am, admittedly, rather in awe of Paul, as an example of what is possible if one demonstrates a little gumption. I have an old Peace Corps advertisement glued into my journal, it says "We need someone with the boldness of a pioneer, the resourcefulness of an inventor, and the faith of a sword swallower." This *is* Paul. For my money—what precious little of it I have—he is the best "volunteer" around. In Raf Raf he has organized *Dar Shebeb*, an activity center for the youth of his community, a haven of art, learning and creativity, populated with fun and energy and Paul, ever-present. Around the village he inspired the youth to pretty-up the place. So small beautification projects are underway, like the weaving of thatch covers to mask the dumpsters and shelter the bus stop. He is active in Amnesty International—gutsy, as expatriates live under the watchful eye of a paranoid regime. Dissension from the rank and file is one thing, but the presence of watchdogs from outside bodes well for no one. Beyond his intrepid support of human rights, Paul is also a producer of progressive Tunisian *malouf*, the traditional music that dwells in the heart of every Tunisian (and battled its way into mine). *Malouf* is typically played at special events, like weddings and circumcision ceremonies, though very rarely recorded.

By way of prolonged exposure, *malouf* is no longer a collision to my Western ears; it has morphed from dissonance into harmony. The recordings of Umm Kulthoum, the Egyptian diva of Arabic song, the legendary Lebanese singer Fairuz and the hugely popular Cheb Khaled of Algeria, are finally accessible to me are. *Darbouka* rhythms pound while sliding musical scales seep into my skin and slink into my heart. I happily croon in the space of this traditional Arabic home, on this beautiful simple beach. Everything comes to a sweet halt.

> My feet meet with sand
> my eyes with sea
> I relinquish all
> but the effort to be.

We sleep out on the beach. During the night, I leave my sleeping bag to walk alone under an inky starlit sky, to let my toes bathe in the gentle surf and to sing at the top of my lungs…because I can. An expression of pure freedom. Unbarred and celebrated joy. We rise early enough to witness the sun begin to peek over Raf Raf's own Rock of Gibraltar, a huge stone monolith that juts dramatically out of the sea some two kilometers from shore.

I decide to sneak into Tunis unannounced with a plan to kidnap Patty. Four louages, four taxis, a fair amount of hoofing in betwixt, accomplished without complaint, as I will never tire of the freedom of mobility I enjoy here. Now, persuading Patty to come may require effort.

She left our beloved medina house when I did and moved to Hay Chalker, a nondescript, one thoroughfare town on the outskirts of the capital. She is making the best of it, but, yikes, boring. This will not be a tough sell. I lift her brass hand of Fatima door knocker: tink-tink-tink. The door opens. Happy shriek, giggles, then Patty says in a flat voice "Your damn bunny is dead." About the bunny, it wasn't the most brilliant idea I have ever had, but some months ago, I chose to honor the occasion of Patty's thirtieth birthday with a pet. I'd found him at Marche Central, in the southwest corner, the area reserved for the slaughter of animals. I had saved him from certain death. I brought him home, placed him in a box, wrapped the box slightly and presented the package to her. As she was opening her gift, the box moved of its own accord on her lap. Patty hurled the box across the room. I take responsibility for concealing a live animal in a box (he was only in there for two minutes before the hurling). He survived and lived (well, until he didn't) free-range in Patty's house in Hay Chalker. The town is, after all, a dreadfully lonely place and Patty needed company. It wasn't always pretty, but they tolerated each other.

Fast forward some weeks after the purchasing of the pet...I was visiting Patty. We were camped out on her floor blathering on endlessly when I noticed, hanging on the back of her door, a silk dress in a familiar shade of blue, though it was shredded almost beyond recognition.

"Is that...is that my dress?" Patty was safeguarding the one and only piece of formal attire I owned, worn only twice. It was in tatters, shortened by several inches, the handiwork of that god-dammed bunny. Karma. Payback. Tit for Tatters. I had it coming. I had nothing, however, to do with the bunny ending up on the neighbor's barbeque.

"Someday, we might just laugh about this...want to come to Raf Raf with me?" It doesn't take a great deal of convincing to get Patty to throw together a bag and skip out five minutes later for our destination. When in our lives will we ever be this free again?

After securing Patty, it is time to acquire provisions. With the New Year approaching, Marche Central is buzzing with women wrapped in white *saf saris* always clenched between teeth, managing *ghouffa*, cash and cumbersome wardrobe, bartering, shuffling along in their *shlekas*, gathering their ingredients for the holiday meals. The smell of fresh greens mingles with the tang of animal and the fusty odor of countless days of squished this and squashed that embedded in the concrete flooring. We load up on ripe succulent tomatoes, fiery peppers, cheese and bread. I shell out seventeen dinars for a kilo of shrimp, up eleven dinars from four weeks ago. Just a few streets over, we visit the olive vendor whose shop is filled with barrels and barrels of multihued olives soaking in fragrant brine. You can sample any or all of them, which I most certainly do. We collect a variety and make one last stop, for toilet paper. Never leave home without it.

Heavy-laden with our booty, we encounter near frenzy conditions at Bab Saddoun, the north *louage* station: too many bodies, too few cars. I enlist the help of a man who "works" there. He's ancient but spry. Over time, he has become the friendly face I anticipate seeing when entering or departing this hub. We share tea on slow days; he hustles seats for me on maddeningly crowded days. This is one of them. He ends up in a nasty confrontation while trying to secure us two seats in the only louage heading to Raf Raf. While I am feeling a little desperate for those seats, they aren't worth conflict.

Raf Raf with Patty and Lisa and Paul is sublime. We spend time in Paul's *Dar Shebab*, playing games with the kids. I don't know why I find it easier to relate to small beings here, as opposed to home where contact with children fills me with dread. Maybe it's the deep chocolate eyes, big as dinner plates, or delicate gold hoops adorning the tiny earlobes of the little girls, or the way they are all curious, but so sweetly timid.

Raf Raf is divine.

We visit.

We dine.

We while away 1989.

Following Raf Raf, my New Year's tour includes a stop in Kairouan to visit Lisa and to at last gain possession of the brilliant red *kilim* I have had in hock for months. With January 15 as motivation, the time for scooping up souvenirs has come. In the early days living in the *souq*, I was easily lured by the carpet vendors along my route, enticed by the rich colors of the *kitfeyas*, the beautifully woven shawls, the *kilims*, hand-knotted rugs with distinctive geometric motifs, fish as well as crescent moons, stars, representing good luck and fertility. Even the least savvy among tourists knows any demonstration of interest will elicit an invitation to buy. In the carpet market, your spark of interest will soon have you escorted into the inner sanctum to sip sickly-sweet minted tea from a shot glass, as rolls of beautifully hand woven carpets unfurl before your eyes, each one more exquisite than the last, piled one atop the other with no end in sight. I *would* buy dozens if my wallet were fat. Beautiful works of art in textile, made by the hands of women, sold by men. Acquiring my souvenir requires that I reconcile myself to that fact and to the fact that I have weeny disposable income. *"Maandeesh shay...hot—ta—shay, w'Allah,"* is my standard admission, annunciated very clearly with great emphasis: "I have nothing—swear to God." Absolutely true. Arab merchants are gracious, true salesmen and persistent with a capital "P." Negotiating, not my forte, is an art to which I have had to become accustomed.

One benefit of my poverty, beyond releasing the stranglehold on my want for things, has been the opportunity to observe the practice of wheeling and dealing. Which brings me to my beautiful red *kilim*, whose negotiation took place over several months. It found me in a shop nestled in the vicinity of Mosque Sidi Sahbi in Kairouan. Over several months on my returns to the holy city, I would go visit it, have it rolled at my feet and drink tea while pondering it and talking dinars with the one who stood between us. This ancient hollow with stacks and stacks of carpets, rolls of *zarbias, marghoums* and *kilims* six deep to the walls was a museum and I, almost a patron.

Tunisian textiles are cultural masterpieces, true gems of utility, master craftsmanship, history, tradition and avocation; informed by mothers to daughters, the expressions of skills honed over lifetimes: I have fallen in love. As I travel hither and yon with more time than money, I mine for ancient textiles, things woven, embroidered and hand pieced, each with a story to tell. And, this *kilim*, this expanse of brilliant red, whose story will be my story, was meant for me.

My passion for textiles of a historical bent has required a right-quick indoctrination into the ways of the economy previously unknown to me. Suffice it to say, my bartering skills are much-enhanced. In fact, in Gafsa they parleyed into a brilliant *Ta'jira* wool shawl deep burgundy with elaborate white cotton ornamentation. Two hundred years earlier, it shielded hair, face and other symbols of femininity as its married host moved through the village streets. In Tunis I was given permission to sift through several trunks locked away in a dark room on the second floor of a collector's home, located deep in the medina. The trunks were filled with elaborately embroidered *qoufiya* caps, covered in pearls, precious stones and golden thread—more than cover for brides or high-society ladies—crowns of achievement. As I ran my fingers over the work, I marveled that such exquisite ornamentation—the domain of kings and queens—is now the province of this realm and I have unbridled access to it. In Douz I found a woolen sack, two meters in length. Filled with grain and slung over the backs of camels, it had become deeply weathered from countless journeys across the sands of the Sahara. Century-old *qmijji* and *jaloua*, bridal tunics with velvet waistcoats and sleeves of satin and gold embroidered silk ribbon, fringed with brightly colored silk bobbles, I found in Sidi Bou Saïd. How could such treasures ever be put up for sale?

With my lovely red *kilim* packaged tightly in brown paper and twine, I leave the holy city for Sousse to observe the turning of the year. More pensive than party animal, I spend mine under a full moon with my toes in the Gulf of Hammamet, contemplating one million troops in the east, at the ready.

CHAPTER 58

Strange encounters of the unwanted kind

There is a CIA operative in my house! Out of the blue, she appears at my door, invites herself in, then sits on my bed. Now she is questioning me. She wants a "read" from someone in the trenches.

"Do you perceive any threat or anti-American sentiment? How about at school? What are people saying about what is happening in Kuwait?" There are so many red flags flying up, I can't get a handle on a one of them. But, here goes.

"Couldn't you have flagged down a volunteer at the embassy commissary the next time one showed up for a burger? Rather than, let's say, put someone at risk in her own site by, let's say, showing up at her house?"

It has already been established that everyone in greater Beja knows of my comings and goings. Even the police keep an account. That enormous American car parked outside my door will not go unnoticed in this neighborhood. Robyn's didn't. But, Robyn brought news of Molly's death. Either way, it is a bad omen.

There is political conflict to the east. All the volunteers have been obsessed with it. Wondered what will come of it. Speculated whether we would be among its fallout. Truth be told, we *are* valuable sources of information, assimilated to some degree and living as we do among Tunisians. I have no objection to sharing what I have or have not observed with regard to perceived threats against Americans...well, this American...I'm the only one around. But, I am angry with Miss Amateur-Hour, whose very presence in my home compromises more than my safety alone. Regardless of the many mindless choices I have made since I arrived here, her breach puts all Peace Corps volunteers at risk.

For the record, short of glorifications of Saddam in newspapers, I have yet to encounter any negativity directed at me or my nationality with respect to events unfolding elsewhere. I have found Beja, in fact, to be an interesting place from which to witness distant and detached support for Saddam. It's the Palestinian crisis that drives hearts and minds to support Saddam who leads its charge under the guise of the mess he's made in Kuwait. We live in a realm not unlike Hamlet's, where appearance and reality are ours to discern. Our eyes see the one of the world's largest democracies rushing to the aid of a tiny monarchy. It's the whole globe versus a dictator who looks an awful lot like a benevolent Rambo. And, Rambo is ready to take them all on...for the Palestinians. It's gosh darn confusing. None of it is likely to be brought into focus by newspapers, or in debates on buses, or under the interrogation of some barefaced CIA operative who shows up at a random door, in a random town, in a random country in Africa. I've been okay being the observer. Any distance I had however, has been annihilated.

Speaking of unpleasant encounters, I have at last had mine with Sofien. Knowing that Tunis will buffer my decision not to return to "the boys," I made him a proposition: I will take over any one of his classes (compliant darlings all) saving him the burden of teaching four sections. He was astonished—completely baffled—that I haven't altogether forgotten about the pummeling. *Oh contraire.* You know what they say about assuming. Case in point: I assumed the boys were angry. No, to be accurate, I assumed the boys were pissed. Then I ran into them in the *souq.* "When will we continue with the course?" they asked. I was stunned. "And what of Chedly?" I had to know. They laughed it off, as if it were a mild joke long dismissed. Turns out, I am the only one that can't shake the incident. It's true. Guilt and mortification cling—I cannot let it go. And because I cannot or will not drop it, what I will do is bow out (i.e., skulk away with my tail between my legs). I would rather bail than construct my return. What would a return even look like? Will the dynamics in that classroom change now that I have a thug at my disposal? There is a really big lesson here, my teachable moment. Problem is I'm not getting it. As my wise friend Tom says of Tunisia, "Knowing that hidden order exists isn't the same as understanding it."

It isn't long before the school director makes an appearance. It is our first meeting. Our first. The conversation lasts about one minute. Isn't really a conversation, as he does all of the talking. His last words are:

"This isn't America." I say nothing. His message, though he does not explicitly state it, is clear: corporal punishment is a sanctioned practice and everyone knows it. Now, get back to work. I am ever struggling with context and judgment. It is fairly difficult to separate emotion from something once it is attached. Nevertheless, I am still trying to think this one through. I don't know what more to do about this.

• • •

In place of my disco boys, I have a class of hecklers who have been without books for over three months. I am now responsible for teaching Sofien's fourth year students. The rising commentary of the evening pushes to the side the writing lesson I've planned. Tonight's outbursts during class include: "Everybody hates George Bush" and "Everybody hates Jews" and "Everybody loves Saddam Hussein." At first there is great entertainment value, looking for my reaction, waiting for my response. One student, Abdeljalil, holds up a newspaper. Prominently featured across the front page is a cartoon of Saddam Hussein, posturing in full military regalia, wielding firepower, biceps bulging. Abdeljalil stands up and very quietly asks "Is America going to war with Iraq?" I do what Dad would have hated me to do…I answer with a question.

"What do you think?" I'm fairly certain I've crossed the boundary, allowing this conversation to proceed into the realm of things political and such. But proceed it does, for an entire evening entirely in English. I am back to work!

Two of my new students walk me home. They sing Tunisian folk songs as we follow the winding road up into Jbel Axdhir. I am well in the world…for this moment. I love Tunisia.

CHAPTER 59

Peace Corps: first casualty of war

الله مصلى و سلم على سيدنا محمد قل لـ
الله أحد الله الصمد ولم تلده ولم يُلد
كان من الرجال أطلع من روس الجبال
بات من النساء أطلع من الكساء بات من
الذراري أطلع من روس البراري أخرج
من اللفريسة بجاه سيدي على بن غيسة.

Omee's blessing

For twenty minutes I have been staring at everything I brought with me and everything I've acquired, some of it packaged in boxes, most of it deposited in the corner of the room. My phone rang at 7:00 this morning. It was Penny White, the Director of Peace Corps operations in Tunisia. For six months I have feared this moment would come, and so it has: we are evacuating…in anticipation of the United States going to war with Iraq…because it could get ugly for Americans in Tunisia.

I spend most of my time with the Smadhis, who do not own a telephone. So it is lucky indeed that I was home this morning to receive the call, the official summoning of the Area Warden. To be clear, the only reason I *am* Area Warden is because I have a telephone, a party-line, which means I am mostly reachable. Now, I have to track down fourteen very phone-less volunteers scattered throughout the northwest and give them their instructions. Peace Corps plans to move us to Nice, France for three weeks. There, we will spend time "training" and wait out the looming United Nations deadline. We are to inform our immediate supervisor of the evacuation, but no one else. We are to bring just one bag. The rest of our property has to be packed up, addressed and ready to ship…if we don't come back. In all the hours of speculation, I had not imagined we might leave for good.

• • •

I am able contact almost everyone through their emergency numbers, except for one. So, I am on my way to Tabarka to get word to him. I am taking my shortwave radio with me—something I never do. I cannot bear listening while last ditch efforts at diplomacy fail, yet I cannot pull myself from it. We are rolling toward conflict. First casualties of war: Peace Corps Islamic countries, Tunisia, Morocco, Mauritania, Tanzania, Pakistan and Yemen.

• • •

In Tabarka, I don't locate the volunteer. It is thought he might be on vacation. These things are so hard to verify. We are required to inform Peace Corps when we leave the country. Otherwise, we are obligated to remain mostly in our sites. But we don't. We are among the best traveled residents in the country. And, we don't often leave word of where we are headed. Our AWOL volunteer could be anywhere in Tunisia. I let Penny White know. Everyone else in northwest is making their way to Tunis. Soon I will be too, but not without seeing the Smadhis first.

They are all home—*il hamdullah*—thank God. Bubba, Omee, Raodtha, Bchira, Sonia, Rejeh, Intessar and Grandma. I tell them that I have to leave the country...today. It is difficult to explain the reasons why. I am not certain about returning. Bubba tries to persuade me to stay. He promises I will be safe right here with them.

"There is no threat to you here. Not with us. Nothing will happen to you. I will take care of you," he tells me.

"The decision to leave isn't mine...it isn't mine to make." This is awful. I didn't know it would hurt so much, didn't know how much I had grown to love them and them me until I realized I turned them into a family of huggers (hugging is not standard practice, ever). I am smothered with love and long embraces by everyone, until finally there is Omee waiting for her turn. She places a carpet in my arms. It is crazy with bright colors and bold geometric shapes, unlike any I have seen.

"For you, from my hands." She made it for me, this treasure beyond all I have coveted in all the shops of my wanderings. She asks me to wait while she goes into the kitchen and returns with a bit of salt and some incense. She clutches them together and rubs my back with her fisted hand and begins to pray. After I leave the incense will be put directly on hot coals. The prayer she whispers is meant to ward off the evil eye, to protect me from accident or tragedy. She asks Bchira to write the prayer on a piece of paper so that I can take it with me, so that the protections will extend to my family at home in America. She carefully passes the incense to Sonia. Next, just as she had the first time we met, Omee cradles my face in her hands and pulls me to her. There are tears rolling down her cheeks. She kisses me four times directly on the mouth and looks deeply into my eyes. I see joy and sadness. She places her hands on my shoulders and this time she prays loudly to Allah to keep me safe, to look after me because she cannot any longer.

Not so long ago, I thought I might not return to the U.S. so enamored of Tunisians and go ahead, lump in all Arabs as well. Yet here I am in tears, wasted once again at the leaving of family—my family that I may never see again. I direct the Smadhis to go to my house in three weeks time and take whatever they want from my 110+ pounds of diddly. With that I leave Beja, light of hand but very very heavy of heart. The door that opened the world to me is slamming shut. This isn't the exit I'd imagined.

CHAPTER 60

Goodbyes

With Omee

Most of the volunteers have made it to Tunis. Three are traveling in Damascus, Syria, including Tom. Their status is unknown. My unreachable arrives very late to Tunis, but arrives nonetheless. Ambassador Pelletreau meets with us briefly. He is hopeful about the United States' relationship with Tunisia and about the possibility of us returning within a month.

"Tunisia has shared a long peaceful friendship with the U.S. and although tensions are running high, there is faith that ties will not be broken." In the immediate moment, we are to maintain a very low profile. Accordingly, we are to travel in groups of no less than four, wear nothing that identifies us as Americans and keep public discussions at a lower than normal speaking level. Additional areas off limits include touristy restaurants, the medina (my former home), the Peace Corps office and areas around mosques, especially during call to prayer.

So where do I go? Right to the medina—by myself—back to Besma's…though I know Besma isn't there. I go to see her Mother. I want an update. But the brother is home, lurking just around the corner, monitoring our conversation. I inquire of the sisters and of the family. She asks me about Beja, about teaching there. We feign a joke about the "less refined" accent in the west. Nothing controversial is said and certainly nothing about the evacuation of Americans from Tunis. I am careful to hold her hand in mine for an extra moment when I kiss her twice on each cheek and say goodbye. I know if he sees the piece of paper I've slipped her, he will take it. It's my mother's address in the U.S. She will pass it on to Besma, if she can. She is my one and only link to my friend.

From Besma's, I walk the narrow corridors to the kasbah up past the Prime Minister's, past his guard, out to the half-circle where Molly was hit by the bus. I've stood here a few dozen times waiting for taxis…a few times more since her accident. I can understand how it happened. It's always chaotic there, bus after bus, taxis and mopeds, commotion, the coming and going of so many people and vehicles converging into one space. I'm so sorry Molly. I miss you.

I walk past the double, Hafsid-style brown doors leading up to the medina house. There are no more Americans living here. I love this house, even though it nearly killed me. I love it. I love the medina too, though the life of my friend was claimed at its gateway. The first time I was led into the labyrinth of the medina, it imprinted distinctly on my memory, a living mixture of everything ancient to now. It is in fact the perfect metaphor for the whole of my experience here, representative of everything that is at first incomprehensible and mysterious, but worth exploring, worth effort, worth even a bit of pain. How could I not come back to the medina to say my goodbye?

The farewell includes one more no-no, a walk past the great Zitouna Mosque…because it is on my route. As luck would have it, just as the cobblestoned Rue de la Kasbah gives way to Rue Jamaa ez-Zitouna, the sky opens with *"Allah hu akbar."* Call to prayer. At least I am not wrapped in an American flag. Rather, I am wrapped in a scarf, concealing as best I can. I am trying to be as nondescript, as anonymous as anyone can be. At least it isn't Friday.

I tuck myself into a doorway to bask in the voices of muezzins rising up from mosques all over the medina. Too many to number are those things that were once foreign, even cataclysmic, that have in time become something else entirely, like the call to prayer. It is not my call, or my prayer. But it certainly is profoundly effective at evoking reverence in me. It re-orients me, pulls me out of myself. Anything that can cut through the chatter of my day (and everyone's for that matter) to focus attention for a moment on God (Allah, the divine, etc.) is okay with me. It is no longer a noise that shatters my peace, but a song that has taken deep root in my soul. I am so glad I've come back.

This medina, the living heart of this country for over twelve hundred years, is not a place I am willing to fear. And while I am on the subject, the same goes for Arabs and Muslims. So I ignore the warnings and linger for a while in the very place I was told not to venture, allowing the sights, smells and sounds to seep into my cell tissue, so that I can take some measure of this dream with me.

I've never been evacuated before. I find it all very interesting, the drama, the confusion, the urgency. Tunis airport is overloaded with Americans, the entire expat community exiting en masse, save our Ambassador and staff and the military that surround them. In addition to bodies, there are a host of cats and dogs, and a great deal of fuss over what to do with them. Our group, plus its surprisingly large menagerie of pets, is being divided in two and will travel separately. I briefly considered bringing Moses home with me. But I chose not to because I am not certain where I will land. He is no longer the pathetic scrawny creature I found under my bed. He is lustrous and fully grown. He will have to find a way to survive without me.

Peace Corps Tunisia alone is being put on "Administrative Hold" in Nice, which leaves open the possibility that I may be able to complete the three months I have left of my service. The evacuees from Peace Corps' other Islamic countries are returning to the U.S. definitively done with their service. Our status depends on "the crisis," which we will wait out while lodged in a hotel on the French Riviera, where all of our meals will be provided, while receiving per diem and French language training. Some crisis.

CHAPTER 61

Nice is Nice

Evacuated Peace Corps Volunteers from Islamic countries
(including me) gather in front of the White House, January 12, 1991

It's been rumored that there is an ice cream parlor in proximity to
our hotel, reason enough to lure four of us out of the sanctuary of
that space and leave behind the television around which we've all collected, from which we can hardly manage to pry ourselves. The buzz
of conversation that normally accompanies the gathering of two or
more volunteers has been absent in the presence of looming war and
in the overt televising of the ramp up to it. We take our silence to the
street where we come face-to face-with finely dressed Europeans in
their squeaky clean surroundings. We are not tourists. We are aliens,
awkwardly out of sync with the world of the French Riviera. The pen-

dulum of culture shock arcs anew. We find a nook from which to continue our blatant staring and completely forget about our ice cream.

Before too long, a large crowd approaches. Hundreds, thousands move toward us chanting slogans for peace and making declarations against the U.S. and against France's President Francois Mitterrand for siding with Bush. There is a group of communists waving red flags. A percussion ensemble marches within the group. One man carries an olive branch. We fall in behind him. The mass of people halts traffic. The crowd grows and grows to over 7,000. Three people climb atop a bus. They unfurl an American flag. They wave it provocatively then proceed to set it alight. I am reminded of an exchange I once had with this jerk I worked with on Mackinac Island. He was a Young Republican, always wearing pink and green and bowties—we were bound to clash sooner or later. Anyway, the subject of our discussion was flag desecration. He could not abide my support for the wife of a certain presidential candidate who burned the American flag out of her deep opposition over the Vietnam War. His passion was intense. The debate escalated. It ended with him slamming me against a wall. Clearly it is a controversial matter, the burning of Old Glory. It is a singularly bold act of defiance (the flag burning, not the body slamming). It screams desperation and a hopelessness I think I can understand. But I guess it all depends on who's holding the match. Because when I witness my flag being burned before my eyes, I find ambivalence I cannot reconcile. This is not a moment I can support. It is a moment, rather, that makes my insides churn. The flag burns slowly while the crowd cheers its destruction. Then they tear the remains to shreds, throw them to the ground and wipe their feet upon them. I pull a piece from under someone's boot and tuck it into my pocket. I am ashamed. This march for peace has me feeling brutally violated.

Today in Paris, New York, Washington, Tokyo, Toronto and other cities around the world, people gather...for Peace.

• • •

Monday, January 14, 1991:

Two PLO officials are assassinated in Tunis.

In Tunis tanks surround the American Embassy.

Peace Corps Tunisia suspends indefinitely.

"Peace Corps Volunteers were withdrawn because of a decision made by the State Department that their lives were at risk from terrorists, not from the government or the people they work with...The risk had just gotten too high in that region of the world."

Paul Coverdell, Peace Corps Director

Denver Post

January 19, 1991

CHAPTER 62

The year 2012

Tunisia, summer 2010

"To those peoples in the huts and villages of half
the globe struggling
to break the bonds of mass misery,
we pledge our best efforts to help them help themselves…"

John F. Kennedy
(in his inaugural address)

The events of 1991 brought to an abrupt end many peaceful missions in Arab countries. In the intervening years, relations between Muslims and non-Muslims, between Arab nations and the United States haven't exactly improved. For too many Americans, "terrorist" is synonymous with Arab or Muslim. It breaks my heart that this is the world I live in, where fear is so deeply entrenched there is quite simply no willingness to understand the other. And it's getting worse. It's madness.

I am very fortunate to have served in an Islamic country. I didn't have enough time, nor could I, to fully grasp the complexity of Islam, but I am eternally grateful that I don't have to live my life ignorant or terrified of it. Fear of Islam had a stranglehold on the American populace long before the Iraq War, long before 9/11 synthesized in our collective conscious that Muslims are people worthy of hating. In my own very small way, I've spent twenty years loosing the grip of that stranglehold, telling my stories to anyone I could, to anyone who would listen long enough to learn that Muslims and Arabs are a people worthy of knowing.

I've been lucky to have been able to return to Tunisia many times over the years. I always go straight to the loving arms of my adopted family, the Smadhis. I've participated in weddings, watched the family grow by many members, returned when there was loss and witnessed, albeit at a distance, as Tunisia recently struggled through a national revolution and began rebuilding a government for the people. It has been my absolute privilege to know and love the people of this country.

A few words about the vehicle that allowed me the opportunity to find my place in the world. Peace Corps might seem like an artifact from the Sixties, but I believe it is as relevant as it has ever been. The United States spends as much on the military as the entire rest of the world combined, so says Time Magazine's Mark Thompson, who goes on to say, quite accurately, that, despite our huge expenditures, we are not feeling a whole lot more secure. We've been at war in two countries, for eight years—one is finally coming to the end. For the other there's no end in sight. At the polar opposite end of the government spending spree is the Peace Corps, with its miniscule budget and hopeful approach, offering Americans from every walk of life the opportunity to promote peace and friendship on behalf of our country and to make a difference in the world.

So just what has this Sixties relic wrought over the past fifty years? I can only measure what I know and to do that I need only look at how the Peace Corps experience influenced the lives of the friends I wrote about in this book. My co volunteers—almost without exception—went on to live exceptional lives of service. They are career inner-city educators and mentors, leaders in non-profits, Foreign Service officers, United Nations officers and international development staffers working in war-torn areas and regions of great poverty and crisis. They live in service of people, positively influencing countless lives each and every day. Multiply that by the 200,000 Americans that have served over the past fifty years. This is the legacy of Peace Corps, not just for two years, but for a lifetime. How's that for changing the world?

As for me, my Peace Corps experience has had a significant impact on my life. I stayed connected to Peace Corps for almost a decade. I worked in recruitment, first assisting in the effort to help recruit the first (high-level business) volunteers to serve in the newly-opened former Soviet States, next as a public affairs officer and finally, I ended my tenure with a second tour as a volunteer, this time to Papua New Guinea to work as a rural community development and eco-tourism development volunteer.

Following Peace Corps, I naturally gravitated to the field of cross-cultural training. I had the opportunity to prepare individuals and families moving out of or into the United States. I would never have had the credibility to speak to things like culture shock and cultural adaptation if I had not experienced them first-hand. Of the over thirty countries I have presented in my trainings, it is the Muslim countries that generate the most anxiety in participants. I have been grateful to have been put in the path of these folks in particular.

The most important (and most challenging) work I have done to date is parenting my two children, Molly—named for my dear friend, and Jimi. My husband shivers just a little when I speak optimistically of the day my children might choose to strike out on a Peace Corps mission of their own. Whether they do or do not make that choice, I hope they will be open; open to cultivating relationships with people who don't look or think like them, and to cultures, ideas and beliefs which differ from their own. I hope they find joy in the rich tapestry that is the world that awaits them. I hope that the world that awaits them is a peaceful one.

"It's opener there in the wide open air.
Out there things can happen and frequently do...
And when things start to happen, don't worry. Don't stew.
Just go right along. *You'll* start happening too..."

Dr. Seuss

GLOSSARY OF TERMS

Allah: Muslim name for God

Dar: house or dwelling

Dar Arby: traditional Tunisian home with a courtyard surrounded by rooms

Ghouffa: a large woven basket used for daily shopping

Hamdullah: Arabic for thank God

Hannute: a local shop or store, generally in a confined or limited space, that sells anything from food staples to household goods

Harissa: a spicy condiment or paste made from hot peppers

Imam: a religious teacher

Kasbah: a fort, citadel or center of government

Louage: shared long-distance taxi

Kilim: a hand-knotted rug

Medina: city or old quarter of Tunisian towns

Minaret: a mosque's tower from which the muezzin calls the faithful to prayer

Mosque: Islamic house of worship

Muezzin: a mosque officially responsible for calling the faithful to prayer

Nakarifi: a small truck, usually with an open bed

N'shallah: Arabic for god-willing

Qur'an: the holy book of Islam

Surah: any chapter of the Qur'an. The Qur'an has 114 surahs or chapters.

Souq: market

Tabbouna: a kind of flat bread

Xubz: bread

Made in the USA
Monee, IL
06 November 2021